S0-BIP-408

FISCAL AUSTERITY AND AGING

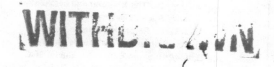

Volume 152, Sage Library of Social Research

RECENT VOLUMES IN
SAGE LIBRARY OF SOCIAL RESEARCH

FISCAL AUSTERITY AND AGING

Shifting Government Responsibility for the Elderly

CARROLL L. ESTES
ROBERT J. NEWCOMER
and ASSOCIATES

A. E. Benjamin
Lenore Gerard
Charlene Harrington
Philip R. Lee
David A. Lindeman
Alan Pardini
James H. Swan
Juanita B. Wood
and with the editorial assistance of
Ida VSW Red

Volume 152

**SAGE LIBRARY OF
SOCIAL RESEARCH**

SAGE PUBLICATIONS
Beverly Hills / London / New Delhi

For information address:

SAGE Publications, Inc.
275 South Beverly Drive
Beverly Hills, California 90212

SAGE Publications India Pvt. Ltd.
C-236 Defence Colony
New Delhi 110 024, India

SAGE Publications Ltd
28 Banner Street
London EC1Y 8QE, England

Printed in the United States of America

Library of Congress Cataloging in Publication Data

Main entry under title:

Fiscal austerity and aging.

   (Sage library of social research ; v. 152)
   Includes bibliographical references.
   1. Aged—Government-policy—United States—Addresses, essays, lectures. 2. Fiscal policy—United States—Addresses, essays, lectures. 3. United States—Politics and government—Addresses, essays lectures.
I. Estes, Carroll Lynn, 1938-   . II. Series.
HQ1064.U5F486   1983   353.0084'6   83-3440
ISBN 0-8039-2074-1
ISBN 0-8039-2073-3 (pbk.)

FIRST PRINTING

To Margretta M. Styles
whose vision and support created
the Aging Health Policy Center
and made this book possible

CONTENTS

FIGURES

TABLES

Tables

PREFACE

The decade of the 1980s is characterized by economic uncertainty and political ambiguity regarding the direction of American public policy for the elderly. Analysis of policy trends during the past decade suggests that two forces will be central in shaping policy in the near future: fiscal austerity and federalism. Inflation, recession, unemployment, tax cuts, reductions in social spending, increases in defense spending, high interest rates, and other fiscal and monetary policies portray in vivid economic terms the impact of austerity. Austerity also has a political face, for it suggests an ideology built on the belief that scarcity of resources should govern public policy. Federalism represents the relationships among governments within the American political system and involves one of the fundamental questions of politics: Who will decide? Issues about the appropriate roles of federal, state, and local governments may influence not only the focus of public choice, but also the nature of the choices that are possible.

The themes that characterize and frame the contemporary U.S. debate over the economy and the roles of federal government as they relate to the aged are incorporated throughout the book. This debate involves the interdependence of the public sector with the market sector and of the market sector with the welfare state. It involves social justice and the rights of citizens as well as vested interests in particular policy decisions. It involves the human consequences for more than twenty-six million older Americans, their families, friends, and future generations of older persons.

In considering these questions, it is our contention that social action and public policy are indivisible from socially constructed and socially maintained ideas that define and provide images of the problems of austerity, of the economy, and of old age in the United States. These ideas are, in turn, shaped and carried forward — not entirely or primarily on the basis of the "facts." Corporate, political, professional, and other interests are brought into play, utilizing the media and economic, political, and ideological resources to frame the limits of what ultimately will be considered acceptable as policy. The weaker the empirical basis of our knowledge concerning a particular problem, the greater the influence of social and political factors in what is accepted as knowledge in the determination of public policy.

In analyzing the economic crisis and American society, Castells (1980; see references in Chapter 11) observed that the new ideology of austerity was needed to rationalize economically difficult times; yet the ideology can have a powerful effect as a divisive tool in pitting youth against age and individuals and families against each other and themselves. This book was undertaken in an effort to contribute to an understanding of the critical questions of aging and public policy in an era shaped by the ideology of austerity. In attempting to inform the public debate, our purpose is not to reiterate the deleterious effects that may be promoted by the use of a concept such as austerity, with its implicit blame on individuals. It is our contention that issues of austerity can be used to mask changes in fiscal conditions, political and corporate decisions, and their impact on the population in general and the elderly in particular.

Organization of the Book

The book is organized to provide the reader a perspective on both the past and the future direction of social policies for the aged and to present our research findings about public programs for the aged and the fiscal condition and political priorities of state and local government. Chapters 1 and 2 begin with an analysis of the origins and perceptions of the values and major issues underlying the development of public policy and aging, including the assignment of governmental responsibility. Chapter 3 gives an historical overview of the development of intergovernmental relations and its significance to aging programs and policies over the past fifty years. Chapter 4 outlines the contemporary debate about the two largest public policies for the elderly — Social Security and Medicare. The next six chapters present empirical data developed in studies of public policies and programs implemented and operated in various forms of federal and state partnership over the period 1974 to 1983. These studies include an examination of the fiscal crisis (Chapter 5), Title XX Social Services and block grants (Chapter 6), Medicaid (Chapter 7), the Older Americans Act (Chapter 8), and the Health Planning and

Development Act (Chapter 9) programs, as well as programs in the private nonprofit sector (Chapter 10). The concluding chapter (11) presents the personal observations of two of the senior investigators who for the past eight years have guided much of the research reported in this volume.

This research is drawn from a series of longitudinal studies conducted by the authors in the Aging Health Policy Center and in the Department of Social and Behavioral Sciences, School of Nursing, University of California, San Francisco. These studies illustrate how governmental responsibility for the elderly and for other needy individuals is being played out, providing an assessment of both the policy shifts emerging in the first half of the 1980s and the long-range impact of shifting governmental responsibility for the elderly.

Acknowledgments

Many individuals, agencies, and private organizations have in some way supported and contributed to the research, thinking, and study involved in the preparation of this book. The interpretations and commentary are those of the authors and should not be attributed to any other individuals or sponsoring agencies.

We are particularly grateful to three federal agencies and to one private foundation for the support of the research that underlies the thoughts and writing in this volume. Three studies funded by the Administration on Aging are: Funding Policies and Performance of State and Area Agencies on Aging (Grant No. 90-A-979); Fiscal Crisis and Tax Revolt: Impact on Aging Services (Grant No. 90-AR-0016); and Health Planning and the Health Care Needs of the Elderly (Grant No. 09-AR-0028). The first study, funded from 1976 to 1981, not only brought our research group into existence, but also focused us squarely on research on issues of federalism and decentralization. Our subsequent research on fiscal crisis, initially funded in 1980, immersed us in issues of austerity rather early. Our research on long term care, and particularly on Medicaid, on the Title XX Social Services program, and on Supplemental Security Income (SSI) has been supported by two federal agencies. The National Center for Health Services Research is currently funding a four-year study of the Correlates of Long Term Care Expenditures and Utilization in Fifty States (Grant No. H504042-02), and the Health Care Financing Administration provides grant support for our three-year research project on Long Term Care and the Impact of State Discretionary

Policies (Grant No. 18-P-97620/9). Both of these studies have shed light on the implications of the fiscal crisis for the important health and social services for the elderly discussed in the book. The Pew Memorial Trust has generously supported a new study now under way on public policy, the private nonprofit sector, and the delivery of community-based long term care services for the elderly. This research has been influential in broadening our grasp of the full extent to which austerity is shaping resource availability at the state and local levels. Thanks also to grant funds from the Pew Memorial Trust for health policy research training, both Pew fellows and faculty have contributed to the writing and review of this volume. Also, we would like to acknowledge the assistance of faculty of the Institute for Health Policy Studies.

Dean Margretta Styles of the School of Nursing and our faculty colleagues in the Department of Social and Behavioral Sciences have inestimably aided our efforts with support, encouragement, and needed resources.

The research staff of the Aging Health Policy Center contributing to these studies over the past eight years includes more than twenty professional staff and research assistants. Three who deserve special acknowledgment are Victoria Peguillan-Shea, Jon Garfield, and Mary Kreger. We are appreciative also of the insightful review and comments provided by Jane Sprague Zones and Lynn Parringer. Patricia A. Saliba has made vital contributions to the coding, management, and analysis of the data sets for virtually all of the studies reported here.

All of the authors of this volume personally owe a great debt to the long hours, late nights, and early mornings of Norton S. Twite, who coordinated and supervised the production of the manuscript, and the able help of Sue Churka-Hyde, Emilie Cruger, and Andrea Olson. Kerry McDermott, Nancy DeMartini, Prima Conde, and Peg O'Neill also deserve thanks for their administrative support of the projects and the book. To Nancy Nienhuis and Elaine Benson, we owe thanks for seeing to it that the affairs of the Center and the Department were smoothly run, giving us the time we needed for this task. Finally, special thanks are due to Duskie Lynn Gelfand, Stacy Newcomer, and Emily Newcomer for the support they gave to their parents during this project.

San Francisco, California   Carroll L. Estes
                                                   Robert J. Newcomer

CHAPTER 1

FISCAL AUSTERITY AND AGING

Carroll L. Estes

Fiscal austerity and old age are inextricably linked. A fiscal crisis at the federal level was formally declared in 1981 by the president, by other politicians, and by conservative economists. The media repeated the fiscal crisis definition over and over again. The public, including millions of elderly, have come to accept this image of reality and are concerned. As such images become widely shared, they take on the character of objective reality, regardless of their basis in fact, because policymakers begin to act as if the image reflects concrete reality. When something as vital as the economy is declared in crisis, the social, economic, and political stakes are high. The content of the defined crisis and the proposed remedies are not so much related to objective facts as to the capacity of strategically located groups and classes to press their views into public consciousness and law.

Not only has a fiscal crisis been declared, there is a growing portrayal of aging in American society as "a problem" — that is, old age and older people are perceived as a problem *to society*. Notions such as the graying of the budget, the graying society, and the demographic revolution encourage the tendency to *link* the economic crisis with old age. The debate over responsibility for the problems of the economy and aging reflects a larger set of power struggles among contending forces in the American body politic. Competing definitions of societal problems are important in framing the debate, specifying the viable options, and delineating the federal role in domestic social programs.

Author's Note: The author wishes to acknowledge the invaluable contributions of Lenore Gerard, Philip R. Lee, and Jane Sprague Zones.

The shape and debate of public policy for the aged can best be understood in light of societal perceptions of old age, of the fiscal crisis, and of federal responsibility. Definitions of the "social problem" of old age and of the appropriate policy solutions to treat this problem have reflected the ups and downs of the U.S. economy and the shifting bases of political power during the past thirty years. The expansion and contraction of old age policy reflect not only the state of the economy but also the strength of political, economic, and ideological interests and alignments that form around it (Weber, 1946; Collins, 1968). Thus, old age policy is one important reflection of the structural arrangements and resource conflicts in the society. When the economy is expanding, optimism abounds and resources for dealing with societal problems tend to increase, as they did for the elderly in the 1960s and early 1970s. Conversely, periods of scarcity tend to produce limited and inadequate (and often punitive) social programs, as in the 1980s. The likely failure of such programs will provide a further rationale for debunking social change efforts and for limiting resource allocations for the disadvantaged (Miller, 1976). Such government policy contractions occur precisely when the disadvantaged are hit hardest by the same deteriorating economic conditions that initially fostered retrenchment policies.

Social Construction of Reality

Societal perceptions of aging and old age emerge through a process of ideological and political struggle. The perceptions of reality that frame opinions and shape the policies that flow from them reflect the dominance of certain values and normative conceptions of social and economic problems and their remedies. The value choices and socially accepted definitions of existing conditions do not, however, derive from consensual agreement of the members of society. Nor are they a result of a benign accommodation among different interests as the pluralists posit (Connolly, 1969); nor, even in the case of old age policies, from the definitions of older persons themselves (Estes, 1974). The perceptions of aging and old age in America flow largely from those who have the greatest power to influence the dominant definition of societal problems and to specify the policy interventions and resource allocations to address those problems (Miller, 1976; Alford, 1976).

In the 1980s, the definition of the problems of the elderly has shifted. More and more, the elderly are blamed for the inadequate situations in which they find themselves by those economic and political interests that have the most to gain from public policies that reduce domestic social spending and that seek to shift public responsibilities to the individual or to other levels of government than the federal level.

As noted, one major perception of reality that is shaping policy debate is the notion that old age and aging are a problem to society. Not only has aging been defined as a problem, but individual older persons have increasingly been labeled in the 1980s as "the problem." The well-meaning attention and concern for the individual elderly persons' health, happiness, life satisfaction, and high morale have played strongly into the propensity to think about the problems of old age as individual problems — to think of the physical, behavioral, and social manifestations of old age as the consequence of inherent biological factors rather than the result of a combination of social, economic, political, and biological factors.

In this philosophical and political environment, the research task among many social gerontologists has been to learn how the aging process works (implicitly taking for granted the existing policies and conditions) and how adult development and adjustment occur in old age under the given policies and conditions. Thus, societal treatment of the elderly (for example, through policies of mandatory retirement and socially created dependency) tends to be taken as given rather than empirically examined for its effect on the aging process and the elderly. Because aging is conceptualized as an individual problem, it appears to occur as a consequence of largely apolitical processes (that is, individual physiological and chronological decline), rather than being shaped by public policies, economic conditions, and the political forces that affect them.

The perception of the aging process as a biological phenomenon lends support to those who argue that society bears little responsibility for what happens to old people. It is consonant with the laissez-faire, survival-of-the-fittest, "every man for himself" concept of society, each individual theoretically having an equal opportunity to succeed. From this perspective, success is seen as the result of individual effort; failure is due not to race, sex, social class origin or other structural factors, but to the lack of individual initiative. This perception also supports the notion that the problems of older persons bear little or no relation to how society treats the aged (with rejection, denial of status, and work loss), but instead, that aging problems are independent of the economic and social order in which old people reside. An extension of this line of thinking is that individual old people must be responsible for themselves.

Another major perception of reality shaping the debate over responsibility for the aged and for other vulnerable groups in society concerns fiscal crisis. A political declaration of fiscal crisis at the federal level has generated a climate of intense psychological uncertainty and vulnerability of the American public to proposals to dismantle major social programs. The crisis definition of the U.S. economy — now incorporated into law through both the Omnibus Budget Reconciliation Act of 1981 (U.S. PL 97-35), through federal budget reductions, block grants, and Medicaid cuts, and the Economic Recovery Tax Act of 1981 (U.S. PL 97-34), through a $750 billion tax cut over a five-year period, as well as the monetary policies of the Federal Reserve Board (high interest and slow growth in money supply) — assured the objective condition of a fiscal crisis in many states by bringing on a recession to control inflation and by refusing to provide for countercyclical aid to state and local governments.

The public perception of fiscal crisis may serve important political and economic interests, depending on how it is incorporated into economic and other public policy. Perhaps the most serious potential threat to the survival of a viable public policy for the elderly is the construction of reality that links the perception of fiscal crisis with an aging society. This perception is promoted by numerous journals and popular periodicals, in portrayals of the "graying" federal budget (health and welfare social benefits for older persons) as a major source of the nation's economic troubles.

Of great concern to the aging will be the outcome of power struggles among contending views concerning the needs of the aged, their rights, and their social responsibilities.

Intense political and partisan issues have arisen in the effort to designate blame for the nation's current economic woes. Starting with the Secretary of the Department of Health, Education and Welfare, Joseph Califano, who in 1979 coined the phrase "graying of the budget," the idea has been advanced by Samuelson (1978, 1981) and others that the aged are "busting the budget" and that expenditures for the elderly are a major reason for U.S. economic problems.

This is most dramatically illustrated by the controversy over Social Security. Related and important constructions of reality of

Reagan administration officials are the notions (1) that Social Security is going bankrupt, that the U.S. cannot afford Social Security in its present form, and that cuts in Social Security are essential and inevitable (Wickenden, 1981; Estes, forthcoming) and (2) that Medicare is being bankrupted because of Social Security's borrowing from the Hospital Insurance Trust Fund to meet financing problems and because of the demographic aging of the population. Although this extreme oversimplification of a very complex set of economic problems is vigorously contested by many Social Security experts, blaming the aged has become a political pastime with immense social, economic, and political interests at stake.

The debate over who is responsible for the elderly reflects a larger set of power struggles among contending economic and ideological forces operating in the broad American body politic. Competing definitions of societal problems and what causes them are important in terms of future directions. Part of the austerity and aging debate is the controversy over policy solutions. It is within the purview of social policy not only to identify problems but also to take action that will ameliorate those problems. One solution reflects the view that the problems of the poor elderly and of other disadvantaged groups cannot be solved with national policies and programs. It is contended that the solutions must come from efforts of state and local governments, initiatives of the private sector, or initiatives of the individual. This perspective is often justified in two ways: first, by the belief that individuals create their own conditions and opportunities and thus have only themselves to blame for the predicaments and, second, by the belief that the cost of government social intervention is, itself, harmful to the productivity and economic well-being of the nation. Under the banner of new federalism, the Reagan administration has invested significant political resources in efforts to reduce federal spending and federal responsibility in areas of domestic social concern.

Public Expenditures

There are five major themes in the debate over government spending and responsibility for the elderly, all of which reflect the broader issues of the perceived crisis in the economy and patterns of public spending.

(1) How much government spending is enough, how much is too much, and what are the determining criteria for the limits to government spending?

(2) How should public resources be allocated between competing areas of the nation's health and welfare, such as defense versus domestic social spending?

(3) How do particular kinds of spending affect other sectors of the economy, raising the issue of efficiency?

(4) What portion of the federal budget should be expended for the elderly?

(5) What is the effect of public expenditure policies (for example, tax cuts and spending) on different classes of citizens, raising issues of equity among the aged?

These questions and issues will not be resolved by the application of objective processes and standards alone. Public expenditure decisions are mediated in the political arena and motivated as much by public expectations and powerful interests as by objective economic measures of the actual capacity and performance of the American economy.

Public Spending Patterns

There are several trends to note in the allocation and distribution of public resources. First, while there has been a great rise in government spending as expressed in nominal terms of total dollars (rising to $925 billion in 1981) for federal, state, and local governments, there has been an observed decline in government spending since 1975 when measured as a percentage of the gross national product (Advisory Commission on Intergovernmental Relations [ACIR], 1980a; Palmer and Mills in Palmer and Sawhill, 1982) or when measured in government expenditures per capita, corrected for inflation (ACIR, 1980a). One analysis of the growth of government spending between 1959 and 1981 shows that, when adjustments are made for economic factors (such as inflation), there has been "only very modest relative growth in federal program activity" (Palmer and Mills in Palmer and Sawhill, 1982, p. 63). It also has been observed that between 1976 and 1979 public social welfare expenditures (including social insurance programs) decreased as a percentage of the gross national product (GNP) and as a percentage of the federal budget (Johnson Foundation, 1982).

This overall trend of declining share of GNP devoted to social welfare, and to the support of state and local infrastructure needs in safety, transportation, and protection services, is expected to accelerate (downhill) if the Reagan administration's proposed domestic spending cuts continue to be adopted by Congress. The magnitude of the reversal in federal, state, and local government fiscal relations proposed by the Reagan administration is best illustrated by a single comparison. If all of the administration's new federalism proposals are adopted and implemented, the federal share of state and local budgets will have been reduced from 25 percent in 1980 to 3 to 4 percent by 1991 (Peterson in Palmer and Sawhill, 1982). The federal role will have been dramatically diminished, and national policies will have been replaced a hundredfold by state and local policies.

Although the eventual fate of the many new federalism proposals by the Reagan administration remains uncertain, the goal is clear — a return to the strict separation of federal from state and local government responsibility. "Dual federalism," a term to denote this strict separation of responsibility, was basically the policy that prevailed from the Civil War of the 1860s to the Great Depression and the advent of the New Deal in 1933 (D. Walker, 1981).

The figures on the growth of government spending raise questions of the limits and balance of government expenditure and the determining criteria for defining those limits. The role of government and of public policy in the austerity of the 1980s is being shaped by four major conservative contentions: (1) that the size of government and government spending (especially at the federal level) is too big (U.S. Congressional Budget Office [CBO], 1982a); (2) that massive tax cuts for corporations and the wealthy are necessary to limit the growth of government and stimulate investment; (3) that general budget deficits are harmful to the economy because they require federal borrowing that raises interest rates and limits the funds available for private (for example, corporate) borrowing; and (4) that increased private sector resources and activity will stimulate economic growth, reduce employment, and solve the nation's social problems.

All of these perceptions are ultimately political in terms of their judgment. The U.S. Congressional Budget Office states: "Whether the described trends are desirable or undesirable, too slow or too fast, enough or not enough, cannot be demonstrated by analysis; rather the answer is a matter for intuition and political judgment" (U.S. CBO, 1982a, p. 5).

In 1982 the U.S. Congressional Budget Office (1982a) undertook a study to examine whether there is any direct relationship between the size of the public sector and the nation's economic performance. The study concluded that although federal deficits and the federal sector have been growing steadily over the past twenty years, "cross-national data do not establish a connection between a pattern of deficits and expenditure growth and a country's economic perform-ance" (U.S. CBO, 1982a, p. 9). Moreover, drawing upon estimates from Palmer and Sawhill (1982), the CBO study reported that since 1966 "the federal sector in relation to the economy has grown only 0.9 percentage points and has remained basically the same size . . . during the last five years" (U.S. CBO, 1982a, p. 17). A comparison of the United States with other industrial countries gives an interna-tional perspective on this issue. Figure 1.1 shows the evolution of government spending (federal, state, and local) among thirteen indus-trial democracies over the period 1960 to 1980. Within a range of a 1980 high of 65.7 percent of gross domestic product in Sweden to a low of 32.7 percent of gross domestic product in Japan, "the United States had one of the smallest and slowest growing public sectors" for the period of 1960 to 1980 (U.S. CBO, 1982a, p. 19).

Thus, the evidence does not support the contention that the gov-ernment is either too large or too small. The failure of the centerpiece of Reagan fiscal policy — the massive tax cut of 1981 — to stimulate the economy raises additional questions about the basic economic assumptions underlying the current policy shifts. In contrast to Re-publican and Democratic administrations in the past, the Reagan administration has not used countercyclical funding or public sector programs to counter the effects of the recession and to stimulate recovery.

Competing Areas of Public Spending

The second issue concerning public expenditure is the major shift in priorities from domestic social to defense spending. This shift was dramatically accelerated by the Reagan administration, although it had been initiated by the Carter administration in the late 1970s.

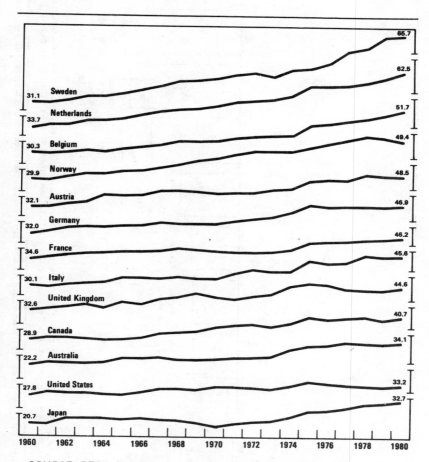

SOURCE: **OECD Economic Outlook,** Volume 31, (July 1982), p. 149.
a. Includes total expenditures for all levels of government.
b. The GDP is a national income concept based on production within the geographic borders of the country; the GNP covers production by and incomes
   to citizens of the country no matter where they may live.

Figure 1.1 Evolution of General Government Expenditures,[a] 1960-1980 (in percentages of GDP[b] at current prices)

Reagan's strategy differs from previous efforts, however, in seeking
"not merely to modify existing trends, but to shift policy into a
fundamentally altered ideological framework" (Reichley in
Pechman, 1981, pp. 260-261).

26

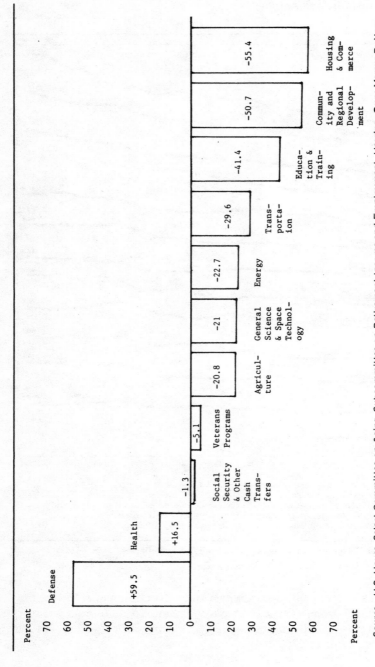

Source: U.S. House, Select Committee on Aging, Subcommittee on Retirement Income and Employment. Hearing: **Guns Versus Butter: How the Military Budget Affects Aging Americans**, July 24. Washington, DC: U.S. Government Printing Office, 1981, p. 20.

Figure 1.2 Projected Expenditure Changes for Fiscal Years 1981-1986 (based on administration's budget requests and projected expenditures in constant 1981 dollars)

The most significant feature of this strategy is "part of a dramatic redefinition of the role of the federal government, involving a far larger commitment to military spending and a corresponding reduction in domestic spending" (Omenn and Nathan, 1982, pp. 1057-1058). The Reagan administration has projected defense spending that totals $1.5 trillion for fiscal years 1982 through 1986 (U.S. House, 1981b). Figure 1.2 shows the projected defense expenditure increases in relation to other budget categories. Virtually all categories of expenditure, with the exception of health, will decrease (most of them significantly) between fiscal year (FY) 1981 and FY 1986, in dramatic contrast to defense spending, which is projected to increase by more than 59 percent during this period.

The magnitude of the shift to defense from social spending is apparent in Figure 1.3, which shows the projected defense expenditures as a portion of the federal budget, both with and without the Social Security trust funds incorporated in the budget. The Pentagon share of the federal budget authority in FY 1982 was shown to be 52 percent ($226 of $435 billion) of the total actual budget, if Social Security were removed. Even with Social Security calculated in the federal budget, the Pentagon share was shown at 32.5 percent (U.S. House, 1981b).

Effects of Specific Types of Spending

The third public expenditure issue concerns the perceived effect on the private sector (or efficiency) of social welfare spending in an era of observed decline in the economy's overall performance as well as decline in state and local fiscal capacity. A major target of budget reductions has been Social Security, which accounts for 60 percent of federal outlays for the elderly. The recent and unprecedented attack on Social Security has involved the philosophical as well as fiscal basis and viability of the program. Social Security expenditures, totaling an estimated $135 billion in 1982, with approximately $92.8 billion in payments to retired workers (U.S. Social Security Administration [SSA], 1982), has been charged with having the effect of reducing the public's reliance on the market, increasing the individual's dependency on the government, and reducing incentives for personal savings that provide a major source of essential investment capital for economic growth (Rahn and Simonson, 1980).

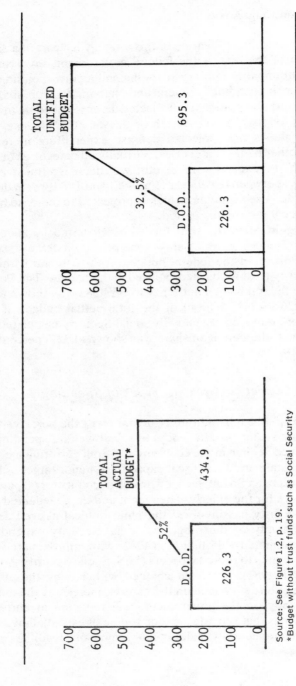

Source: See Figure 1.2, p. 19.
*Budget without trust funds such as Social Security

Figure 1.3 Pentagon Share of Federal Budget Authority, FY 1982 (in billions of dollars)

Recent policies of retrenchment have been advanced through "gloom and doom" prognostications concerning the economy, and exhortations to sacrifice (by enduring high unemployment, high interest rates, and tax advantages to the wealthy, for example) in order to "get the economy going again." The confluence of the definitions of crisis with an attack on the legitimacy of support for the elderly is evident in the debate about Social Security. Here, the power struggles among contending interests are clearly seen, with conservative rhetoric adopting images of the aged as bankrupting society and harming the economy. Sharply contrasting views and statistics have been presented by the Study Group on Social Security (Wickenden, 1981), Myles (1981), and others (Ball, 1982).

While fears have been aroused, the public appears resistant to accepting the conservative view as a basis for significant cuts in Social Security. In poll after poll, the elderly are seen by the public as a deserving group (Cook, 1979; Harris, 1975; National Council on Aging [NCOA], 1981) and especially so where Social Security is concerned. The "high endorsement for government's involvement in assuring the economic security of older persons" (Klemmack and Roff, 1981, p. 594) is a consistent finding in research over the years. The Harris poll (NCOA, 1981) reports strong public opposition to reducing the benefits for current retirees (92 percent oppose) and strong opposition to benefit reductions for future retirees (85 percent oppose). Clear majorities support tax increases and general revenue financing, if necessary, for Social Security; they also oppose raising the retirement age — even though 54 percent of those 18 and over had "hardly any confidence" in Social Security's capacity to fund their own retirement.

Share of Federal Budget
Allocated to Elderly

Some public officials and economists have voiced alarm about the fourth expenditure issue — the aging "share" of the federal budget. Current federal expenditures related to aging are reported to exceed one-quarter of the budget and to be moving toward a projected one-third of the budget in the future. It is important to understand what these figures represent. Table 1.1 shows major categories of federal outlays that benefit the elderly at 26.4 percent for 1981 and estimates of 26.9 percent for FY 1982 and 27.7 percent for FY 1983.

TABLE 1.1 Federal Outlays[a] Benefiting the Elderly

Program[b]	FY 1981 (Actual)			FY 1982 (Estimate)			FY 1983 (Estimate)		
	Millions	% of Elderly Budget	% of Total Budget	Millions	% of Elderly Budget	% of Total Budget	Millions	% of Elderly Budget	% of Total Budget
Totals[b]	173,345	100.0	26.4	195,150	100.0	26.9	209,585	100.0	27.7
OASDI (Social Security)	$ 97,096	56.0	14.8	$109,708	56.2	15.1	$121,221	57.8	16.0
Medicare	35,752	20.6	5.4	41,833	21.4	5.8	46,916	22.4	6.2
Other retired disabled and[c] survivors' benefits	22,847	13.2	3.5	24,562	12.6	3.4	22,197	10.6	2.9
Medicaid	5,967	3.4	0.9	6,345	3.3	0.9	6,365	3.0	0.8
Housing	3,562	2.1	0.5	4,087	2.1	0.6	4,293	2.1	0.6
Supplemental Security Income	2,598	1.5	0.4	2,654	1.4	0.4	3,069	1.5	0.4
Other federal health care	2,229	1.3	0.3	2,516	1.3	0.4	2,741	1.3	0.4
Older Americans Act programs	993	0.6	0.2	905	0.5	0.1	758	0.4	0.1
Food stamps	906	0.5	0.1	899	0.5	0.1	660	0.3	0.1
Miscellaneous	701	0.4	0.1	829	0.4	0.1	751	0.3	0.1
Title XX Social Services[d]	595	0.3	0.1	647	0.3	0.1	445	0.2	0.1
ACTION	85	0.1	0.0	87	0.0	0.0	88	0.0	0.0
National Institute on Aging	70	0.0	0.0	76	0.0	0.0	81	0.0	0.0
White House Conference on Aging	4	0.0	0.0	2	0.0	0.0	0	0.0	0.0

SOURCE: U.S. Office of Management and Budget, Health and Income Maintenance Division. Reprinted in U.S. White House Conference on Aging, *Final Report: 1981*, Vol. 1. Washington, DC: WHCoA, 1982, p. 13.

a. Reflects outlays, including effects of proposed legislation, for recipients aged 65 and over in most cases. These are estimates based on federal agency information, which may be administrative counts, samples, or less accurate estimates from federal, state, and program staff. Other federal programs that assist the elderly (e.g., consumer activities, USDA extension services, national park services) have been excluded due to data limitations.

b. Totals may not add due to rounding.

c. Includes veterans compensation and pensions.

d. Includes energy assistance.

The Senate Special Committee on Aging has, however, examined these expenditures and observed that if "expenditures for all partially self-funded programs (i.e., Social Security and Medicare) are excluded from 1982 Federal spending estimates, about 4 percent of the Federal budget would be devoted to programs assisting the Nation's elderly" (U.S. Senate, 1982b, pp. 4-5).

The largest expenditure category for the elderly is, of course, Social Security. Considering the four human service programs of particular importance — Medicare; Medicaid; Title XX Social Services, now a block grant; and the Older Americans Act — there are vast disparities in the distribution of public spending for the elderly. Physicians, hospitals, and nursing home services have overwhelmingly dominated in the expenditure of funds, with over seventy times more dollars now spent annually on health than on social services for the aged (Newcomer et al., 1982). Although these expenditures benefit the elderly because they help assure needed access to care, the money goes largely and directly to hospitals and physicians. In addition, the rapid increase in Medicare expenditures has been due primarily to medical inflation, not to increased utilization of services by the elderly.

Effects of Public Policies on Different Classes of Citizens

In spite of federal efforts and expenditures, poverty among the elderly has not been eradicated. After years of declining poverty, the poverty rate of older persons is on the rise again — rising precipitously from 14 percent in 1978 to 15.7 percent (or 3.9 million people) in 1980. More recent data are not yet available, but it is likely that the trend has continued. Women, blacks, and other minorities are the most disadvantaged, with 38 percent of aged blacks and 30.8 percent of Spanish-origin aged living at extreme poverty levels (U.S. House, 1982). Moreover, half of all the aged poor are single women (never married or widows) who live alone (Orshansky in U.S. House, 1978). This overall poverty rate of 15.7 percent reflects the official poverty standard of $3941 for individuals 65 years of age and over in 1980. Recognizing the arbitrarily low level of this poverty threshold, many have suggested that thresholds of 125 percent and 150 percent of the poverty standard be employed in order to include the near-poor elderly. These near-poor levels merely add an additional $20 to $40 per week to the official poverty index in order to calculate the total poor and near-poor elderly population.

Current old age policy in the United States reflects a two-class system of welfare with benefits distributed on the basis of legitimacy rather than on the basis of need (Tussing, 1971). Old people may have more legitimacy relative to other disadvantaged groups in society competing for scarce public funds (Cook, 1979), but old age neither levels nor diminishes social class distinctions (Nelson, 1982; Estes, 1982; Crystal, 1982). Social class and economic resources in old age are largely determined by lifetime conditions and labor force participation established before retirement age (A. Walker, 1981).

Both income and service policies in the United States reflect different classes of "deservingness" in old age (Nelson, 1982; Titmuss, 1965). Public policies for the aged who are considered "deserving" differ from those for the aged who are considered "undeserving." Three classes of the aged are entitled to some type of government program: (a) the middle and upper-class (the deserving nonpoor) aged; (b) the downwardly mobile, newly poor in old age (the deserving poor); and (c) the aged who have always been poor (the undeserving poor; Nelson, 1982).

The aged who are not poor have the resources to permit access to public and private services without the necessity of government intervention. They also receive a disproportionately high share of the benefits from the largest federal programs for the aged (such as Social Security, Medicare, and retirement tax credits). Most social service policies tend to favor the newly poor in old age, largely because they are thought of as both deserving and deprived (Nelson, 1982). Services have been designed largely to assist the recently deprived aged in maintaining their lifestyles, rather than to provide the more crucial life-support services (such as income) needed by the poor aged. The aged who have been lifelong poor are assisted largely through inadequate income-maintenance policies, such as Supplemental Security Income (SSI), Medicaid (which is highly variable from state to state), food stamps, and the Social Security minimum benefit (now available only to current, not future, beneficiaries).

Deservingness in old age income policies is firmly based on the principle of differential rewards for differential achievements during a lifetime. For those individuals who had been casually employed or who had low lifetime earnings covered by Social Security (mainly women and minorities), the minimum benefit in the past guaranteed a basic monthly payment of $122. The successful Reagan administration and congressional cutback effort targeted at eliminating the Social Security minimum benefit for all future beneficiaries (U.S. PL 97-35, 1981) is illustrative of the trend to eliminate the "undeserving" aged from the receipt of Social Security benefits. Proponents of this policy change have argued that those who require income support beyond what they have actually earned in the labor market ought to look to the means-tested SSI program or other state discretionary welfare programs for relief (U.S. House, 1981a).

The important point is that most, if not all, of the policies that deal with the "undeserving," poorest aged involve state discretionary policy — that is, responsibility is in the hands of the states (Estes, 1982). The eligibility and benefits under these policies depend on the variable willingness and fiscal capacity of states to fund programs at the state level. Not only are these state discretionary programs different from state to state; they are easily politicized and are more economically vulnerable and variable than uniform federal policies.

Despite an enormous investment of public resources in health care, serious problems still exist in the equitable distribution of these resources. There continue to be class, racial, and regional disparities in the benefits of publicly financed health care (Institute of Medicine [IOM], 1981). The Medicare program is an example. While most aged are eligible for Medicare, research has shown that Medicare benefits are provided disproportionately to the upper and middle classes and to whites rather than to the lower classes and blacks, who suffer a greater burden of illness and disability (Davis, 1975). Inequities in Medicare benefits appear on the basis of income, race, and region. In the southern region of the United States, where 56 percent of the nation's aged nonwhites reside, the disparities between white and nonwhite Medicare beneficiaries persist (Ruther and Dobson, 1981). Furthermore, upper- and middle-class aged can afford to supplement these benefits with private health insurance, and they are better able to meet the increasing costs of copayments and deductibles under Medicare than are the lower-class aged. The Reagan administration and Congress have adopted policies in the Omnibus Budget Reconciliation Act of 1981 (U.S. PL 97-35) and the Tax Equity and Fiscal Responsibility Act of 1982 (U.S. PL 97-248) that will cut Medicare and Medicaid and increase the hardship of medical expenses for the poor elderly.

The effect of the most recent policy shifts in the United States toward slowing the growth in federal Medicaid costs, block grants, and reduced social spending will be to increase existing inequities in programs for the poor across the states. The block grants of the 1970s and 1980s have eased the constraints of categorical funding and of federal requirements, resulting in increased discretion for state government decision making in multiple programs that affect the most economically disadvantaged and vulnerable elderly. A reduction in the federal share of Medicaid, as well as fiscal cutbacks at the state and local levels of government, has resulted in a number of restrictions on services and eligibility in the Medicaid program (see Chapter 7 for discussion). The Medicaid program has widely varying eligibility criteria that are influenced both by political attitudes toward welfare and fiscal capacity (Bovbjerg and Holahan, 1982). Because of the relationship between state welfare criteria and Medicaid eligibility, it was estimated before the first Reagan administration cuts that only about one-half of all people living below the poverty level were eligible for Medicaid (U.S. CBO, 1981; Rowland and Gaus, 1981).

In evaluating the effects of public policy on different classes of citizens, it is important to consider both direct government expenditures, such as Social Security and Medicare, and indirect government expenditures such as federal tax policy (Nelson, 1982). Tax savings can be regarded as a federal expenditure because a reduction in tax liability results in losses in federal revenue (U.S. CBO, 1982b). Both Wilensky (1982) and Nelson (forthcoming) have shown that while direct federal expenditures benefit the poor and low-income individuals, indirect federal expenditures (such as tax credits and tax subsidies) favor the middle- and upper-income groups. In 1982, $43 billion in indirect federal expenditures were allocated largely to middle- and upper-income elderly (Nelson, forthcoming). This alone could pay for the estimated $12.7 billion in "welfare" expenditures for older people, because it is more than three times the total of the elderly's share of program costs for Medicaid, SSI, Title XX, and food stamps.

Bawden and Levy (in Palmer and Sawhill, 1982) analyzed the effects of 1981 federal tax and transfer program changes on different groups, finding that the major reductions initiated by Congress in 1981-1982 are in programs that benefit low-income people (such as food stamps, child nutrition, and welfare). As shown in Table 1.2, approximately 60 percent of the cuts in federal expenditures in FY 1982 were taken from the means-tested programs that comprised only

TABLE 1.2   Estimated Reductions in FY 1984 Outlays for Payments to
Individuals and Families Resulting from 1981 Congressional
Actions

Program, by Type	FY 1984 Baseline Outlays (in billions)	Change in 1984 Outlays (in billions)	%
Social insurance and others			
Social Security (OASDI)	$189.5	$− 3.7	− 2.0%
Unemployment compensation	23.3	− 2.4	−10.3
Trade adjustment assistance	0.7	− 0.5	−71.4
Medicare	67.7	− 1.0	− 1.5
Guaranteed student loans	4.9	− 0.8	−16.3
Subtotal	286.0	− 8.4	− 2.9
Low-income assistance			
Food stamps	14.6	− 1.6	−11.0
Child nutrition program	5.0	− 1.4	−28.0
AFDC	9.8	− 1.3	−13.3
Student financial aid	4.8	− 1.2	−25.0
Medicaid	22.9	− 1.0	− 4.4
Low-income energy assistance	2.9	− 0.8	−27.6
Housing assistance	11.5	− 0.3	− 2.6
Veterans income security	15.4	− 0.1	− 0.6
Supplemental Security Income	8.0	0.3	3.8
Subtotal	94.9	− 7.4	− 7.8
Total	381.0	−15.8	− 4.1

SOURCE: L. Bawden and F. Levy's estimates based on methodology described in Chapter 3 of
The Reagan Experiment. Ed. J.L. Palmer and I.V. Sawhill. Washington, DC:
Urban Institute, 1982, p. 469.

one-quarter of the federal budget (Bawden and Levy in Palmer and
Sawhill, 1982).

An analysis of FY 1983 budget reductions in programs serving
older Americans by the U.S. Senate Special Committee on Aging
(1982) indicates a similar pattern in which the Reagan budget proposed larger cuts (almost two times larger) in the low-income assistance programs for the elderly than in those for the non-means-tested
programs (see Table 1.3).

While programs for the poor, particularly the working poor, have
been drastically cut or eliminated, tax benefits to the middle- and
upper-income strata have been significantly increased. The largest
relative declines in income, resulting from the combined effects of the
tax, welfare, and food stamp changes of 1981, will hit the working poor
the hardest (Bawden and Levy in Palmer and Sawhill, 1982).

TABLE 1.3   Impact of Proposed FY 1983 Reagan Budget Reductions in Programs Serving Older Americans

Non-means-tested Programs	*Millions*
Social Security disability	$ 59.0
Civil Service retirement	$ 489.0
Military retirement	$ 56.0
Veterans disability compensation	$ 146.0
Railroad retirement	$ 80.0
Transportation	$ 467.4
Medicare	$ 2,498.0
Older Americans Act	$ 77.5
USDA commodities	$ 9.2
Subtotal	$ 3,882.1
Low-income Assistance Programs	
Supplemental Security Income	$ 286.0
Veterans pensions	$ 62.0
Food stamps	$ 2,300.0
Low-income energy assistance	$ 575.0
Medicaid	$ 2,911.0
Senior community services employment	$ 277.1
Social services block grant	$ 426.0
Community Services Block Grant	$ 248.0
Legal services	$ 241.0
Housing	$ 428.0
Weatherization	$ 144.0
Subtotal	$ 7,898.1
Total	$11,789.2

SOURCE: U.S. Senate, Special Committee on Aging. *The Proposed Fiscal Year 1983 Budget: What It Means for Older Americans.* Washington, DC: U.S. Government Printing Office, March 1982.

References

Advisory Commission on Intergovernmental Relations (ACIR). *Recent Trends in Federal and State Aid to Local Governments.* Washington, DC: ACIR, 1980a.
———. *Significant Features of Fiscal Federalism, 1979-80.* Washington, DC: ACIR, 1980b.
Alford, R. *Health Care Politics.* Chicago: University of Chicago Press, 1976.
Ball, R. M. *The Financial Condition of the Social Security Program.* New York: Study Group on Social Security, 1982.
Bovbjerg, R. R., and J. Holahan. *Medicaid in the Reagan Era.* Washington, DC: Urban Institute, 1982.

Collins, R. "A Comparative Approach to Political Sociology." In *State and Society*. Ed. R. Bendix et al. Boston: Little, Brown, 1968.

Connolly, W. E. *The Bias of Pluralism*. New York: Atherton, 1969.

Cook, F. L. *Who Should Be Helped? Support for Social Services*. Beverly Hills, CA: Sage, 1979.

Crystal, S. *America's Old Age Crisis*. New York: Basic Books, 1982.

Davis, K. "Equal Treatment and Unequal Benefits: The Medicare Program." *Milbank Memorial Fund Quarterly/Health and Society*, 53, No. 4 (1975), 449-488.

Estes, C. L. "Community Planning for the Elderly: A Study of Goal Displacement." *Journal of Gerontology*, 29, No. 6 (November 1974), 684-691.

———. *The Aging Enterprise*. San Francisco: Jossey-Bass, 1979.

———. "Austerity and Aging." *International Journal of Health Services*, 12, No. 4 (1982), 573-584.

———. "Social Security: The Social Construction of a Crisis." *Milbank Memorial Fund Quarterly/Health and Society*, forthcoming.

Harris, L. *The Myth and Reality of Aging in America*. Washington, DC: National Council on the Aging, 1975.

Institute of Medicine. *Health Care in a Context of Civil Rights*. Washington, DC: National Academy Press, 1981.

Johnson Foundation, Inc. *Welfare Policy in the United States*. Racine, WI: Johnson Foundation, 1982.

Klemmack, D. L., and L. L. Roff. "Predicting General Comparative Support for Government's Providing Benefits to Older Persons." *Gerontologist*, 21, No. 6 (1981), 592-599.

Miller, S. M. "The Political Economy of Social Problems: From the Sixties to the Seventies." *Social Problems*, 24, No. 1 (1976), 131-141.

Myles, J. F. "The Aged and the Welfare State: An Essay in Political Demography." Paper presented at the International Sociological Association, Research Committee on Aging, Paris, July 8-9, 1981.

National Council on the Aging (NCOA). *Aging in the Eighties: America in Transition*. Report of a 1981 poll by Louis Harris & Associates. Washington, DC: NCOA, 1981.

Nelson, G. "Social Class and Public Policy for the Elderly." *Social Science Review*, 56, No. 1 (1982), 85-107.

———. "Tax Expenditures for the Elderly." *Gerontologist*, forthcoming.

Newcomer, R. J., C. Harrington, C. L. Estes, and P. R. Lee. "State Adjustments in Medicaid Program Policies and Expenditures: Implications for Health and Human Services for the Elderly." Working Paper No. 20. San Francisco: Aging Health Policy Center, University of California, 1982.

Omenn, G. S., and R. P. Nathan. "What's Behind Those Block Grants in Health?" *New England Journal of Medicine*, 306 (April 29, 1982), 1057-1060.

Palmer, J. L., and I. V. Sawhill, eds. *The Reagan Experiment*. Washington, DC: Urban Institute, 1982.

Pechman, J. A., ed. *Setting National Priorities: The 1982 Budget*. Washington, DC: Brookings Institution, 1981.

Rahn, R. W., and K. D. Simonson. "Tax Policy for Retirement Programs." In *Retirement Income: Who Gets How Much and Who Pays?* National Journal Issues Book. Washington, DC: Government Research Corporation, 1980.

Ross, D., and W. Birdsall. *Social Security and Pensions: Programs of Equity and Security.* Special Study on Economic Change. Washington, DC: U.S. Congress Joint Economic Committee, 1980.

Rowland, D., and C. R. Gaus. "Medicaid Eligibility and Benefits: Current Policies and Future Choices." Paper presented at the 1981 Commonwealth Fund Forum, Lake Bluff, Illinois, August 9-12, 1981.

Ruther, M., and A. Dobson. "Equal Treatment and Unequal Benefits: A Reexamination of the Use of Medicare Services by Race, 1967-1976." *Health Care Financing Review,* No. 36 (1981), 55-83.

Samuelson, R. J. "Busting the U.S. Budget: The Costs of an Aging America." *National Journal,* 10, No. 7 (1978), 256-260.

———. "Benefit Programs for the Elderly Off Limits to Federal Budget Cutters?" *National Journal,* 13, No. 40 (October 1981), 1757-1762.

Titmuss, R. "The Role of Redistribution in Social Policy." *Social Security Bulletin,* 28 (June 1965), 14-20.

Tussing, A. "The Dual Welfare System." In *Social Realities.* Ed. L. Horowitz and C. Levy. New York: Harper & Row, 1971.

U.S. Congressional Budget Office (CBO). *Medicaid: Choices for 1982 and Beyond.* Washington, DC: CBO, 1981.

———. *Balancing the Federal Budget and Limiting Federal Spending: Constitutional and Statutory Approaches.* Washington, DC: CBO, 1982a.

———. *Tax Expenditures: Budget Control Options and Five-Year Budget Projections for Fiscal Years 1983-1987.* Washington, DC: CBO, 1982b.

U.S. General Accounting Office. *Perspective on Income Security and Social Services and an Agenda for Analysis.* Washington, DC: GAO, 1981.

U.S. House, Select Committee on Aging. Hearing: *Poverty Among America's Aged,* August 9. Washington, DC: U.S. Government Printing Office, 1978.

U.S. House, Committee on Ways and Means, Subcommittee on Social Security. Hearing: *Elimination of Minimum Social Security Benefit Under Public Law 97-35,* September 10. Washington, DC: U.S. Government Printing Office, 1981a.

U.S. House, Select Committee on Aging, Subcommittee on Retirement Income and Employment. Hearing: *Guns versus Butter: How the Military Budget Affects Aging Americans,* July 24. Washington, DC: U.S. Government Printing Office, 1981b.

U.S. House, Select Committee on Aging. *Every Ninth American.* Washington, DC: U.S. Government Printing Office, 1982.

U.S. Public Law 97-34. Economic Recovery Tax Act of 1981. Washington, DC: U.S. Government Printing Office, 1981.

U.S. Public Law 97-35. Omnibus Reconciliation Act of 1981. Washington, DC: U.S. Government Printing Office, 1981.

U.S. Public Law 97-248. Tax Equity and Fiscal Responsibility Act of 1982. Washington, DC: U.S. Government Printing Office, 1982.

U.S. Senate, Committee on Governmental Affairs. Hearings: *President's Federalism Initiative,* February 4 and March 11, 16, 18. Washington, DC: U.S. Government Printing Office, 1982a.

U.S. Senate, Special Committee on Aging. *The Proposed Fiscal Year 1983 Budget: What It Means for Older Americans.* Washington, DC: U.S. Government Printing Office, 1982b.

U.S. Social Security Administration (SSA). Office of Governmental Affairs. *Annual Report to the Congress for Fiscal Year 1981*. Baltimore: U.S. Department of Health and Human Services, 1982.

Walker, A. "Towards a Political Economy of Old Age." *Ageing and Society*, 1, No. 1 (1981), 73-94.

Walker, D. *Toward a Functioning Federalism*. Cambridge, MA: Winthrop, 1981.

Weber, M. "Class, Status and Party." In *From Max Weber: Essays in Sociology*. Ed. and trans. H. H. Gerth and C. W. Mills. New York: Oxford University Press, 1946.

Wickenden, E. *Thoughts on the First Concurrent Budget Resolution*. New York: Study Group on Social Security, 1981.

Wilensky, G. R. "Government and the Financing of Health Care." *Government and Health*, 72, No. 2 (May 1982), 202-207.

Wilensky, H. *Welfare State and Equality: Structural and Ideological Roots of Expenditures*. Berkeley: University of California Press, 1975.

CHAPTER 2

GOVERNMENTAL RESPONSIBILITY
Issues of Reform and Federalism

Carroll L. Estes
Lenore Gerard

Decentralization of program and fiscal responsibility is a central part of contemporary conservative philosophy, as are efforts to reduce the federal role and responsibility for social needs. The notion of federalism that underlies the present-day decentralization debate is as old as the U.S. itself (Beer, 1982), and controversy about its form and function is heard among officials and citizens at all levels of government. Five consistent and important themes have emerged concerning the role of government: (1) the delineation of national, state, and local responsibilities; (2) the capacity and structural incentives of government (and of different governmental levels); (3) equity and the role of government; (4) accountability; and (5) democratic participation and the distribution of power. The purpose of this chapter is to describe these central issues, which are basic to consideration of the shifting of governmental responsibility for the elderly as examined in subsequent chapters of this book.

The intensity of the contemporary debate about the appropriate role of the government and of the private sector is illustrated by the large number of political observers and policymakers calling for major reforms in the scope and direction of federal domestic social policy. One interesting categorization of the contemporary perspectives on

Authors' Note: The authors wish to acknowledge the invaluable contribution of A. E. Benjamin.

reform of the federal aid system has been developed by Nathan (1982, p. 235), who identified four leading schools of thought:

(1) The "Henny Penny School of federalism" which holds that the sky is falling, thus we urgently need to adopt basic institutionalized and programmatic reforms.

(2) The block grant approach, which began under Nixon and is now proposed to be extended into new . . . functional areas.

(3) The turn-back school of federal aid reform, which is almost as old as money and equally hard to deflate.

(4) The idea that budget reduction is reform, which may indeed be the real Ronald Reagan position on the federal aid system.

Nathan (1982) notes that the Advisory Committee on Intergovernmental Relations (ACIR) represents a view of intergovernmental relations as a significant problem in light of which the federal government has even been described by Walker (1981) as a "Leviathan run amuck." The perception that the federal government is "the problem" has, like all such perceptions and definitions, enormous political and economic consequences — depending on whose definition prevails. Beer (1982) observes that, beginning with the Nixon administration, intergovernmental "reform" through new federalism was nothing less than the first major attempt to repeal the Great Society. In Nixon's time, however, the objective was "not so much to reduce overall public expenditure as to decentralize the decisions that directed it" (U.S. House, 1981a, p. 197).

One of the crucial issues in the ongoing struggle over governmental reform has been whether budget cutting is the sole aim of the reform or whether a reconsideration of organization and shared responsibility is included. Nathan (1982) and others (Nathan et al., 1982; Omenn and Nathan, 1982) have challenged the idea that cutbacks in funding are in themselves a viable reform at a time when there is a need for federal leadership and responsibility in the interest of the national welfare. Among those who agree that reform should not constitute merely cutbacks and more state discretion is the intergovernmental lobby, consisting of elected officials of state and local governments such as governors, mayors, county supervisors, city managers, and state legislators. They argue for a clearer definition of the federal role and responsibility in key areas of national concern, most often in the basic areas of income and health policy — the need for which they argue is triggered largely by economic policies and other circumstances that are beyond the control of state and local government (U.S. House, 1981a; Matheson, 1982).

Defining National, State, and Local Responsibilities

The issue of reform raises the fundamental question of national purpose and goals. What are the national goals and how can these goals be achieved (Rivlin in U.S. House, 1981a)? This question has arisen sharply in the debate on national health and welfare policies, particularly with regard to the Medicaid and Aid to Families with Dependent Children (AFDC) programs. There has been a continuing dispute about whether a new federalism strategy can in fact realize national goals other than those related to a reduced federal role in domestic social policy. Reagan and Sanzone (1981, p. 148) have identified as a major myth the "belief that national goals can be achieved by decentralizing subnational choice and policy priorities within broad federal parameters." This they call the "myth of decentralization."

One of the classical arguments used by statesman Daniel Webster in favor of national (or central) responsibility is summarized by Beer (1982, p. 18): "Where the effects of government activity within one jurisdiction [e.g., a state or locality] spill-over into other jurisdictions, there is a case for central intervention to promote this activity if it is beneficial, or to restrain it if it is harmful." Advanced by Webster as a criterion of what is in the national good, this spill-over argument was joined by another line of reasoning to justify federal action. "The other consideration," Webster stated, "is that the United States have the means [while] the states have no abundant and easy source of public income" (Beer, 1982, p. 18). His point was "to show what the federal government must do by demonstrating what the states cannot do" (Beer, 1982, p. 17). Further, Webster argued that the Constitution was not a compact between the states, or of the governments of the states, but rather among "the people of the United States in the aggregate." It is "the people's constitution, the people's government, made for the people, made by the people and answerable to the people" (Beer, 1982, p. 20).

As described by Samuel Beer (1982, p. 20), today's federal system is the result of "three waves of centralization, launched respectively

by Abraham Lincoln, Franklin Roosevelt, and Lyndon Johnson."
Each emerged in the context of crises of the past: Lincoln's, from the
crisis of sectionalism; Roosevelt's, from the crisis of industrialism;
and Johnson's, from the crisis of racism. Each gave rise to a distinctive public philosophy shared by a broad coalition, and each shaped
intergovernmental roles in a different fashion.

Between 1861 and 1930, in a period of "dual federalism," the
dominance of the federal government was distinguished primarily by
its role in the military, foreign policy, monetary, and banking areas
(Walker, 1981). The national government served as a regulator of the
economic system, leaving most public services to the states. As
described in Chapter 3, this relatively separate pattern of federal
responsibility was to be altered considerably over the following four
decades.

Some of the major arguments justifying the evolving federal role
have been that federal grants (1) provide for an equalization in the
level of public services among states and localities; (2) provide for a
level of services that the national interest requires; (3) reflect the
capacity of the national government to collect taxes; and (4) involve
national administrators, raising the overall level of performance and
competence (Hale and Palley, 1981).

The economic recession and crises of the 1970s and 1980s present a
challenge to the federal system precisely at the time when the functions of the three levels of government have been described as "no
longer distinguishable" (Hale and Palley, 1981). There has been re-
newed political and ideological conflict about what are appropriately
private versus public societal concerns and responsibilities — this
following an almost two-decade hiatus in serious debate about national purpose and federal aid in a constitutional context (Walker,
1981). According to Walker, the necessity for rethinking federalism
has been prompted by many factors: Issues in the private sector have
become politicized; an increasing array of social as well as economic
issues have become politicized at the national level; there is an
increasing influence of lobbyists and interest groups on the federal
government; electoral participation is decreasing; and there is too
much lawmaking and too little congressional oversight. According to
the ACIR, all of these factors are said to have led to an increasingly
overburdened and dysfunctional federalism "wherein intergovernmental relations have become more pervasive, more expansive and
less manageable, less effective, and above all less accountable"

(Walker, 1981, p. 225). Thus, on entrance into the decade of the 1980s, actors from the intergovernmental lobby were articulating their strategy for change in the direction of fewer federal strings and clarity in the assumption of national responsibility by the federal government.

Contrary to this strategy for change is the Reagan administration's new federalism initiative, which, in its most extreme form, challenges the idea that there is a national responsibility for meeting the basic human needs in health, income, housing, or welfare. As envisioned by David Stockman, director of the Office of Management and Budget, the new federalism strategy would put an end to the idea that citizens have "any basic right to legal services or any other kinds of service" (Stockman in U.S. Senate, 1982a, p. 363).

A companion goal of Reagan administration proposals is apparently abandonment of what are perceived to be redistributive policies of federal programs that address inequities across age, sex, racial, ethnic, or geographic boundaries. As bluntly stated by Stockman (in U.S. Senate, 1982a, p. 68), the federalism initiative with its focus on decentralizing decision making in the nation's welfare system "would put an end to any hope, at least within this century, to the grand redistributionist dreams of the guaranteed annual income advocates."

While much of the testimony to date favors a decentralization strategy with an emphasis on state-level decision making, two fundamental, overriding concerns have emerged: First, how uniformly committed will the states be to equity, social justice, and racial equality; second, do the states have the fiscal capacity and adequate resources to deal effectively with their program responsibilities and to assume full responsibility for a range of programs in welfare, education, transportation, social services, and health?

Fiscal Capacity and Structural Incentives of Government

Closely linked to the issues of what should be the national, state, and local responsibilities are issues of the capacity of respective governmental levels to undertake particular types of responsibility. For allocations of authority among governmental levels to work, it is important that governments possess those capacities appropriate to their responsibilities. Governments must possess the revenue capacity, the capability to plan and manage policies and programs, and the political will necessary to carry them out. There are great differences in the fiscal capacities of different states to support programs. For example, because state governments do not tax as heavily as — or generally possess a tax structure as progressive as — the federal government, their capacity for generating new revenues is limited (Reagan and Sanzone, 1981). Many states, moreover, are viewed as having inadequate administrative "infrastructures," as being short on sophisticated management techniques, and as having limited capabilities in the conduct of policy analysis and planning.

There is also some evidence that state and local governments may have less political will to make decisions in the "public interest" than the federal government. The wide variations across states in health policies (on Medicaid, for example) suggest significant inequities in program outputs (such as infant mortality) across states. The argument is not that, if freed from federal constraints, every state would establish standards for health programs that are certain to fall below former federal standards. Rather, it is that some states will surely exceed some federal standard, but that others (perhaps many others) will fall far below what is generally considered adequate. Many argue also that state governments are more susceptible to interest group pressures and narrow conceptions of the public good.

Two authors, David and Kantor (1981), have provided additional insight into the meaning of federalism and the outcomes that would be anticipated under conditions of increased decentralization. They point out that federalism is a source of "policy bias" — that federalism is more than a process of intergovernmental decision making (about which interest group theorists have written so much). Federalism policies, such as those that give increasing responsibility through decentralization, bias the types of substantive policies that are likely to receive support at different governmental levels. This occurs because "federalism . . . is not only a system of distributing power . . . and specifying jurisdictions . . . it is also a constitutive arrangement which defines the ecological systems within which the government units must make decisions on questions of substantive policy" (David and Kantor, 1981, p. 6). They point to the interests that emerge not only from a process of decision making but also from the contextual structure of the political system itself.

Policy bias can also be understood by an examination of the economic systems that operate on and influence different levels of government, particularly the different positions of federal, state, and local governments in this respect (David and Kantor, 1981). Cities operate in a competitive market environment and thus favor policies that promote developments of a revenue-producing nature. The key issue here is that, because of their competitive market environments and their limited influence on the domestic economy, cities will tend not to respond to redistributive policy issues. It is the federal government, on the other hand, that has the opportunity (and greater degree of autonomy) to be responsive to redistributive policies pertaining to social welfare.

It is important to consider the constraints operating at different levels of government that are likely to influence policy outcomes. The flexibility of private business to relocate their firms and the potential economic impact of their decisions impose tax limits that insulate local tax systems from political challenge and render them particularly vulnerable to the economic constraints and needs of private corporations (Alford and Friedland, 1975; Friedland et al., 1977; Estes, 1979). Can states or localities, given their uneven revenue-producing capacity and natural resources (see Chapter 5), meet the demands for an equitable — as well as efficient — system of services in health, housing, transit, and social welfare for the elderly or for others?

In 1978, states (taken as a group) spent a higher percentage of their budgets on health care than did the federal government, even while absolute federal expenditure for health grew to more than double state and local health expenditure combined (Clarke, 1981). Additional indication of state capacity is the considerable increase in the conduct of policy analysis and its use in policy deliberations and decisions (Lee and Staffeldt, 1977). Regarding inequities and political will, however, little counterevidence has emerged to challenge the argument that the states are highly vulnerable to special interest groups (such as insurance companies, hospitals, and physicians) and that the result is wide program variation across states, usually in response to provider — not consumer — interests (Vladeck, 1979; Estes and Lee, 1981).

Considerations of state capacity to assume responsibility for the elderly (and particularly for the long term care policies for the near-poor and poor elderly) must acknowledge the fiscal context within which state and local governments are operating, the interrelationship between state and federal economic conditions and policies, and the real (and growing) revenue disparities across different states and geographic regions (U.S. House, 1981a). The contention of the National Governors' Association (U.S. Senate, 1982a) that income security should be a federal responsibility is predicated on solid recognition of these facts. Significantly, as Governor Matheson of Utah has stated, states are not in control of the key economic policies that vitally affect poverty and the levels of unemployment (and thus benefit demands) in the states. Further, resources are unequally distributed across the states. Some have argued that a hands-off federal aid policy is irresponsible, given that the states and the welfare of state residents may be drastically affected by changes in industrial and manufacturing bases, in gas and oil prices and demand, and in federal policies associated with them or with other aspects of the economy.

Equity and the Role of Government

In examining the basic failures of federalism, the ACIR has also raised the question of whether the "federal aid system as a whole protects the interests of the needy or equalizes levels of public service" (U.S. House, 1981a, p. 38). Basic questions of equity tend to be ignored as special interest lobbies and bureaucrats garnish benefits for their particular goals.

Issues of social justice, equity, and the federal role are not new ones in American history but have been restimulated by the new federalism strategy advanced under the Reagan administration. Two earlier periods of crisis in American society, in the 1930s and the 1960s, witnessed unprecedented federal intervention in areas previously left to he private sector or to state and local government. "Live memory of the Great Depression created a broad consensus that the state must assume responsibility for maintaining prosperity as well as for protecting individual citizens against the inevitable insecurities of life in a market economy" (Tobin, 1981, p. 11). In addition to protecting the individual, federal intervention has also been justified as a means of achieving a stable and growing economy. In this regard, the federal role in assuring a minimum level of health and welfare arises from the needs of society to maintain a population of sufficient health and well-being to carry out its work and to maintain a minimum standard of living to assure the maintenance of the social and political order (Piven and Cloward, 1982; O'Connor, 1973; Wilensky, 1975).

Thus, the issue of equity has been defined as relevant both to the collective social good and to the good of the individual.

Many have argued that the federal government is in a more fiscally advantageous position for promoting redistributive objectives (Reagan and Sanzone, 1981; David and Kantor, 1981). The preceding discussion on fiscal capacity and structural incentives of different levels of government raises several important questions concerning the issue of equity and government responsibility: How does policy structure affect equity? Does state discretion augment inequities to an unacceptable degree in particular areas? How do state and local fiscal conditions and capacity affect equitable treatment of all citizens?

Equity is directly related to the concept of distributive justice. Historically, resources have been distributed (or rationed) on the basis of different criteria, such as deservingness, supply and demand of the market, and people's needs (Chapter 3 discusses the historical response and constraints of government intervention for the aged population in this regard). Rawls's (1971) concept of social justice is based on the criteria of need — that is, that resources should be allocated to those individuals who have the greatest need. However, in the United States two divergent views have continually struggled against one another for supremacy. First is the notion that an individual has an equal opportunity to acquire a fair share. Second is the notion that an individual has an inalienable right to a reasonable share of a nation's wealth (Ryan, 1982). In other words, regardless of the vicissitudes of life that may impinge on opportunity, many Americans have defined certain "rights" of citizenship, such as health care, education, adequate income, or fair employment (Reagan and Sanzone, 1981). Health care, in particular, has continued to be a salient policy issue because, unlike many others, it directly involves matters of life and death.

Consistent with the deliberations reflected in the preliminary draft report of the President's Commission for the Study of Ethical Problems in Biomedical and Behavioral Research (U.S. President's Commission, 1982), equity in health care arises as an important societal consideration for at least two reasons: welfare and opportunity. Welfare is involved, for it is assumed that "health care promotes personal well being" and avoids the "loss of life." The same could be said of income. Opportunity is involved because health is necessary to enable the pursuit of one's opportunities and life's plans. As the President's Commission observed, "a society's commitment to health care [equity] reflects some of its most basic attitudes about what it is to be a member of the human community" (U.S. President's Commission, 1982; Scitovsky, 1982). In noting that "society has a moral obligation to insure equitable access to health care for all at burdens that are not excessive," the Commission did not argue, however, that this responsibility inherently lay with government (Scitovsky, 1982). Equity of access is defined here as the distribution of services on the basis of people's need rather than on the basis of race, income, or place of residence (Aday, 1980).

A central equity issue is the assurance of equal treatment and equal access of all members of the society to at least a minimal level of health and welfare across the varying political, economic, and cultural boundaries that characterize the more than 38,000 jurisdictions composed of states, counties, cities, and townships in the United States. Although the differential treatment of the poor and nonpoor was somewhat abated by the Great Society commitment to access and equity, genuine substantial concern with these issues had all but vanished from federal public policy by the mid-1970s (Lewis, 1982). The impact of inflation on medical care prices and government spending has shifted the policy focus from access to cost containment. As Vladeck (1981, p. 78) observes, "There is no question but that, to date, cost containment narrowly defined has had a disproportionately adverse effect on the poor and members of minority groups."

Significant consequences of and concerns about block grant decentralization are the implications for equity. The wide discretion that block grants and broad legislative powers provide the states is likely to augment inequities in the same programs across the different states. This, in turn, makes it impossible to assure uniform benefits for a targeted population (such as poor elders or children) across different jurisdictions with so many varying state approaches. The result of the large-scale shift to block grants in health and social services, combined with the across-the-board expenditure reductions for fiscal years 1982 and 1983 for the block-granted programs, has been increased pressure on state and local governments to underwrite program costs at a time when many states, cities, and counties are also under extreme pressure to curb rising expenditures. Because the most disadvantaged (including the poor aged) are heavily dependent on state-determined benefits such as Medicaid, block-granted social services, and SSI supplementation, they are particularly vulnerable to swings and cutbacks in state policies during periods of economic austerity.

Reflecting this concern, the issue of "equal access to care of minimal quality across communities and states provided much of the impetus for state and then federal involvement in social services" (Gutowski and Koshel, 1982, p. 312). The central point is that the states have unequal resources and political dispositions that result in persons with similar problems being treated differently in different states (Nathan et al., 1982; Reagan and Sanzone, 1981; Estes, 1979).

Accountability

Many are concerned that national objectives and priorities (and liberal gains of the past) may be lost with the devolution of authority unless specified and regularized mechanisms of accountability are instituted. Schultze (1971) goes further to argue that incentives are required to ensure decision making at subnational levels compatible with central program goals. The challenge and the central dilemma of decentralization are striking a balance between the degree of state and local discretion necessary to plan responsively for and meet the needs of the population, and the requisite accountability to ensure performance congruent with national objectives concerning those needs (Estes and Noble, 1978).

To be accountable is to be capable of providing a reasonable explanation of what actions have been undertaken and what resulted. In this context, accountability will not be satisfied with a simple dollar or effort input-output analysis; it requires an analysis of effect, effectiveness, and impact as well. In a broad sense, "accountability can encompass such issues as fiscal responsibility, equitable treatment, the correspondence of programmatic focus and legislative intent, the quality of program management and implementation, and the effectiveness of the program" (U.S. General Accounting Office [GAO], 1982b, p. 91).

Accountability can occur on several levels, involving the federal, state, or local government, in which different types of grants operate, and the service providers who receive the grants. Accountability also requires a determination of political priorities and a balance of national objectives with state and local performance (Chelimsky, 1982). The extent to which federal accountability is possible depends in part on the structure of financing associated with given funding streams and programs.

Accountability is different for each of the three major grant types:

(1) *Categorical grants* provide funding for specialized purposes and narrowly defined activities; the federal role in administering them is active (for example, specifying application requirements, negotiating awards, monitoring the progress of the funded activities, and evaluating effects).

(2) *Block grants* provide funding for a wide range of activities within a broadly defined functional area. The federal role is minimized, and considerable discretion is given to the recipient government in identifying problems, designing programs, and allocating resources.

(3) *General revenue sharing* provides funding to local governments for almost any use, including initiating new programs, stabilizing local taxes, and generally supporting government programs. The federal government imposes almost no conditions on the recipients beyond requirements to hold proposed-use hearings, conduct audits, and comply with civil rights requirements.

As described in Chapter 3, the first major attempt to slow the growth of categorical programs and to shift the emphasis to general purpose state and local government was the Nixon administration move to initiate block grants and revenue sharing in the 1970s. This shift from categorical to block grant funding was extended by the Omnibus Budget Reconciliation Act of 1981 (U.S. PL 97-35), which consolidated more than fifty categorical and two former block grants into nine new block grant programs.

The discretion and funding available to state governments through these block grants affect available resources for programs of import, including the provision of community mental health services, home health services, emergency medical services, and hypertension control. The nine new block grants created in 1981 differ from the earlier ones in their increased emphasis on state flexibility and discretion in planning, spending, and reporting. In contrast to some of the earlier block grants (such as Community Development Block Grants), all of the block grants adopted in 1981 designated state, not local, governments as recipients.

In keeping with the Office of Management and Budget (OMB) policy of exercising as little federal control over the 1981 block grants as possible, the Department of Health and Human Services (HHS) has minimized its oversight and regulatory authority, essentially allowing grantees discretion in the form and content of applications and annual reports. Further, federal agencies have been silent on the subject of whether national cross-cutting requirements such as fair labor standards and political activities constraints apply to the new grants.

Two methods aimed at achieving accountability have been targeting and evaluation. While the Omnibus Budget Reconciliation Act of 1981 (U.S. PL 97-35) contains definitions of target populations, it generally does not link these to a specific requirement to target funds (U.S. GAO, 1982b). Naming target populations in the legislation does not assure that funds will be used for those populations unless specified by federal regulation. In six of nine block grants, targeting is discretionary and ambiguous. Only three block grants — Home Energy, Community Services, and Maternal/Child Health — clearly identify and target funds on the basis of low-income criteria. Furthermore, efforts to assess targeting nationwide are likely to be impaired by the variable quality and scope of data reported across states. In the absence of uniform data, it will be difficult to determine the amount of targeting implemented on a nationwide basis under these block grants.

Evaluation activities have traditionally been the primary federal mechanism for achieving accountability. However, both the block grant changes in 1981 and the new federalism philosophy raise a question about what the federal evaluation role will be. The 1981 act shifts the decision for evaluation to the states, but it in no way assures that states will, in fact, assume this responsibility (U.S. GAO, 1982b).

The Reagan administration's model of accountability assigns the decision and responsibility for assuring appropriate and equitable use of national public funds to the states and localities. There appears to be minimal interest at the federal level in the accountability of grantees directly to the federal government, even as it remains unclear what precisely the federal oversight role will be under the 1981 block grants. The OMB has suggested that because the block grants represent a major shift of responsibility and accountability to the states, "there is far less need for extensive federal data collection, monitoring and evaluation systems" (Stockman in U.S. Senate, 1982a, p. 112; U.S. GAO, 1982b).

Since the new block grants do not require uniform national standards for evaluation or data collection, it is improbable that national studies of the use and impact of the allocations of federal tax monies will be undertaken. In two of the block grants — Social Services and Education — evaluation activities are considered to be administrative costs and therefore must compete with other needs.

Thus, the question is raised of whether there will be an authoritative source of nationwide data on the nature of the block-granted programs, the levels and types of services funded, and their impact on the problems they are intended to resolve (U.S. GAO, 1982b). Meaningful policy analysis and the assessment of the impact of policy shifts may further be impaired by recent and proposed reductions in federal research expenditures, national data base resources, and statistical programs (U.S. House, 1982a, 1982b).

Power and Participation

The allocation of governmental responsibility for the elderly raises important questions about how power is distributed and exercised — that is, issues of democratic participation. One of the major arguments of contemporary would-be reformers is that centralized government has distanced itself from the people. Nixon's new federalism of the 1970s and Reagan's new federalism of the 1980s both have utilized the imagery of returning power to "the people" by shifting government responsibilities "closer" to home through decentralized, block-granted programs and reduced governmental intrusion. While the key questions involve who benefits and who loses from such reforms, there are also important questions about who makes the decisions and how democratic and participatory are the processes invoked with decentralization. Is more democratic participation automatically associated with the transfer of primary program responsibility from the federal to the state and local levels?

Both revenue sharing and block grants have redistributed political power, largely diminishing that held by national policymakers in Congress (who more closely controlled the categorical programs), while increasing that of public officials at the state and local levels. Less obvious, perhaps, but even more important, these decentralized programs also shift power from Congress more directly to the White House (Nathan et al., 1975; Banfield, 1961). As the 1980s have shown, the power of the presidency and its Office of Management and Budget should not be underestimated. To the extent that decentralization policies tend to shift control over the fate of programs and resources affecting the states and communities from Congress to the White House, the decentralization ideology of increased citizen participation may be more mirage than reality.

The redistribution of power among federal, state, and local officials that results from new federalism policies is an issue of major political importance. Equally important is the degree to which decentralization may increase the politically motivated, rather than the need-based, determination of priorities and resource allocations and thus augment private special interest influence. This would occur at the expense of broader-based political parties or citizen groups, which may have more power on a national scale than in the multiple jurisdictions and geographic units involved in decentralized programs.

Lowi (1971) has argued that the decentralization of power to localities functions primarily to remove the policy process from the focus of large national movements, resulting in a transfer of public conflict to private arenas in which national movements have little influence and critical moral issues and goals may be more easily converted into negotiable and administrative issues. Lowi's key argument is that decentralization tends to plug government into the interest group system, resulting in maintenance of the status quo. Further, Lowi credits decentralization with fostering the development of the trade association type of interest group in order to regularize relations among competitors in the same industry or profession and to protect their interests so that they are not compromised through nonnational, decentralized policies and activities. Trade associations supplant the uncertainty of unregulated competition with the certainty of closed and protective administrative processes, jointly worked out with government officials. However, Lowi notes that the danger of such trade organizations and of the multiple, varied, decentralized, and almost invisible ways of working their influence is that important value questions may be removed from public view and settled privately.

From this perspective, the problem is that decentralization may actually discourage public participation, with public policy formed largely through the partnership of nonelected state and local administrators together with private sector representatives and agencies. To the extent that block grant and other decentralized policies are formulated by bureaucrats, lobbyists, and other private interests, decentralization actually reduces political (electoral) accountability for public policy. In sum, while the principle of decentralization has been lauded as enhancing pluralistic political participation, automatic assertions appear unwarranted concerning the fairness and equal opportunity that decentralization affords for that participation.

Much of the literature on public and private responsibility and new federalism deals with political issues, beliefs, and ideologies and their relationship to the tension in intergovernmental relations, power conflicts between levels of government, and different goals of interest groups and private citizens. Although Reagan and Sanzone (1981) stress the importance of an empirical examination of federalism because its conceptualization has been ambiguous, complex, and contradictory, the literature reflects relatively little attention to objective evaluation of policy outcomes and the impacts of federalism. It is the aim of the remaining chapters to provide an empirical basis for examining the content and consequences of evolving federal, state, and local policies, particularly as they relate to the health and well-being of the elderly.

References

Aday, L. A., R. Andersen, and G. V. Fleming. *Health Care in the U.S.: Equitable for Whom?* Beverly Hills, CA: Sage, 1980.

Alford, R., and R. Friedland. "Political Participation and Public Policy." *Annual Review of Sociology,* 1 (1975), 429-479.

Banfield, E. C. *Political Influence.* New York: Macmillan, 1961.

Beer, S. M. "Federalism: Lessons of the Past, Choices for the Future." In *Federalism: Making the System Work.* Ed. S. M. Beer et al. Washington, DC: Center for National Policy, 1982.

Break, G. F. *Financing Government in a Federal System.* Washington, DC: Brookings Institution, 1980.

Chelimsky, E. "Making Block Grants Accountable." In *Policy Studies Review Annual,* Vol. 6. Ed. R. C. Rist. Beverly Hills, CA: Sage, 1982.

Clarke, G. J. "The Role of the States in the Delivery of Health Services." *American Journal of Public Health,* 71, No. 1, Supplement (January 1981), 59-69.

David, S. M., and P. Kantor. "Urban Policy in the Federal Systems: A Reconceptualization of Federalism." Paper presented at the annual meeting of the American Political Science Association, New York, September 25, 1981.

Davis, K., and C. Schoen. *Health and War on Poverty: A Ten-Year Appraisal.* Washington, DC: Brookings Institution, 1978.

Estes, C. L. *The Aging Enterprise.* San Francisco: Jossey-Bass, 1979.

———. "Social Security: The Social Construction of a Crisis." *Milbank Memorial Fund Quarterly/Health and Society,* forthcoming.

——— and P. R. Lee. "Policy Shifts and Their Impact on Health Care for Elderly Persons." *Western Journal of Medicine,* 135, No. 6 (1981), 511-517.

Estes, C. L., and M. L. Noble. "Paperwork and the Older Americans Act: Problems of Implementing Accountability." Staff information paper for use by the U.S.

Senate Special Committee on Aging. Washington, DC: U.S. Government Printing Office, 1978.

Friedland, R., R.R. Alford, and F.F. Piven. "The Political Management of the Urban Fiscal Crisis." Paper presented at the annual meeting of the American Sociological Association, Chicago, September 1977.

Gutowski, M.F., and J.J. Koshel. "Social Services." In *The Reagan Experiment.* Ed. J.L. Palmer and I.V. Sawhill. Washington, DC: Urban Institute, 1982.

Hale, G.E., and M.L. Palley. *The Politics of Federal Grants.* Washington, DC: Congressional Quarterly Press, 1981.

Institute of Medicine. *Health Care in a Context of Civil Rights.* Washington, DC: National Academy Press, 1981.

Lee, R.D., and R.T. Staffeldt. "Executive and Legislative Use of Policy Analysis in the State Budgetary Process." *Policy Analysis,* 3, No. 3 (1977), 395-405.

Lewis, I.J. "Evolution of Federal Policy on Access to Health Care, 1965-80." Paper presented at the New York Academy of Medicine, April 29-30, 1982.

Lowi, T. *The Politics of Disorder.* New York: Basic Books, 1971.

Matheson, S.M. Presentation at the 14th Annual Conference of State Medicaid Directors, Salt Lake City, April 26, 1982.

————. "'Reforming' the Federal Grant-in-Aid System for States and Localities." In *Policy Studies Review Annual,* Vol. 6. Ed. R.C. Rist. Beverly Hills, CA: Sage, 1982.

————, A.D.C. Manvel, and S.E. Calkins. *Monitoring Revenue Sharing.* Washington, DC: Brookings Institution, 1975.

Nathan, R.P., et al. "Initial Effects of the Fiscal Year 1982 Reductions in Federal Domestic Spending." In *Reductions in U.S. Domestic Spending: How They Affect State and Local Governments.* Ed. J.W. Ellwood. New Brunswick, NJ: Transaction, 1982.

National Council on the Aging (NCOA). *Aging in the Eighties: America in Transition.* Report of a 1981 poll by Louis Harris & Associates. Washington, DC: Author, 1981.

Nelson, G. "Social Class and Public Policy for the Elderly." *Social Science Review,* 56, No. 1 (1976), 85-107.

O'Connor, J. *The Fiscal Crisis of the State.* New York: St. Martin's Press, 1973.

Omenn, G.S., and R.P. Nathan. "What's Behind Those Block Grants in Health?" *New England Journal of Medicine,* 306 (April 29, 1982), 1057-1060.

Palmer, J.L., and I.V. Sawhill, eds. *The Reagan Experiment.* Washington, DC: Urban Institute, 1982.

Piven, F.F., and R. Cloward. *The New Class War.* New York: Pantheon, 1982.

Rawls, J. *The Theory of Justice.* Cambridge, MA: Harvard University Press, 1971.

Reagan, M.D., and J.G. Sanzone. *The New Federalism.* New York: Oxford University Press, 1981.

Ryan, W. *Equality.* New York: Vintage, 1982.

Schultze, C.L. "The Role of Incentives, Penalties and Rewards in Attaining Effective Policy." In *Public Expenditures and Policy Analysis.* Ed. R.H. Haveman and H. Margolis. Chicago: Markham, 1971.

Scitovsky, A. "Equity of Access to Health Care." Paper presented at the University of California, San Francisco, November 1982.

Tobin, J. "Reaganomics and Economics." *New York Review of Books,* December 3, 1981.

U.S. Congress, Joint Economic Committee. *The 1982 Joint Economic Report on the February 1982 Economic Report of the President*. Report No. 97-436. Washington, DC: U.S. Government Printing Office, 1982.

U.S. Congressional Budget Office (CBO) *Balancing the Federal Budget and Limiting Federal Spending: Constitutional and Statutory Approaches*. Washington, DC: CBO, 1982a.

————. *Tax Expenditures: Budget Control Options and Five-Year Budget Projections for Fiscal Years 1983-1987*. Washington, DC: CBO, 1982b.

U.S. General Accounting Office (GAO). *Early Observations on Block Grant Implementation*. Washington, DC: GAO, 1982a.

————. *Lessons Learned from Past Block Grants: Implications for Congressional Oversight*. Washington, DC: GAO, 1982b.

U.S. House, Committee on Government Operations. *Current Condition of American Federalism*. Washington, DC: U.S. Government Printing Office, 1981a.

U.S., House, Select Committee on Aging, Subcommittee on Retirement Income and Employment. Hearings: *Guns Versus Butter: How the Military Budget Affects Aging Americans*, July. Comm. Pub. No. 97-306. Washington, DC: U.S. Government Printing Office, 1981b.

U.S. House, Committee on Government Operations. *Reorganization and Budget Cutbacks May Jeopardize the Future of the Nation's Statistical System*. Report No. 97-901. Washington, DC: U.S. Government Printing Office, 1982a.

U.S. House, Committee on Post Office and Civil Service, Subcommittee on Census and Population. Hearing: *Impact of Budget Cuts on Federal Statistical Programs*, March 16. Washington, DC: U.S. Government Printing Office, 1982b.

U.S. House, Select Committee on Aging, and U.S. Senate, Special Committee on Aging. Joint Hearing: *Impact of the Federal Budget on the Future of Services for Older Americans*, April 1. Washington, DC: U.S. Government Printing Office, 1982c.

U.S. President's Commission for the Study of Ethical Problems in Biomedical and Behavioral Research. Unpublished draft. Washington, DC: The Commission, 1982.

U.S. Public Law 97-35. *Omnibus Budget Reconciliation Act of 1981*. Washington, DC: U.S. Government Printing Office, 1981.

U.S. Senate, Committee on Governmental Affairs. Hearings: *President's Federalism Initiative*, February 4 and March 11, 16, 18. Washington, DC: U.S. Government Printing Office, 1982a.

U.S. Senate, Special Committee on Aging. *The Proposed Fiscal Year 1983 Budget: What It Means for Older Americans*. Washington, DC: U.S. Government Printing Office, 1982b.

Vladeck, B.C. "The Design of Failure: Health Policy and the Structure of Federalism." *Journal of Health, Politics, Policy and Law*, 4, No. 3 (Fall 1979), 522-535.

————. "Equity, Access, and the Costs of Health Services." *Medical Care*, 19, No. 12, Supplement (December 1981), 69-80.

Walker, D. *Toward a Functioning Federalism*. Cambridge, MA: Winthrop, 1981.

Wilensky, H.L. *The Welfare State and Equality: Structural and Ideological Roots of Public Policy Expenditures*. Berkeley: University of California Press, 1975.

CHAPTER 3

INTERGOVERNMENTAL RELATIONS
Historical and Contemporary Perspectives

Philip R. Lee
A. E. Benjamin

Primarily because of the relationship of old age and poverty, aging policies have been an essential element in intergovernmental relations since the founding of the republic more than 200 years ago. In its early years the United States followed the welfare traditions of England, based on the Elizabethan Poor Laws. Indeed, some of that legacy persists. It was not until the 1930s that aging policy became a major element in domestic social policy, particularly through Old Age Assistance and Social Security. In 1965, Medicare and Medicaid were added, and in the 1970s social services began to assume a growing role. In this chapter we trace the origins of aging policy in the United States, its gradual evolution prior to the Great Depression and the advent of the New Deal, and its emergence as an area of great controversy in the 1980s as fiscal crisis besets all levels of government and the private sector.

The Early Days of the Republic: A Limited Role for Government

Public policies affecting the elderly, particularly policies related to income support or public assistance, trace their origins to the Elizabethan Poor Law of 1601 in England. The Poor Law was based on five principles that remained the norm for public assistance in the United States until the 1930s: (1) local financing and administration;

(2) minimization of costs; (3) workfare; (4) separate consideration of the deserving and the undeserving poor; and (5) recognition of two types of relief: outdoor relief or aid given in the home of the poor, and indoor relief or institutionalization (Advisory Commission on Intergovernmental Relations [ACIR], 1980a).

Welfare laws in both England and the United States were designed for three categories: children, the able-bodied, and indigent adults. The impoverished elderly were also included because there were no other special provisions for their care (Williamson, 1982). The burden of providing for the poor was placed on the lowest governmental unit in the United States — the town in New England and the parish in the South. Policies affecting the elderly were consistent with other national policies. Federalism in the United States initially stressed the independence of each level of government from the other, incorporating the idea that some functions, such as foreign policy, were the exclusive province of the central government. Other functions, such as police protection, were viewed as the responsibility of state and local government (Reagan and Sanzone, 1981; Hale and Palley, 1981).

Although outdoor relief was the primary method of public assistance in the seventeenth century, it was gradually replaced with indoor relief (the almshouse) in the eighteenth and nineteenth centuries. As industrialization and urbanization began to take hold in the United States (ACIR, 1980a), more punitive attitudes developed toward the poor, including the elderly. The local community usually assumed responsibility for the needy if families were unable to do so. Sometimes the poor were boarded out or received limited provision at home. They could also take shelter in public almshouses, which had existed since colonial times. Evidence indicates that before the Civil War about 16 to 25 percent of the people in almshouses were 60 years of age or older (Achenbaum, 1978).

Although local government was to bear the primary public responsibility for the aged and the poor, it was the family that, in fact, bore most of the financial, legal, and moral responsibility. Laws modeled after the Elizabethan Poor Law of 1601 and an act passed by the Massachusetts Bay Province in 1692 made family members legally and morally responsible for their poor and infirm kin, including the elderly. By 1860, eighteen of the nation's thirty-three states had enacted laws designed to deal with dependency of family members of all ages. Initially, the aged were not considered as a separate category of dependents. Gradually, however, some states began to distinguish between old age dependency in particular and poverty in general in laws affecting family relationships (Achenbaum, 1978).

Prior to the Civil War the elderly were expected to work or in other ways remain socially and economically active as long as they were physically able to do so. Neither structural factors, such as mandatory retirement laws, nor social prejudices denied citizens the right to engage in any profession, trade, or vocation because of age (Achenbaum, 1978). Laws disqualified citizens from voting and holding many public offices because they were too young, not too old. Indeed, the Constitution established minimum ages for election to Congress and the presidency, but it placed no maximum age restrictions for elected or appointed officials at the federal level. States enacted laws establishing minimum ages for governors and state legislators. Unlike the federal government, however, a number of states imposed limits on the number of years a person could serve as a justice, and some set a maximum age of 60 or 70 years for judges and justices of the peace.

Although Achenbaum (1978) identifies the period of 1865 to 1914 as one of transition in attitudes and policies affecting the elderly, Fischer (1978) finds evidence of changes as early as 1770 to 1820. He notes the abolition of the special status accorded elders in "seating the meeting," in the enactment of the first mandatory old age retirement laws (1777-1818), in the pattern of age reference revealed by census data (1787-1850), in the age bias of costumes (1790-1820), in the changing language of age relations (1780-1820), in the inheritance of property (1775-1810), and in the descent of names (1780-1820).

During the early years of the republic, the federal government played a limited role in domestic social policy, concentrating primarily on foreign policy, national defense, and efforts to stimulate commerce. The states also played a limited role in public assistance policies until New York State enacted the County Poor House Act of 1824, which transferred responsibility for public assistance from the towns to the counties. Other northern states rapidly followed suit (ACIR, 1980a). The evolution of state aid to the poor was gradual, exhibiting the incrementalism that has characterized domestic social policy throughout the history of the United States. One of the few areas of direct action by the states related to the "unsettled poor" (those who did not meet the residency requirements of any local jurisdiction). Even in this area of aid, however, the states were careful not to impinge on the responsibility and authority of local governments.

The Civil War to the Great Depression: The Growing Role of the Federal Government and the Development of Dual Federalism

The Civil War of the 1860s brought a dramatic change in the role of the federal government in many aspects of American life. Not only did the federal government engage in a Civil War to preserve the Union; its role was extended broadly to strengthen the public and private sectors and to accelerate national development. Among the important developments that began with the Civil War were federal land grants to the states (first for education and later for agricultural experiment stations) and for the development of the railroads. Federal land grants for the railroads were initially made only to the states, but later they were made directly to the railroads. The era ushered in by the Civil War, which was to last until the Great Depression in the 1930s, has been described as one of dual federalism because of the growing role of the federal government in areas previously left entirely to the states (Walker, 1981; Reagan and Sanzone, 1981).

Other changes afoot in America were industrialization, immigration, urbanization, and the opening up and development of the West. With these movements came changing attitudes and changing policies that were to affect the elderly. Mandatory retirement began to impoverish growing numbers of the elderly; changes in family structure and residence patterns began to alter how the generations related to each other; and the growth of large corporations with their demands for efficiency and productivity from workers were other factors affecting the elderly (Fischer, 1978; Kutza, 1981).

The family remained the primary source of support for the dependent elderly, but local governments, local charities, and local voluntary organizations began to play a role. Although state and local legislatures raised funds for jails, for mental hospitals, and for hospitals for those with communicable diseases, governments did not create separate institutions for the elderly. As a result, almshouses became increasingly populated by the destitute elderly. Indeed, some almshouses were converted into homes for the aged. By 1910, roughly

45 percent of the native-born and 70 percent of the foreign-born inmates of almshouses were at least 60 years old. Although an increasing percentage of those in almshouses were elderly, prior to World War II less than 2 percent of those aged 60 years or older lived in poorhouses (Achenbaum, 1978).

After the turn of the century, a number of public policy developments at the state level began to reflect a growing awareness of the problems of the destitute elderly. In Massachusetts the first public commission on aging was established in 1909, and a major survey of the economic conditions of the aged was undertaken there in 1910. The first state old age pension system was instituted in Arizona in 1915, and in 1923, Montana and Nevada became the first states to provide public assistance to the elderly outside of the poorhouse. By 1934, prior to enactment of Social Security, twenty-eight states had policies of aiding the elderly poor in their homes (ACIR, 1980a).

Although many European countries developed the foundations for a modern welfare state between the 1880s and the 1920s, it remained a radical idea in the United States until the Great Depression of the 1930s. The welfare state, as it emerged in Europe, provided predictable, publicly funded benefits to people in need without imposing a means test or other restrictions. Developing European programs of social insurance were intended to cover the risks to a national population from work injuries, sickness and disability, diminished earnings in old age, and unemployment (Skocpol and Ikenberry, 1982).

While compulsory old age, sickness and disability, and unemployment insurance were condemned in the United States, two politically popular forms of relief were growing. The first was disaster relief for farmers; the second, the even more popular veterans' benefits. Indeed, by the early years of the twentieth century, the veterans' benefits program in the United States had become the largest pension system in the world (Skocpol and Ikenberry, 1982). Veterans' benefits were first authorized by Congress in 1862; the numbers pensioned grew rapidly immediately after the Civil War and then stabilized.

After the turn of the century, a system of Universal Service Pensions was established, and by presidential order, in 1904, all veterans were granted pensions on the basis of service alone (Morison and Commager, 1962). From the 1880s until near the beginning of World War I, veterans' pensions were by far the largest single item in the federal budget. In most years between 1880 and 1900, veterans' pensions consumed 20-30 percent of the federal budget (Skocpol and Ikenberry, 1982). In some years, veterans' pensions accounted for more than 40 percent of the federal budget (Fischer, 1978). Not only did the federal government provide veterans' benefits, but they were also provided by most states. By 1910 nearly every state was providing some kind of benefit for veterans of the Civil War, as well as the Indian, Mexican, and Spanish American wars (ACIR, 1980a). During this period "every second native white man over sixty-five was receiving a pension" (Rubinow, 1913, p. 407). Aged white persons in the South excluded, Rubinow (1913) estimated that two-thirds of native white persons over age 65 were receiving a federal pension.

Veterans' benefits, as opposed to public assistance payments for the poor, were a clear case of rewarding those considered deserving, in contrast to the undeserving, whose primary source of relief was the local almshouse. After World War I veterans' benefits grew, and in 1920 the federal government enacted a new retirement plan for federal civil servants. The plan for the civil servants was a compulsory old age and disability insurance program financed by employee and government contributions. Following the federal lead, a number of states and municipalities enacted retirement plans for government employees. Those most likely to be included were firemen and policemen. Private pension plans for retired employees of private industry were also expanding during this period of relative prosperity.

During the period from the Civil War to the Great Depression, a number of factors contributed to the lack of development of welfare state policies similar to those that developed in most industrializing European countries. One of these factors was veterans' benefits (Skocpol and Ikenberry, 1982). Four other factors, identified by Morison and Commager (1962), stand out as important: (1) the tradition of rugged individualism that disposed the public to associate welfare legislation with socialism; (2) the tradition of the classless society, in which each person or each economic group was supposed to fend for itself; (3) the constitutional limitations and restrictions on federal action, which were interpreted strictly and narrowly by the Supreme Court; and (4) the existence of a federal rather than a centralized state. It took the Great Depression to overcome some of these formidable barriers to welfare state policies.

The Great Depression and the New Deal: Transforming the Federal Role – The Emergence of Cooperative Federalism

The Great Depression and the New Deal dramatically enlarged the role of the federal government and altered the relationship between the federal government and the states. Action was taken by the federal government to save the banks, support small business, provide direct public employment, stimulate public works, regulate financial institutions and business, restore consumer confidence, and provide Social Security in old age. The role of the federal government was transformed in the period of a few years. That transformation began with the Federal Emergency Relief Act of 1933. The act was important in shaping subsequent federal welfare policy in four ways: (1) through a new definition of the federal role; (2) through a significant alteration in intergovernmental relations; (3) through a pervasive, official philosophy that such federal measures would function only temporarily; and (4) through emphasis on federal aid to "employables" rather than to "unemployables" (ACIR, 1980a).

It was not the plight of the elderly but the plight of the large number of unemployed and the conditions of large and small businesses resulting from factors beyond their control that were to be the basis for the dramatic shift in federal welfare policy in the 1930s. Although the unemployed were the stimulus, the elderly were to be very much part of the changing federal role, as President Franklin D. Roosevelt made abundantly clear in an address to Congress on June 8, 1934. In announcing his intention to appoint a special commission to advise on ways of protecting Americans against threats to their economic security in 1934, the president said:

> If, as our Constitution tells us, our federal government was established among other things, "to promote the general welfare," it is our plain duty to provide for that security upon which welfare depends. . . . I am looking for sound means which I can recommend to provide at once security against several of the great disturbing factors in life — especially those which relate to unemployment and old age [Franklin D. Roosevelt in Achenbaum, 1978, p. 131].

It was little more than a year later that President Roosevelt signed the Social Security Act of 1935, which was probably the most important piece of social legislation ever enacted in the United States. The enactment of the Social Security Act marked the beginning of what has been termed "cooperative federalism." The act firmly established the principle of federal aid to the states for welfare assistance (initially provided in the Federal Emergency Relief Act of 1933) and provided the structure for old age insurance, and unemployment insurance, as well as grants for public health and social services. Of particular significance in terms of impact on the balance of power between the states and the federal government was the decision to include both federal aid to state programs providing support for the elderly and a federally financed and administered program of old age assistance.

Title I of the Social Security Act provided grants to the states for old age assistance. The title delineated the requirements for such grants in aid, and it provided for broad state discretion (Title I, Social Security Act, 49 Stat. 620, 1935). A state's old age assistance program had to be mandatory and in effect in all counties or other subdivisions within the state. States could not transfer all the responsibility to localities but had to provide some of the funds for aid to the elderly. States were permitted, however, to pay woefully inadequate amounts to the needy. In addition, federal funds could not be used to pay for grants to the elderly in public institutions. Title I, a prime example of cooperative federalism, was to serve as the basis for state assistance to the elderly for almost forty years.

After enactment of the Social Security Act in 1935, states hurried to qualify for the federal grants for the elderly, the blind, and dependent children. By February 11, 1936, when the first public assistance funds became available, thirty-nine plans representing twenty states and the District of Columbia had been approved by the Social Security Board. By June 1939 a total of 135 public assistance plans for fifty-one jurisdictions had been accepted (ACIR, 1980a). The Social Security Act represented a radical departure from past policy. Not only was the federal government a major partner in public assistance payment for the elderly poor; it required that programs be in effect throughout the state, that assistance must be in the form of money payments, and that individuals denied eligibility must be given a fair hearing (Altmeyer, 1962).

Title II of the Social Security Act provided for old age insurance through the establishment of an Old Age Reserve Account by the

Department of the Treasury. Both employees and employers were to contribute equally a prescribed percentage of the first $3000 of the wage earner's salary to the Old Age Reserve Account. The federal government would appropriate the funds needed to provide for current old age benefits. While the eventual goal was to provide universal coverage, the law initially excluded farm laborers, domestic servants, and government workers. Although payments were not initially scheduled to begin until 1942, amendments in 1939 permitted initial payments to retired workers in 1940. The 1939 amendments extended coverage to additional employed workers and provided payments not only to retired workers but to their wives and dependent children as well. In addition, benefits were granted to widows and dependent children of Social Security beneficiaries.

The Social Security Act was limited in its coverage of employee groups to those in business and industry; its financing was considered regressive by European standards; and its payments were small at the outset. The enactment of the Social Security Act was, nonetheless, a remarkable accomplishment, as Fischer (1978, p. 184) notes:

> But the most astonishing fact about Social Security was not that it passed in so conservative a form, but rather that it passed at all in so conservative a nation. With its enactment the American republic collectively acknowledged that survival was a basic human right, and that the supply of the minimal means of subsistence to every needy individual was a social obligation.

After the enactment of Social Security in 1935, there were a number of modest changes in 1939, 1950, 1952, 1954, 1956, 1958, and 1960. Two important administrative changes were made during those years. In 1939 the Federal Security Agency (FSA) was established to administer the Social Security Program, public assistance, public health, and education programs. In 1953 the FSA was accorded cabinet status, becoming the Department of Health, Education, and Welfare.

The Great Society: Expanding the Federal Role from Cooperative to Creative Federalism

In the 1960s there was a second transformation in the role of the federal government in dealing with domestic social issues. Civil rights, medical care, minimum wages, elementary and secondary education, early childhood development, air and water pollution, and poverty were among the areas receiving attention. Indeed, there was hardly an area of domestic policy that did not engage the attention of federal policymakers in Congress and the executive branch during this period. The most significant change in terms of the elderly was enactment in 1965 of Medicare and Medicaid. However, many other programs serving the needs of the elderly, including the Older Americans Act, were enacted during this period.

During the Johnson presidency the traditional federal-state relationship was extended to include direct federal support for local governments (cities and counties), nonprofit organizations, and private businesses and corporations for carrying out health, education, training, social services, community development, and other social programs. The term "creative federalism" was used by President Johnson to describe this surge of federal activity in domestic programs. The primary means used to forward the goals of creative federalism were grants-in-aid. Over 200 new grant programs were enacted during the five years of the Johnson presidency. In 1962, prior to the initiation of the Great Society programs, it is estimated that there were 160 federal formula and project grants (Peterson in Palmer and Sawhill, 1982). By 1967, there were 379, and by 1971 the number had reached 530 (ACIR, 1980b). Among the many new programs affecting the elderly, only Medicare was directly administered by the federal government. Federal aid to states and local governments grew from $7 billion in 1961, the beginning of the Kennedy-Johnson presidencies, to $20.3 billion in 1969, the end of that era (ACIR, 1980b).

The enactment in 1965 of Medicare and Medicaid, as Titles XVIII and XIX of the Social Security Act, ushered in a new era of public involvement in the provision of health care, particularly for the elderly. The two programs differ sharply in their financing, eligibility, and benefit provisions, but have shared (until recently) a willingness to pay for health care (and especially medical care) with little attention to the nature of the delivery system into which public funds are pumped. Medicare, created as a federally operated insurance program for persons aged 65 and over, was administered as part of the Social Security contributory system. The program provides mandatory federal insurance for hospital care and voluntary federal insurance for physician services, as well as limited skilled nursing home care (see Chapter 4). Medicaid was conceived on public welfare principles, and designation of Medicaid eligibility is based on highly complex means tests that vary across the fifty-four states and territories with established programs (Davidson and Marmor, 1980). Medicaid provided the states considerable discretion regarding allowed benefits and eligibility both within and outside the public assistance (categorically) eligible. Medicaid is important to the low-income elderly because of the range of benefits that may be available under its provisions; most important, the program accounts for more than half of all public and private expenditures for nursing home care (see Chapter 7).

The Economic Opportunity Act of 1964 presented another significant legislative initiative of this period. Although it did not achieve many of its early goals, it did have a major impact on public policy and the public's perception of the poverty problem. It also served to catalyze efforts to legislate a national policy on aging. This and other New Frontier and Great Society social welfare policies served (1) to legitimate a clientele group based on advanced aged, just as the Office of Economic Opportunity (OEO) and its predecessor, Mobilization for Youth, were aimed primarily at the young; (2) to dramatize socioeconomic deprivation in America; (3) to define the federal government's role in providing opportunities for the impoverished to improve their lot; (4) to institutionalize a reform model based on the assumed benefits of the rational planning and coordination of social services; and (5) to decentralize responsibility for making the program work. The policy of universal eligibility without regard to differential need included in the Older Americans Act of 1965 was a consequence primarily of OEO's claim already to be serving the poor. To avoid a duplicative approach to the aged, the Older Americans Act addressed not just the poor, but all the aged (Estes, 1979).

Although the Johnson years witnessed the development of a wide array of new policies and programs, the basic structure of public assistance remained unchanged. Indeed, in 1967 restrictive policies related to public assistance (particularly AFDC) were enacted requiring state work training programs for all able-bodied adults (including mothers of young children). The states were also required to provide day care for children of working mothers. These were the most stringent requirements that Congress had imposed on the states in relation to public assistance. The primary cause of the congressional alarm was the rapid increase in the AFDC rolls — from 3.1 million in

1960 to 5.3 million in 1967. During this same period, the number of old
age assistance recipients declined by 24,000. These restrictions did
little to stem the rapid growth in AFDC recipients; at the start of the
1970s, their number was only 300,000 shy of 10 million (ACIR, 1980a).
The explosive growth in the number of public assistance recipients,
the inequities among states, and the perceived failures of the welfare
system set the stage for the efforts at welfare reform and new
federalism that were to emerge in the 1970s.

In terms of future policy development affecting the elderly and the
respective roles of the federal government and the states, the 1960s
were a watershed period. Although many fundamental constitutional
issues related to the federal role were determined in the 1930s through
extension of the commerce and welfare clauses of the Constitution,
the full policy implications were not apparent until the 1960s when, it
was observed,

> the American federal system entered a new phase. Through a series
> of dramatic enactments, the Congress asserted the national interest
> and authority in a wide range of governmental functions that until
> then had been the province, exclusively or predominantly, of state
> and local government. The new legislation not only established
> federal-state-local relations in entirely new fields and on a vast scale
> but it established new patterns of relationships as well [Sundquist in
> ACIR, 1980b, p. 27].

Federal Policy in an Era
of Limited Resources:
New Federalism as Practiced
by Nixon, Ford, and Carter

Two major themes were to emerge early in the administration of
President Nixon: welfare reform and new federalism (Table 3.1).
Surprisingly for some, a Republican president proposed not only a
guaranteed federal income "to those American families who cannot
care for themselves in whichever states they live" (Nixon, 1969, in
ACIR, 1980b, p. 17), but also recommended the first steps in federaliz-
ing public assistance. The program, the Family Assistance Plan
(FAP), finally failed in Congress after three years of consideration and
conflict.

President Nixon also coined the term "new federalism" to describe the efforts of his administration to move away from the federal

categorical programs of the Johnson years toward the transfer to state and local governments of federal funds with as few federal strings as possible. This was done through general revenue sharing and block grants (Table 3.1). Although the Nixon administration attempted to implement its new federalism policies across a broad front, progress was made primarily in the fields of community development, manpower training, and social services, where block grants were made and broad authority to state and local governments was granted.

Categorical grant programs in other areas continued to expand despite attempts by both Nixon and Ford administrations (1969-1977) to transfer program authority and responsibility to the states and to reduce the federal role in domestic social programs. Many of these programs were of direct or indirect benefit to the elderly.

Although President Nixon failed to achieve the goals of his basic welfare reform proposal and had only limited success with his new federalism initiatives, there were three major policy developments in the early 1970s that were to have a significant impact on the elderly: the enactment of the Supplementary Security Income (SSI) program as part of the 1972 Social Security Amendments, enactment of Title XX (Social Services) of the Social Security Act in 1974, and liberalization of the eligibility for food stamps in 1971.

The SSI program, passed in 1972 and implemented in 1974, was significant in providing a guaranteed minimum income for the deserving poor who were aged, blind, or disabled. The program federalized state welfare payments and instituted national standards of income and resources. According to one analysis of the SSI program, the "primary motivation for the radical income guarantee was the preservation of Social Security" (Burke and Burke in Hudson, 1981, p. 170). The rationale was to protect the contributory and wage-related principles of Social Security from the stigmatizing effects of needs-tested income programs for America's poor — especially the retired low-wage earner or surviving dependents who had not "earned" the benefits. Under SSI provisions, states are required by law to maintain income levels of former public assistance recipients transferred to the SSI program. Many states provide a supplementary payment to eligible individuals in addition to the basic federal SSI payment. Currently about half the states do so "by amounts ranging from $10 to above $261 per person for individuals living independently" (U.S. House, 1982, p. 165). Since aged SSI recipients are largely poor and very old, this program has been extremely important

TABLE 3.1   Historical Phases of American Federalism

Historical Phases	Legislation of Importance to Elderly
DUAL FEDERALISM (1789-1930)	
Separated powers and responsibility of federal, state, and local governments	Shift of responsibility from township to county (1824), Veterans pensions, almshouses (local)
COOPERATIVE FEDERALISM (1931-1960)	
Shared responsibilities among federal, state, and local governments for all functions	Social Security Act of 1935; Kerr-Mills Amendment, 1960; National Housing Act of 1937
CREATIVE FEDERALISM (1961-1969)	
Redefined the federal-state partnership to include expanded fiscal federal support for state and local governments (cities, counties, school districts), nonprofit organizations, private business and corporate sector	Medicare, 1965; Medicaid, 1965; Older Americans Act, 1965
NEW FEDERALISM (1970-present)	
Transferred federal revenue to state and local governments with no strings, greater decentralization and devolution of power to state and local governments	Social Security Act Amendments, 1972; Supplementary Security Income, 1972; State and Local Fiscal Assistance Act, 1972; Older Americans Act amendments, 1972, 1973; Comprehensive Employment Training Act, 1973; Legal Services Corporation, 1974; Title XX Social Services, 1974;
Devolution of federal responsibilities for health, education, and welfare, shifted responsibilities to state and local governments with reduced federal commitment to domestic social spending and increase in military budget	Omnibus Budget Reconciliation Act, 1980, 1981; Economic Recovery Tax Act, 1981; Tax Equity and Fiscal Responsibility Act, 1982

SOURCE: Historical Phases derived from D. B. Walker. *Toward a Functioning Federalism.* Englewood Cliffs, NJ: Winthrop, 1981.

in helping people living on the margins to exist independently in the community.

The enactment of Title XX Social Services in 1974 was not designed specifically to benefit the elderly. While Title XX granted broad discretion to states regarding services for which they wanted to spend these funds, Congress imposed a requirement that at least 50 percent of state Title XX funds be expended for services to recipients of AFDC, SSI, or Medicaid. In 1981, however, the Omnibus Budget Reconciliation Act (U.S. PL 97-35) eliminated this and other federal provisions designed to assure that a proportion of funds are expended on low-income persons. While it is difficult to determine precisely who benefits from Title XX social services nationally, it has been observed often that the "elderly are by no means the dominant beneficiaries of the increased flexibility states have in setting recipient eligibility for social services" (Schram, 1980, p. 229).

The expansion of the food stamp program in 1971, which led to its explosive growth in the 1970s, was in large part related to the furor that had developed in the late 1960s and early 1970s because of findings related to widespread hunger and malnutrition in the United States. The food stamp program was primarily of benefit to AFDC families and the working poor. Like Title XX, it was not a program designed primarily to benefit the elderly.

The 1970s saw a rapid proliferation of various programs serving the elderly. Except for SSI and food stamps, most of these provided services of one sort or another. In 1977, the House Select Committee on Aging noted that "There are between 50 and 200 federal programs providing 'major assistance' to the elderly" (U.S. House, 1977, p. 139). Among the many federal programs, the Select Committee identified 47 major programs benefiting the elderly; others put the number as high as 134 (Stanfield, 1978). We identified at least 80 programs in the 1978 *Catalog of Federal Domestic Assistance* that we believed benefited the aged directly or indirectly (Lee and Estes in Estes, 1979).

Federal policies and programs meant to serve the elderly directly or indirectly were classified by the 1977 House Select Committee on Aging as follows:

- income maintenance,
- employment and volunteer service,

- housing,
- health care,
- social service programs,
- transportation, and
- training and research programs.

Of particular concern in our studies have been the income maintenance, health care, and social services programs. The elderly may be
eligible for the programs because of their age, because they are poor,
or because they are designated as beneficiaries (of Social Security, for
example). They may also benefit if they live in an area served by a
particular program or if they have a special problem, such as unemployment.

The departments and agencies that play a major role in programs
for the aged, in addition to the Department of Health and Human
Services, include Agriculture (food stamps), Housing and Urban
Development (housing for the elderly and handicapped, housing subsidies), and the Veterans Administration (compensation and pensions, medical care). Others that play a role in administering or
monitoring some of the many federal programs of potential benefit to
the aged include the Transportation, Labor, Energy, Treasury, and
Commerce departments, the Small Business Administration, AC-
TION, the Civil Rights Commission, and the Civil Service Commission.

Even more important for the elderly than the changes in SSI, food
stamp and social service, and other service programs were amendments to the Social Security Act in 1972 and 1977. In 1972 Social
Security payments were indexed to inflation, resulting in a rapid
increase in payments during the middle and late 1970s. The changes
contributed to a threefold increase in Social Security expenditures
between 1966 and 1976, from approximately $20 billion to $80 billion
(Derthick, 1979; Brodsky, 1982).

Public expenditures for health care also grew dramatically during
this period, increasing from just over $10 billion in 1965 to more than
$60 billion by 1976. The public share of total national health expendi-
tures, which had been just over 25 percent in 1965, grew to more than
42 percent ten years later. The National Health Planning and Development Act of 1974 (U.S. PL 93-641) was one federal response to
this dramatic rise in health care costs. The act created a national

network of new health systems agencies. These agencies were to devise local health plans that would balance local needs and resources and to implement a "certificate of need" process intended to curb the construction of medical facilities, and thus their costs. The failure of Congress to establish strong federal standards or to link financing to this regulatory process, however, assured that this version of state and local health planning would prove an unlikely tool for cost containment.

Although the 1970s brought significant improvements in the retirement benefits for the elderly and the disabled, the decade also saw the emergence of a growing controversy over Social Security. For the first time, substantial long-term deficits were projected in 1974. To attempt to deal with both long-range and short-range problems, Congress further revised Social Security in 1977. Social Security contributions by employees and employers were significantly increased in January 1979. After that date the system in effect provided benefits on the basis of average indexed monthly earnings. Dollar amounts were protected against the hazards of inflation as they had been since 1972 (Lee and Estes in Estes, 1979).

By the early 1980s there was a growing mood of pessimism about the government's ability to deal with the record high rates of inflation that followed the OPEC oil price hikes in 1979. There was a growing tide of antigovernment sentiment among many, expressed clearly by former Senator James Buckley (ACIR, 1980a, p. 29):

> The major complaints that we hear these days — complaints about the size and complexity and cost of the federal establishment, the arrogance and inefficiency of runaway bureaucracies, the growing apathy of the American public — all are in significant degree manifestations of a single phenomenon: the withering away of a system of federalism in which a hierarchy of governmental responsibility is clearly recognized and respected.

Conservative politicians were not the only ones expressing concern about the state of federalism. The ACIR (1980b) issued a major report in 1980 in which it identified four major problem areas: administration, cost, effectiveness, and accountability. There were many other critics, in and out of government. None was more forceful in his criticism of the federal role in domestic affairs than the former governor of California, Ronald Reagan, who was elected president in

November 1980. Few who voted for the future president anticipated the dramatic policy shifts that were to follow, or the effects of those policies.

Part of the explanation for the new federal politics of the 1980s is to be found in the state and local politics and economics of the late 1970s. From the mid-1960s to the mid-1970s there had been a steady growth in expenditures by state and local government. Part of that growth was related to carrying out federally funded programs such as those related to employment and training. Others involved state and local expenditures that responded to federal incentives in project and formula grants. Between 1965 and 1975 real per capita spending by state and local governments had risen 44 percent (Peterson in Palmer and Sawhill, 1982).

The mid-1970s witnessed an abrupt halt to the increase in state and local government spending, and by the late 1970s the fiscal crisis that began in such cities as New York and Cleveland had spread to many states and localities. The result was the now-famous taxpayer revolt that began in California with the enactment of Proposition 13 and continued with other taxing and spending limitations in states throughout the country. Initially property taxes were cut, then state income taxes were indexed to prevent the rapid increase in taxes with inflation, and finally restrictions were placed on state expenditures (Swan et al., 1982; Peterson in Palmer and Sawhill, 1982). The cuts were to place state and local governments in a vulnerable position in relation to possible federal funding reductions and, more important, to the effects of the recession that was to begin in the summer of 1981. The stage was set for a reexamination of the relation of the federal government to state and local governments. How would the aged fare in this reassessment?

Radical Reform or Incrementalism?
New Federalism and the Reagan Policies

Following his inauguration in early 1981, President Reagan proposed major, indeed radical, shifts in public policy. The new policies included:

    (1) decentralization of domestic social programs to the states, with decreased federal funding for most social programs;

(2) decreased regulation and increased stimulation of market forces and competition;

(3) increased military expenditures;

(4) massive tax cuts; and

(5) reduction in the size of the federal government.

The Reagan administration accelerated the degree and pace of change in policy that had been developing since the early years of the Nixon presidency. New federalism is at the heart of the Reagan administration's domestic social policies. Its tenets were reflected initially in the Omnibus Budget Reconciliation Act of 1981, which (1) consolidated many categorical programs in health, education, social services, community development, and training into block grants, and (2) extended state discretion under the Medicaid program, while also reducing the federal share of Medicaid expenditures.

In his 1982 State of the Union address, President Reagan left no doubt that he intended to proceed on the course he had set in the first year of his administration. The President proposed a "swap" and a turnback in which the federal government would assume responsibility for funding Medicaid while turning back Aid to Families with Dependent Children (AFDC), food stamps, and forty other grant-in-aid programs to the states (Wade, 1982). Although this proposal is unlikely to be implemented in the near future, it represents an important example of the politics of federalism in the 1980s.

The new federalism initiative proposed by the president would begin in 1984 and would consist of two major parts. First, the swap would involve a tradeoff in which the federal government would assume full responsibility for the Medicaid program and state governments in turn would take full responsibility for welfare (AFDC) and food stamps. Second, the "program turnbacks" (involving areas of transportation, community development, education, social services, and general revenue sharing) would assign to the states some forty-three categorical and block grant programs and in exchange would offer "super" revenue sharing to the states, so that all decisions concerning these program areas would be made at the state level. Under the Reagan proposal, a so-called trust fund of $28 billion would be established, beginning in 1984, to finance continued participation in the grant programs that are scheduled to be phased out. The $28 billion would be constant for four years, after which the trust fund would be gradually phased out (U.S. White House, 1982; U.S. Senate, 1982).

The states did not accept the Reagan proposals, primarily because most governors did not find the transfer consistent with their view of federal responsibility for fiscal and monetary policies that affect the economic well-being of the nation. State officials argued that principles of federal responsibility should be applied to new federalism policies and federal-state relationships (Matheson, 1982). Federal officials supporting the program exchange have attempted to build on the popularity of the aged and on the fears of state officials regarding the growing costs of Medicaid. The Medicaid-AFDC swap would shift the rising cost of the welfare of the elderly population (incurred through the Medicaid program) to the federal government (U.S. Senate, 1982). Arguments favoring the transfer of federal programs to the states are very similar to those used by President Nixon more than a decade ago in support of his new federalism initiatives.

In response to the Reagan administration's new federalism proposals, the ACIR has three proposals for reforming federalism: (1) decongestion, a better assignment and reordering of government functions, urging a centralization of fiscal and administrative responsibilities for a "cluster of national responsibilities, chiefly welfare programs and income and employment security" (Walker in U.S. House, 1981); (2) full devolution of a range of other program responsibilities to the states in which the federal government role is fiscally modest or in which the federal aid outlay is small; and (3) consolidation into block grants of those remaining categorical grants that operate in program areas that are of an intergovernmental nature (Walker in U.S. House, 1981).

The debate over federalism and shifting roles of various levels of government has taken place within a context of economic hardship, and the consequences for government of recent economic problems cannot be overestimated. The recession of 1981-1982 has added millions to the ranks of the poor and the unemployed. It is estimated that 8 million unemployed workers have lost private health insurance coverage as a result of their loss of employment during the recession. If dependents are included, those who have lost health insurance increase by 10.7 million. Although unemployment has increased the number of persons without health insurance coverage, over 20 million more lack it for a variety of other reasons (Rivlin in U.S. House, 1983).

The recession has also reduced revenues at all levels of government, particularly for Social Security. For example, for every one million workers laid off for one month in 1980, it is estimated that the Social Security trust funds lost $100 million in contributions (Ross and Birdsall, 1980). The loss of revenues through both unemployment (decreasing payments into the system) and inflation (increasing payments out of the system through cost of living increases) has created serious short-term financing problems that have rekindled fears that the system is going bankrupt.

In this changing economic and policy environment, local governments are at risk because they will have to assume fiscal responsibility for health care for the growing numbers of poor, including the elderly needing community based long term care services. Local governments will generally finance care for the poor through the use of local property taxes, placing the fiscal burden on a much more limited revenue base than is available to the state or federal government. Moreover, local governments will have to pay the total cost of care, whereas if the population were Medicaid-eligible, for example, the federal government would be covering at least one-half of the costs (Newcomer et al., 1982). Although state cutbacks in Medicaid, social services, and other programs are consistent with new federalism policies, evidence suggests that the states are responding more to fiscal conditions now prevailing or anticipated than to changes in federal Medicaid policies, (Feder et al. in Palmer and Sawhill, 1982; Lee and Estes in Estes, 1981).

Although various policy alternatives may seem clear, the specific effects of these alternatives on aging policies and programs are not so clear. It is not at all certain, for example, what impact the attempts by President Reagan to alter the federal role in domestic programs, particularly through new federalism swaps and turnbacks, would have on the elderly. Nor is it clear what the alternatives proposed by the ACIR would do in terms of equity, social justice, effectiveness of program implementation, or program costs.

What is clear is that government at all levels is currently faced with a fiscal crisis, defined primarily in terms of rising costs to public treasuries and reduced revenues. Proposed solutions, meanwhile, are framed in terms that do not address in any comprehensive fashion the sources of demand on the public purse. Indeed, solutions to the cost crisis tend to be limited to policies that ultimately result in the withdrawal of benefits from those recipient populations whose needs justified government intervention in the first place. The elderly in this environment, particularly the poor elderly, are placed in an increasingly vulnerable position.

References

Achenbaum, W. A. *Old Age in the New Land: The American Experience since 1970.* Baltimore: Johns Hopkins University Press, 1978.

Advisory Commission on Intergovernmental Relations (ACIR) *The Federal Role in the Federal System: The Dynamics of Growth. Public Assistance – The Growth of a Federal Function.* Washington, DC: ACIR, 1980a.

———. *The Federal Role in the Federal System: The Dynamics of Growth. A Crisis of Confidence.* Washington, DC: ACIR, 1980b.

Altmeyer, A. J. *The Formative Years of Social Security.* Madison: University of Wisconsin Press, 1962.

Brodsky, D. "Raising the Social Security Retirement Age: A Political Economy Perspective." Paper presented at the annual meeting of the Gerontological Society of America, Boston, November 1, 1982.

Buckley, J. L. "The Trouble with Federalism: It Isn't Being Tried." *Commonsense: A Republican Journal of Thought and Opinion,* 1 (Summer 1978), 11-12.

Davidson, S. M., and T. R. Marmor. *The Cost of Living Longer.* Lexington, MA: D. C. Heath, 1980.

Derthick, M. *Policy-Making for Social Security.* Washington, DC: Brookings Institution, 1979.

Estes, C. L. *The Aging Enterprise.* San Francisco: Jossey-Bass, 1979.

Fischer, D. H. *Growing Old in America.* Oxford, England: Oxford University Press, 1978.

Hale, G. E., and M. L. Palley. *The Politics of Federal Grants.* Washington, DC: Congressional Quarterly Press, 1981.

Hudson, R. B., ed. *The Aging in Politics.* Springfield, IL: Charles C Thomas, 1981.

Kutza, E. A. *The Benefits of Old Age: Social Welfare Policy for the Elderly.* Chicago: University of Chicago Press, 1981.

Matheson, S. M. Presentation at the 14th Annual Conference of State Medicaid Directors, Salt Lake City, April 26, 1982.

Morison, S. E., and H. S. Commager. *The Growth of the American Republic,* Vol. 2. New York: Oxford University Press, 1962.

Newcomer, R. J., C. Harrington, C. L. Estes, and P. R. Lee. "State Adjustments in Medicaid Policies and Expenditures: Implications for Health and Human Services for the Elderly." Working Paper No. 20. San Francisco: Aging Health Policy Center, University of California, 1982.

Palmer, J. L., and I. V. Sawhill, eds. *The Reagan Experiment.* Washington, DC: Urban Institute, 1982.

Reagan, M. D., and J. G. Sanzone. *The New Federalism.* New York: Oxford University Press, 1981.

Ross, D., and W. Birdsall. *Social Security and Pensions*. Staff Report: Special Study on Economic Change. Washington, DC: U.S. Congress, Joint Economic Committee, October 1980.

Rubinow, I. M. *Social Insurance*. New York: Arno, 1913.

Schram, S. F. "Title XX Implementation and the Aging." In *The Aging in Politics*. Ed. R. B. Hudson. Springfield, IL: Charles C Thomas, 1980.

Skocpol, T., and J. Ikenberry. "The Political Formulation of the American Welfare State in Historical and Comparative Perspective." Paper presented at the annual meeting of the American Sociological Association, San Francisco, September 7, 1982.

Stanfield, R. L. "Services for the Elderly: A Catch 22." *National Journal*, 10 (1978), 1718-1721.

Swan, J. H., C. L. Estes, J. B. Wood, M. Kreger, and J. Garfield. *Fiscal Crisis: Impact on Aging Services*. Executive Summary of Final Report. San Francisco: Aging Health Policy Center, University of California, 1982.

U.S. House, Select Committee on Aging. Hearings: *Fragmentation of Services for the Elderly,* April 7. Washington, DC: U.S. Government Printing Office, 1977.

U.S. House, Committee on Government Operations. Statement of D. B. Walker. Hearings: *Current Condition of Ameican Federalism,* April, May, and June. Washington, DC: Government Printing Office, 1981.

U.S. House, Committee on Ways and Means. *Report on Programs*. Ways and Means Committee Print: 97-29, February 18. Washington, DC: U.S. Government Printing Office, 1982.

U.S. House, Committee on Energy and Commerce, Subcommittee on Health and Environment. Hearings: *Health Insurance and the Unemployed,* January 24. Washington, DC: U.S. Government Printing Office, 1983.

U.S. Public Law 93-641. National Health Planning and Development Act of 1974. Washington, DC: U.S. Government Printing Office, 1974.

U.S. Public Law 97-35. Omnibus Reconciliation Act of 1981. Washington, DC: U.S. Government Printing Office, 1981.

U.S. Senate, Committee on Governmental Affairs. Hearings: *President's Federalism Initiative,* February and March. Washington, DC: U.S. Government Printing Office, 1982.

U.S. White House. "Tentative Administration Decisions on Federalism Initiative." Unpublished draft, June 22. Washington, DC: U.S. White House, June 22, 1982.

Wade, R. C. "The Suburban Roots of New Federalism." *New York Times Magazine*, August 1, 1982, pp. 20, 21, 39, 46.

Walker, D. *Toward a Functioning Federalism*. Englewood Cliffs, NJ: Winthrop, 1981.

Williamson, J. "Public Policy and Regulation of the Elderly Poor Prior to the Rise of the Welfare State." Paper presented at the Society for the Study of Social Problems, San Francisco, September 1982.

CHAPTER 4

SOCIAL SECURITY AND MEDICARE
Policy Shifts in the 1980s

Charlene Harrington

Gains in Social Security and Medicare benefits for the aged are now threatened by a variety of political and economic forces, as these programs have been targeted for major budget reductions. Beginning in 1981, policy changes have occurred in both programs, and recent changes are designed to reduce Social Security and Medicare expenditures. This chapter examines these shifts in public policy, the major proposals being debated for the Old-Age, Survivors, and Disability Insurance (OASDI), Supplemental Security Income (SSI), and Medicare (Title XVIII) programs and their impact on the aged.

Social Security

The Social Security program (Old-Age, Survivors, and Disability Insurance, OASDI) is composed of the Old-Age Survivors Insurance (OASI) and the Disability Insurance (DI) programs (U.S. Senate, 1982a). In 1981, the OASDI program provided a total of $145 billion in benefits, of which $127.0 billion went to 31.6 million older persons and their dependents in the OASI program, and the remainder to beneficiaries of the DI program (U.S. Senate, 1982b; U.S. SSA, 1982a). The current program is financed out of a Social Security payroll tax, which has a flat rate (10.80 percent of wages in 1982, 5.4 percent each

Author's Note: The author wishes to acknowledge the invaluable contribution of Carroll L. Estes in the preparation of this chapter, and particularly for her work on the social construction of a crisis in Social Security.

paid by employee and employer) paid up to an earnings ceiling of $32,400 (U.S. Social Security Administration [SSA], 1982c).

The Social Security financing system has been criticized because of its regressive tax, which falls heaviest on those with low incomes. On the other hand, it has been called progressive in terms of benefits, because benefits are not distributed solely on the basis of "earned" benefits (there are some redistributive effects). There are gaps in the program for those who have not been in the wage force contributing to the system through payroll taxes. While there are wage-earning limitations for beneficiaries, no such limitations exist for other pension sources. Debate occurred over payroll tax or general fund financing to ensure greater equity for low-income groups.

Of the total income in the United States for persons aged 65 and older, 43 percent was obtained in 1980 from Social Security, 18 percent from other retirement pensions, 15 percent from interest on savings, and 16 percent from earnings (U.S. Senate, 1982b). Social Security was received by nine out of ten elderly persons in 1980 (U.S. SSA, 1980b). Even though the OASI program benefits millions of aged and their dependents, the benefit levels are low — averaging only $387 per month in 1982 — so that many found the income inadequate (U.S. SSA, 1982a). The 24 percent of the aged population dependent upon Social Security and/or Supplemental Security Income as their only source of income found themselves in poverty — the actual median annual income was $3248 in 1980 (U.S. Senate, 1982b). Other aged persons, not eligible for Social Security benefits because they did not pay into the system, are forced to rely on Supplemental Security Income.

Conservative economists have argued that funds currently paid into the system are being used to pay for current beneficiaries rather than reserved or invested for the use of the payees in the future. On the other hand, Myles (1981) points out that the pay-as-you-go basis for the Social Security program was the result of a political decision with specific benefits: that is, early start-up of the retirement system and prevention of the buildup of huge public capital funds in the program.

The Board of Trustees of the Social Security fund reported in 1980 that if spending continued, the fund would be insufficient to pay benefits by late 1981 or 1982 (U.S. General Accounting Office [GAO], 1980). In 1981 public awareness of the problem grew as administration and congressional reports announced the crisis in 1982 and 1983 and others claimed the program was bankrupt. Since the number of older persons will increase by 8 million people in the next twenty-five years and the proportion of working population to aged will decline, short-term and long-term financing problems are viewed by critics of the program as serious (Hudson, 1978). Myles (1981) and Estes (1983) argue that the current "crisis" in the Social Security system is more myth than reality, designed to discredit the program. While Social Security has short-term financing problems, these are exaggerated as part of an ideological attempt by some to constrain the growth of the federal program and promote the growth of private pension programs (Myles, 1981).

Behind the heated political debates about Social Security financial problems were areas of common agreement. There was consensus that a real short-term financing problem existed in the OASDI fund, estimated to be about $180 billion between 1983 and 1990 (U.S. Senate, 1982b). The depletion of the OASI trust funds was, in part, due to the poor performance of the economy in recent years. The unanticipated record high unemployment reduced the flow of payments into the system, estimated to account for a loss of $100 in contributions for every one million workers laid off for one month in 1980 (Ross and Birdsall, 1980). The high inflation of the 1970s also resulted in higher payments out of the system than anticipated (Estes, 1983). There were a number of proposed solutions to the short-term problem — inter-funding or other borrowing for the short run, increasing payroll taxes at an earlier period, or reducing benefits (U.S. Senate, 1982b).

Second, as the OASI and DI trust funds were expected to improve after 1990, the Medicare Hospital Trust Fund is expected to have problems because of the rapid inflation in hospital costs — 10-19 percent annually (U.S. Senate, 1982b). If these rates of medical care cost increases continue, the deficits in the Hospital Trust Fund would jeopardize both Social Security and Medicare after 1990. Another issue raised by some is the long-term financing for OASI and DI when those born during the postwar baby boom reach retirement age. While some regard the demographic data as a signal of alarm for the working population, others have argued that the proportional financial burden will not change much because there will be fewer children to support (Ball, 1982; U.S. Senate, 1979).

The various options under discussion for solving the financial problems of the system are highly charged, with most organizations and representatives of the elderly opposed to any benefit reductions. Other political groups are opposed to any basic changes in the system, advocating general fund financing like that of most other industrialized nations. Others, opposed to payroll tax increases, general fund financing, or interfund borrowing, advocate benefit reductions. Probably no policy decisions of the 1980s will be as controversial or have as great an impact as those involving the Social Security system.

Income protection for those persons who can no longer support themselves through work because of a disability is provided mainly by two major public programs: Disability Insurance (DI) and Supplementary Security Income (SSI). These two programs support almost 5 million beneficiaries, more than half of whom are 55 years of age or older. The combined payments for DI and SSI disability were $21 billion in 1980 and are estimated to be $27 billion in 1983 (U.S. Senate, 1982c). Although the DI trust fund has been regarded as financially sound, disability programs have been under severe attack over the years for allegedly creating work disincentives in the system. As a result, Congress passed the 1980 Disability Reform Amendments, which mandated significant changes in the management and eligibility controls under both the DI and the SSI programs. The 1980 amendments, among other things, require the Social Security Administration to conduct periodic investigations of disability beneficiaries. Of particular concern, however, has been the arbitrary and capricious nature of the procedural process of reviewing thousands of deserving individuals (U.S. Senate, 1983). In addition to this type of program control, a provision in the Omnibus Reconciliation Act of 1981 places a cap on the amount of disability benefits received so that the combined benefits from federal, state, or local government do not exceed previous earnings.

In 1981 several changes were made to address the short-term financing problems of Social Security by reducing benefits. The minimum Social Security benefit was eliminated in July 1981 (U.S. PL 97-35), but it was subsequently restored for current beneficiaries only (HR 4331) after strong protests by concerned individuals and groups. Student benefits under Social Security were phased out with the 1981 legislation. In addition, HR 4331 authorized the Old Age Survivors Insurance (OASI), the Disability Insurance (DI), and the Medicare trust funds to borrow among themselves for a one-year period, to delay cash flow problems while a more permanent solution was found.

For more than a year the Social Security system was under review by President Reagan's National Commission on Social Security Reform. The Commission considered such solutions as potential financing changes, increasing the age for full benefits, and financing from general tax revenues, among others (U.S. GAO, 1980; U.S. Senate,

1982b). After weeks of intense debate, in January 1983 the National Commission on Social Security Reform forwarded a proposal (approved by twelve of fifteen members) to Congress for debate. The Commission's proposal was considered a bipartisan compromise package supported by congressional leaders and the president to raise $169 billion to cover the deficit expected by the end of the decade (New York Times, 1983). Agreeing to the general principle that no alteration should be made in the fundamental structure of the Social Security program, the Commission rejected proposals to make Social Security (1) voluntary, (2) based on paid contributions, (3) fully funded, or (4) means-tested. While agreeing on the basic principles, the Commission recommended a number of changes in the program that would address the short- and long-term financing problems, shown on Table 4.1.

The Commission's proposal included one major approach to increase revenues by $40 billion by accelerating the planned future payroll tax increases from 5.4 percent to 5.7 percent in 1985-1987 (U.S. National Commission on Social Security Reform [NCSSR], 1983; ASN Care Reports, 1983). A second major change proposed was the postponement of the automatic cost of living increase for a six-month period and the shift of the annual computation period for the cost of living adjustment from the first to the third quarter of the year (U.S. NCSSR, 1983). This second part of the proposal would generate a reduction in benefits expected to save another $40 billion.

Another part of the Commission's proposal recommended that Social Security benefits be subject to federal income taxes for individuals with incomes of $20,000 or more (excluding Social Security), increasing revenues by $30 billion. Also, newly hired federal employees and employees of nonprofit organizations would be required to join the Social Security program, raising $20 billion. In addition, withdrawal from the system by state and local employees would be prohibited. Self-employment tax rates would be increased to the level of other businesses, except for deduction allowances. The U.S. Treasury would also be required to pay $18 billion to the Social Security fund for credits owed to military personnel (U.S. NCSSR, 1983). One other major proposal, to extend the retirement age for Social Security to age 66, was not approved by the Commission but had the support of some leaders.

While many of the provisions were controversial and opposed by various groups, Congress passed a compromise package in March 1983 with many of the key provisions proposed by the Commission,

TABLE 4.1   Highlights of Social Security Recommendations by the National Commission on Social Security Reform, and the Social Security Act Amendments of 1983

Proposal	Short-Term Savings, 1983-1989 (billions)	Long-Range Savings (% of payroll)	Actual Amendments of 1983 and Savings
Cover nonprofit/new federal employees[a]	+$ 20	+ .30	X
Prohibit withdrawal of state/local government workers	+ 3	—	X
Postpone COLAs by 6 months	+ 40	+ .27	X
Eliminate windfalls for persons with limited coverage	+ .2	+ .01	X
Continued benefits on remarriage for disabled/divorced widow(ers)	− .1	—	X
Tax benefits for higher-income persons	+ 30	+ .60	X
Index wages for deferred widow(er)s' benefits	− .2	− .05	X
Permit benefits for divorced aged spouse	− .1	− .01	X
Increase benefits for disabled widow(ers) aged 50-59	− 1	− .01	X
Accelerate tax-rate schedule	+ 40	+ .02	X
Revise tax basis for self-employed	+ 18	+ .19	X
Reallocate OASDI tax rate between OASDI and DI	—	—	X
Allow interfund borrowing from HI by OASDI	—	—	X
Credit OASDI trust funds for cost of gratuitous military service wage credits/past unnegotiated checks	+ 18	—	X
Shift to wage indexing if fund ratio drops under 20%	—	—	X
Increase delayed retirement credit	—	− .10[b]	X
Additional long-range changes[c]	—	+ .58	X
Total Effect	+$168	+1.80	$165.3

SOURCE: Adapted from *Report of the National Commission on Social Security Reform* (Washington, DC: The Commission, January 1983), by *Aging Services News*, 132 (January 25, 1983), 7, and U.S. Public Law 98-21, Social Security Act Amendments of 1983.

a. Includes effect of revised tax schedule.

b. Assumes that retirement patterns would be only slightly affected by this change.

c. Commissioner agreed to disagree on one-third of long-range solution — whether to increase taxes or age of eligibility.

including increases in future payroll taxes for 1984, 1988, and 1989. While the enacted postponement of cost of living increases is detrimental to many aged with low incomes, other provisions are extremely positive in terms of correcting some long-standing problems.

Certainly, the decision to retain the basic structure of the program is a welcome relief to many older people who had been led to believe that the entire Social Security system was in danger of collapse. Even though it was not recommended by the Commission, Congress did raise the age for full retirement benefits from 65 beginning in the year 2000 until it reaches age 67 in the year 2027. And Congress removed Social Security from the unified federal budget beginning in 1992.

The Social Security Amendments of 1983 (U.S. PL 98-21) proposal includes some corrective legislation to address the problems of older women. Currently, older women living alone account for three of every four aged units living below the poverty level. In part, older women living alone are poor because they live longer and tend to have small incomes (U.S. Senate, 1982b). In addition, full-time homemakers do not receive Social Security credits for their work, but rather are tied to the earnings of their husbands. Widows and divorced women married fewer than ten years are particularly disadvantaged in terms of Social Security benefits. Congress made policy changes that would continue to pay benefits for spouses who remarry, permit divorced spouses to receive benefits whether or not the insured spouse has retired, provide indexing for survivor benefits by wages instead of prices, and gradually increase benefits for disabled widows and widowers aged 50-59 to the level payable to widows and widowers at age 60 (New York Times, 1983; U.S. NCSSR, 1983). While these changes were beneficial, additional changes could be made to correct inequities for older women, which remains a critical issue for attention in the 1980s (Kahne, 1983).

Supplemental Security Income

Supplemental Security Income (SSI), Title XVI of the Social Security Act, is a federally funded program that provides income maintenance to persons who are over 65, blind, or disabled and whose income and assets fall below federal poverty standards. SSI, an income-maintenance program, was established in 1972 to federalize the Old Age Assistance program and to cover those individuals who have little or no Social Security or other income. While no major federal-level policy changes are anticipated for the SSI program in the near future, this program should be of special interest to students of public policy for the elderly. The gradual decline in the number of aged beneficiaries, the erosion of state SSI supplementation benefits, and SSI benefit inequities among states all require special attention.

In 1981 a total of 4 million people received federally administered SSI payments, of whom 2.2 million were disabled, 1.7 million aged, and 700,000 blind (U.S. Senate, 1982b). Persons aged 65 and over received $234 million in federally administered SSI payments — $173 million in federal and $61 million state supplementation in 1981 (U.S. Senate, 1982b). The maximum benefit in January 1982 was $265 for an individual and $397 for a couple (U.S. Senate, 1982b).

Two changes were made in the SSI program in the Omnibus Budget Reconciliation Act of 1981. The first altered the accounting period for calculating benefits from anticipated income for the future quarter to actual income from the previous month. The second change was to allow for reimbursement to state vocational rehabilitation agencies for successful rehabilitation of former SSI recipients (U.S. PL 97-35, 1981). Although there was some discussion about removing the automatic cost of living adjustment (indexing provisions tied to the consumer price index), no changes were made.

There are several major problems with the current SSI program. The first is that once the minimum federal payment level is established, states have complete discretion in establishing state supplemental payment (SSP) levels and standards. While most states provide basic state supplementary benefits for aged individuals living alone, the following states provided no optional state supplementation for basic needs in 1980: Arkansas, Kansas, Louisiana, Mississippi, Ohio, Tennessee, Texas, and West Virginia (Rigby and Ponce, 1980). The states that do provide basic supplemental funds vary greatly in the amount provided. The federally administered SSI/SSP average payments to the aged range from $85 in Maine to $231 in California in 1983 (U.S. SSA, 1983). These differences create substantial inequities for the aged, based on a number of factors, such as geographic and living arrangement differences. While states are permitted by federal law to provide for emergency or special conditions, twenty states do not even provide such state supplementation for emergency or for other special needs (Rigby and Ponce, 1980).

Most states with supplemental payments, in response to fiscal problems during recent years, have not increased the level of supplements to keep pace with inflation (see Chapter 7 and Harrington et al., 1983). In part, this accounts for the decline in the number of aged SSI eligibles from 2.28 million in December 1974 to 1.68 million in December 1981 (U.S. SSA, 1983, 1982b). Other factors that account for the decline are not clear, but they are under study by various research groups (Harrington et al., 1983).

States have the option of either administering the SSI program directly or having the federal government administer the program. In the twenty-five states that administer their own programs, the average level of state-administered state supplementation benefits varied from $20 in Wyoming to $206 in Virginia for those aged individuals living independently and alone in 1980 (U.S. SSA, 1983). State administration of the SSP programs was selected by some states to allow for greater control and stringency in administation of benefits (Rymer, 1977). If the program were entirely administered by the federal government, the differences among states would be eliminated (Rymer et al., 1977).

When the SSI program was developed, it established mandatory minimum state supplementary payments for states to maintain individual recipients of aid to the aged, blind, and disabled at their December 1973 income level, so that no individuals would receive decreased benefits under the new program. States were, however, allowed to have more restrictive standards for Medicaid eligibility than the minimum SSI levels, so sixteen states adopted more restrictive standards (Muse and Sawyer, 1982). These policies thus allow for substantial inequities among states in Medicaid benefits for the aged.

Disincentives for the aged to live with relatives or friends are built into the federal statutes (Rigby and Ponce, 1980). If a beneficiary lives with relatives or friends, the individual's SSI benefits are reduced by one-third. This discourages group and family living arrangements that could assist the aged to live independently. Such a policy may encourage institutionalization and cost the government more in the long run through other funding sources such as Medicaid.

The most serious problem with Supplemental Security Income levels is that, even with state supplementation, they are still inadequate to meet the basic minimum living standards for food, clothing, shelter, and heat in all but a few exceptional states. SSI income levels were not sufficient to keep nearly 16 million older persons out of poverty in 1980 (U.S. Senate, 1982b). While SSI recipients often are eligible for Medicaid, eligibility and benefits vary significantly among states. As noted previously, sixteen states chose to set Medicaid eligibility standards at more restrictive levels than those for SSI. This means that some functionally disabled and ill aged who must purchase health and social services are not able to do so within the limited SSI income received. The National Commission on Social Security recommended that the federal SSI levels be increased by 25 percent to bring the cash benefits in line with the poverty level (U.S. Senate,

1982b). In view of the perceived budget crisis, increasing the SSI level is not a likely political reality.

Medicare

Although the President's Medicare budget proposal for 1984 is $64.9 billion, compared to $57.3 billion in 1983, substantial budget cutting for Medicare has been proposed for fiscal year (FY) 1984 over the amount that would otherwise be required to maintain existing Medicare program benefits (U.S. Office of Management and Budget, [OMB], 1983). Since the federal budget has a serious deficit and Medicare program expenditures are continuing to grow faster than the rate of inflation, Medicare continues to be a major focus for cost-containment efforts (Freeland and Schendler, 1981). Many policymakers view extensive Medicare reductions as an absolute necessity.

The federal government has two basic policy options for reducing the Medicare program budget: (1) reducing the eligibility and/or benefits directly affecting beneficiaries or (2) reducing the reimbursement rates directly affecting providers. What follows is a discussion of possible policy and budget options for the future and their potential impact on the aged.

As described in Chapter 3, Medicare was enacted in 1965 as Title XVIII of the Social Security Act. Medicare was designed to provide health insurance to most individuals aged 65 and over, to disabled persons under 65 who meet certain criteria, and to certain workers and their dependents for special treatment. In 1981, 29 million eligible persons, 90 percent of whom were aged, received Medicare benefits and services amounting to $44.8 billion, averaging $2400 per person for the 18.2 million users (Waldo and Gibson, 1982).

Medicare is federally administered and financed for all persons eligible for Social Security payments, without respect to income. The program has two components. Part A (the Hospital Insurance Program financed with Social Security trust funds through employer and employee contributions) covers inpatient hospitalization, skilled nursing care, and home care that is medically necessary. Beneficiaries must pay deductibles before Medicare will reimburse for services; they also must pay copayments for those services over the reimbursement limits. Part B (the Supplementary Medical Insurance Program for physician services, outpatient therapy, medical equipment, and home health visits) is a voluntary program, financed through federal revenues and monthly premium charges for enrollees (Muse and Sawyer, 1982). Both Parts A and B require beneficiaries to pay various deductibles and coinsurance charges.

Although Medicare is the primary health insurance program for the elderly, it covered only 44 percent of the total per capita health care costs of the elderly in 1978. Twenty-nine percent of the total bills were paid out-of-pocket by the aged and the remaining 27 percent by private insurance (Fisher, 1980). This is due, in large part, to the failure of Medicare to cover long term care services, out-of-institution drugs, dental care, eyeglasses, hearing aids, and other important services to the aged. Of the total Medicare expenditures for 1981, almost three-quarters (72 percent) were spent on hospital services and one-quarter (22 percent) on physician services. Medicare expenditures were negligible in covering nursing homes (less than 1 percent), home health (1 percent), and other services (4 percent) in 1981 (Waldo and Gibson, 1982). The strict enforcement of Medicare rules has severely limited coverage to services classified primarily as acute care for persons who can be rehabilitated. Those nursing home services (extended care) that reduce acute care stays are the only nursing home services allowed. These federal limitations were imposed on the initial Medicare legislation to control program costs (Vladeck, 1980).

MEDICARE CHANGES FOR 1982

Fiscal year 1982 marked the first time that major cuts were made in the federal financing of the Medicare program. Under the 1981 Omnibus Budget Reconciliation Act, a projected savings of $1.5 billion was to be achieved by increasing the cost-sharing liability of the elderly. The hospital deductible (Part A) was raised from $40 to $45 (about 12 percent), and the Part B physician deductible was increased from $60 to $75 (25 percent). The savings from all of the 1981 changes were projected at $817 million by FY 1983 (U.S. PL 97-35, 1981).

These increased charges to Medicare beneficiaries were added to an already sizable out-of-pocket liability for the aged and disabled, including Part B premiums, copayments, and deductibles of 20 percent on allowed charges above the amount Medicare paid to physicians. An estimated 50 percent of physicians charge beneficiaries more than Medicare pays; that is, they do not accept Medicare payment directly as full payment for services, termed "assignment" (U.S. Senate, 1982d). The elderly now spend about 19 percent of their total income on medical care (U.S. Senate, 1982b). As these cost shifts to beneficiaries increase, the proportion of income spent on medical care is expected to rise (Fisher, 1980; U.S. Senate, 1982b).

MEDICARE CHANGES FOR 1983

The Tax Equity and Fiscal Responsibility Act of 1982 (U.S. PL 97-248) made two types of Medicare changes: those that affect beneficiaries and those that affect providers.

Beneficiary Effects. For the first time, annual automatic increases in the Part B deductible were initiated, and the Part B premium was set at a constant percentage of program costs (U.S. PL 97-248, 1982). Medicare was shifted from the first to the second payer of health costs and employers are now required to offer the same health benefits to workers aged 65-69 and their dependents as to younger workers (U.S. PL 97-248, 1982).

While these changes increased beneficiary costs, two other changes represent important improvements. First, federal employees were required to buy into the Medicare program for hospital insurance (previously they were exempt from such requirements), providing needed revenues for the Medicare fund. Second, benefits were added to provide humane and less costly care for the terminally ill, including nursing care, therapies, medical social services, home health aides, medical supplies, physician services, short-term hospital care, and counseling. Five percent copayments were placed on hospice care and drugs (Commerce Clearing House [CCH], 1981-1983, pars. 24,268 and 24,539).

Provider Effects. Many of the reimbursement changes implemented in 1983 were long-overdue attempts to control the inflationary reimbursement policies of the past. These include setting hospital budget targets for expenditures, denying duplicate payments for outpatient services, eliminating the private room subsidy, discontinuing unnecessary payments to physician surgical assistants, terminating special nursing salary costs in hospitals, suspending payment for ineffective drugs, deleting payment for antiunion hospital activities, and other changes. Limits on total Medicare payments for ancillary costs were set for the first time (U.S. PL 97-284, 1982). A 9.7 percent cap was placed on overall hospital rate increases per discharge with incentives to stay under the ceilings. These cost-saving efforts were projected to save $6.3 billion over three years (U.S. PL 97-248, 1982).

While many of these changes were necessary, there is little evidence that providers, either hospitals or physicians, will absorb the cuts in reimbursement. Rather, it is more likely that providers will shift many of the costs that Medicare saves in provider payments directly to individual elderly beneficiaries, to private paying consumers, and to third-party insurers. Also, a greater number of physicians may refuse to accept what Medicare pays (assignment), requiring more and more Medicare beneficiaries to pay for greater proportions of their care directly to their physicians.

The legislation to reduce inflationary reimbursement rates to providers is designed to control costs. The traditional principle of provider reimbursement in the Medicare program has been based on paying the "usual and customary" price charged for services after they have been provided. Proposals to encourage prepayment for care to organizations called health maintenance organizations (HMOs) are designed to encourage providers to stay within a fixed budget and to reduce unnecessary utilization of costly hospital services. Additional changes were implemented in 1983 to encourage the expanded enrollment and use of HMOs by the aged. This approach is designed to offer a competitive alternative to the traditional fee-for-service system.

MEDICARE PROPOSALS FOR 1984

Key components of the administration's 1984 Medicare proposals include (1) increased copayments and deductibles, (2) catastrophic insurance, (3) vouchers, and (4) prospective reimbursement (particularly for hospitals). Another proposal that has been discussed (but that was not in the President's 1984 budget message) is making Medicare a means-tested program instead of a universal entitlement program.

INCREASED COPAYMENTS AND DEDUCTIBLES

Medicare proposals for 1984 would increase hospital copayments so that the elderly would continue to pay the full cost of the first day of care as they currently do (estimated to be about $350); they would also pay 8 percent of the deductible for the second through the fifteenth day (about $28 per day) and 5 percent of the deductible for the sixteenth to the sixtieth day. After sixty days of hospital care, catastrophic coverage would pay the remainder of the bills. This proposal is estimated to save $710 million in 1984 (U.S. OMB, 1983). The estimates are that only 170,000 Medicare patients per year are in the hospital longer than sixty days.

In addition, beneficiaries receiving Medicaid coverage would be required to pay $1 to $2 per day for hospital care, and $1 to $1.50 for outpatient visits, saving another $9.3 billion during the coming fiscal years. The proposal also requests freezing Part B premiums at the present level until 1984. This would mean cancellation of the already enacted Part B premium increase set for July of 1983 (U.S. OMB, 1983; Health Policy Week [HPW], 1983).

Another major change proposed in the 1984 budget is taxation of health insurance benefits paid for workers by their employers. Individuals (who currently have unlimited tax deductions) could deduct no more than $70 per month in insurance benefits, and families could deduct up to $175. This reduction of the tax subsidy for health insurance is expected to generate $2.3 billion in savings, because about 30 percent of workers are now above these levels (U.S. OMB, 1983).

The effects of increased cost sharing for beneficiaries must be viewed in the context of steady increases in the copayments and deductibles for the Medicare program in the last three years. Between 1980 and 1981, Part A and Part B out-of-pocket expenses increased by 13.3 percent and 14.5 percent respectively (Olson, 1982). Since 1981, substantial increases were made with a 12 percent increase in Part A, a 25 percent increase in Part B for FY 1982, and a 4 percent increase in Part B initially scheduled to begin in July 1983. These increases are in addition to the already sizable amount the elderly spend on Medicare costs, about 56 percent of the total cost, either directly out-of-pocket or through private insurance (Fisher, 1980). The costs for Part B physician services are a particular problem, because beneficiaries are responsible for 20 percent of Medicare's allowable charges and for any other charges above the amount Medicare will pay. Since physician fees have risen and Medicare "allowable" payment rates have not increased comparably, beneficiaries must cover growing costs and may become impoverished in doing so. The increased costs for premiums, copayments, and deductibles may make Part B coverage unaffordable for many older people (Cantwell, 1981). Some 460,000 older people are not now covered for Part B, and this number is expected to increase as the cost of premiums increases (Olson, 1982).

The rising copayments and deductibles have increased the cost of private supplemental insurance — creating "Medigap" (Feder et al., 1982) and further reducing the number of elderly who can afford to purchase insurance. Between 1981 and 1982 rate increases in these supplementary insurance programs rose from 27 percent to 40 percent in some areas (U.S. Senate, 1982a). One state reported premium increases of over 250 percent between 1970 and 1980. In 1979 more than 19 million private policies were held by about 16 million elderly (Carroll and Arnett, 1981), although no more than 6 percent of medical care costs are covered by private insurers. Those with supplemental insurance, which partly or fully cover the gaps in Medicare payments for services, had a higher probability of utilization of Medicare services (Long and Settle, 1982b).

The most serious aspect of increasing copayments and deductibles or shifting costs to beneficiaries is the disproportiate impact on the poor aged (Dallek and Parks, 1981). The Medicare use of flat fee schedules, rather than a sliding fee schedule, places the greatest burden for increases on those who are least able to afford them. The Medicaid program pays for the Medicare deductible and coinsurance for individuals who are poor enough to be eligible for Medicaid. However, only 13 percent of those on Medicare are also covered by Medicaid (Feder et al., 1982; Fisher, 1980).

Davis (1975) showed that the uniform cost-sharing provisions for the elderly on Medicare may be largely responsible for the greater utilization of Medicare services by high-income beneficiaries. Significant differences were found in the reimbursement amounts for physician and other medical services between low- and high-income elderly. These variations are not explained by differences in education or areas with greater medical resources. Significant differences also existed in the payment for physicians and other services by race, with services for blacks receiving lower payments (Davis and Schoen, 1978; Davis et al., 1981; Long and Settle, 1982a). While disparities in use and reimbursement of services by race decreased between 1967 and 1976, the differences continued to be noteworthy (Ruther and Dobson, 1981).

In summary, the policies of increasing the copayments and deductibles are likely to have an extremely negative impact on Medicare beneficiaries who are poor or near-poor, including large numbers of women and minorities (Roemer, 1975). The inequities for those who can least afford cost sharing will increase, with possible serious consequences for this group in terms of delayed or no medical care when necessary. Graduating cost-sharing arrangements by income would bring greater equity to the program. It has been argued that an overall ceiling should be placed on the amount required as reasonable out-of-pocket payment for both Part A and Part B to provide protection against excessive financial burdens for the aged (Davis, 1975).

CATASTROPHIC INSURANCE

To offset the proposed Medicare copayment cost increases, catastrophic insurance is proposed after sixty days of hospitalization. For example, this plan could reduce costs for a typical six-month illness from an estimated $19,000 to $1,580 (HPW, 1983). While the advantages of adding catastrophic coverage for Medicare beneficiaries in hospitals are obvious, this benefit will cover very few individuals, because less than half of 1 percent of beneficiaries ever use all sixty days of their hospital benefits (Feder et al., 1982). The increase in costs for catastrophic coverage would be more than offset by the decreases in Medicare costs due to the copayment and deductible changes.

VOUCHERS

Although one voucher proposal was defeated for 1983, another has been presented by President Reagan in his 1984 budget message. A pure voucher is a fixed dollar subsidy, regardless of the service purchased or the expenditure for services (Sloan, 1981; Enthoven, 1979). The voucher would be used to purchase private insurance or membership in a health plan. If the premium exceeded the value of the voucher, the individual Medicare beneficiary would pay the difference out-of-pocket. If the premium were less than the voucher, the beneficiary or the government could receive a refund.

The voucher shifts the responsibility for purchasing health services and the financial risk to consumers, with some risk given to the participating insurance companies or health plans. It has been argued that such proposals have potentially negative consequences for consumers. Consistent with the administration's interest in competitive health plans, the major purposes of the voucher plans are to make consumers more cost-conscious and to motivate them to shop for the lowest-priced insurance or services. One issue has been that voucher proposals are not generally concerned with altering conditions of providers or supply, but only with consumer demand (Davis, 1981).

There are three problems with the voucher proposals. First, consumers, including older people, typically tend not to be fully informed of their choices, of costs prior to purchase, or of the consequences of various alternatives. This has been particularly true of physician prices (Cantwell, 1981). Thus, consumers may fall victim to unscrupulous insurance companies that provide low-quality and/or inappropriate services. Shifting responsibility to the individual older person without adequate information or experience in selecting the most cost-effective plans could negatively affect the aged. Problems with purchasing supplemental insurance (Medigap) illustrate the difficulties that the aged have already experienced (U.S. House, 1979; Merritt and Potemken, 1982).

Second, the majority of Medicare beneficiaries are already paying a sizable proportion of their income for health care (estimated to be 19 percent of their total income), a proportion almost equal to their costs before Medicare was initiated. (U.S. Senate, 1982b). With only about 50 percent of the physicians accepting Medicare assignments (that is, accepting as payment in full the amount that Medicare determines to be reasonable), many (if not most) Medicare beneficiaries are already paying physician bills directly, usually being reimbursed by Medicare for only part of the cost. As a result, many beneficiaries are already cost-conscious about their bills. In all likelihood, the voucher proposal will have the same deleterious effects on the poor, minorities, and those living in high-cost geographical areas that the increased copayment and deductible proposals are expected to have.

Third, long term care services probably would not be included in voucher programs, continuing the lack of coverage for the health services most needed by older Americans. Vouchers would in all probability further ingrain the current separation of the financing for acute care and physician services (now covered by Medicare) from that for long term care services (now covered by Medicaid and private payers).

Demonstration projects to examine the effects of vouchers on a voluntary basis are currently under way. Only on the basis of careful research and evaluation of outcomes of such demonstration projects will it be possible to determine whether this proposed option can achieve the goals desired without creating detrimental effects for the beneficiaries, particularly for the sickest and poorest.

While efforts to increase Medicare enrollment in HMOs have been expanded in recent years, the voucher proposals encourage further HMO enrollment. HMO services are those offered by organizations on a prepaid basis at a set rate for each individual enrolling in the plan, placing providers "at risk" for covering the cost of health care within a fixed financial limit (Luft, 1981). In the past, HMO providers have been given the option of receiving payment for Medicare beneficiaries on either a retrospective reasonable cost basis or on a capitated basis. Most providers have elected the former method, since they receive higher reimbursement. By increasing the payments for HMO Medicare enrollees to 95 percent of the fee-for-service rate, recent federal legislation has attempted to provide an incentive for capitation payments, beginning in 1983 (U.S. PL 97-248, 1982). While many HMOs have opened enrollment to Medicare providers, few older persons have enrolled nationally. In 1980 data show that 391,082 Medicare beneficiaries were enrolled in 236 HMOs and prepaid health plans (PHPs) throughout the country, representing only about 2 percent of the overall Medicare beneficiaries (U.S. Department of Health and Human Services [DHHS], 1980).

The enrollment of Medicare beneficiaries in HMOs has been small for several reasons. One is that many Medicare beneficiaries are reluctant to change their primary practitioners. HMOs generally do not direct special marketing efforts toward the aged or Medicare recipients, but tend rather to accept present enrollees who become Medicare beneficiaries at age 65. Currently, there are few incentives either for providers to market to the aged or for Medicare beneficiaries to join HMOs. If the federal government intends to use HMOs as a cost-containment approach for Medicare beneficiaries, attention will have to be given to current factors that have kept enrollment low.

PROSPECTIVE HOSPITAL REIMBURSEMENT

In a recent report to Congress (U.S. DHHS, 1983), the secretary of the Department of Health and Human Services outlined the basic problems of the reimbursement system under Medicare that contributed to the high growth rates in hospital expenditures. First, the cost-based reimbursement system for hospitals paid hospitals for whatever they spent. Therefore, hospitals had incentives to increase their expenditures in order to increase their revenues from Medicare. This in part accounts for an increase in Medicare hospital expenditures by 19 percent during the past three years (U.S. DHHS, 1983; Coelen and Sullivan, 1981). Second, hospital reimbursement paid for whatever hospitals legitimately claimed as costs for a particular service. These costs varied tremendously among hospitals — for example, $1500 to $9000 for an average heart attack or $2100 to $8200 for a hip replacement (U.S. DHHS, 1983). Medicare, therefore, does not pay comparable prices for comparable services. Finally, the Medicare reimbursement system has been retrospective on a fee-for-service basis. Since hospitals were paid after services were rendered, the prices were not fixed and could be increased as expenditures are increased. Prices were also set for each service so that there were incentives to increase the number and type of services provided to increase revenues.

The Tax Equity and Fiscal Responsibility Act of 1982 (U.S. PL 97-248) changed the Medicare reimbursement procedures to set (1) limits on total hospital inpatient costs per discharge with adjustments to reflect each hospital's case mix (the composition and complexity of the hospital patient population in a given year); (2) a limit on the annual rate of increase of total costs per discharge; and (3) a small incentive payment for hospitals that are below both of the allowed rate increase limits. Certain problems are created by these provisions. First, the existing differences in costs per discharge were perpetuated, up to the maximum limit (U.S. DHHS, 1983). In fact, the high-cost hospitals were actually at an advantage because they received the same rate of increase, but the increase was calculated on a larger base. While the low-cost hospitals were given an incentive, there was nothing in the law to prevent these hospitals from increasing their expenditures up to the limit and retaining the full amount.

A number of states have had mandatory prospective payment systems that have been evaluated. Table 4.2 shows the growth rates for community hospitals in all states between 1975 and 1980. States with mandatory programs had about 2 percent lower growth rates than the U.S. average (Coelen and Sullivan, 1981; U.S. DHHS, 1983; U.S. GAO, 1980). Studies of these systems show that prospective rate setting is effective in reducing costs, although hospitals paid on a per day basis tend to increase the length of stays, and those paid on a per admission basis without case mix adjustment tend to encourage selection (skimming) of inexpensive cases. Several new projects are now being undertaken by the Health Care Financing Administration to test different prospective approaches, such as those in Massachusetts (Harrington et al., 1983; Glenn and Brazda, 1982; Intergovernmental Health Policy Project, 1982).

TABLE 4.2   U.S. Community Hospitals, 1975-1980: Percentage Increase
Expense per Adjusted Admission for States with and without
Mandatory Hospital Rate Setting

Rank	State	Cumulative Increase	Annual Increase	
1	Alaska	149.67%	20.08%	
2	District of Columbia	123.12	17.41	
3	Nevada	111.88	16.20	
4	New Mexico	111.71	16.18	
5	Montana	109.36	15.93	
6	Wyoming	108.14	15.79	
7	Hawaii	107.54	15.72	
8	Utah	104.99	15.44	
9	Kansas	100.13	14.88	
10	North Dakota	97.30	14.56	
11	Colorado	96.97	14.52	
12	South Dakota	96.18	14.43	
13	Maine	96.08	14.42	
14	California	95.23	14.32	
15	Oklahoma	94.57	14.24	
16	Missouri	93.22	14.08	
17	Idaho	92.37	13.98	
18	Arkansas	90.78	13.79	
19	Illinois	90.13	13.71	
20	Iowa	90.00	13.70	
21	West Virgina	89.81	13.67	
22	Oregon	89.34	13.62	
23	Texas	88.20	13.48	
24	Virginia	88.04	13.46	
25	Wisconsin	87.93	13.45	Mandatory*
26	Alabama	87.73	13.42	
27	Ohio	86.57	13.28	
28	Minnesota	85.14	13.11	
29	South Carolina	84.52	13.03	
30	Pennsylvania	84.48	13.03	
31	Louisiana	83.95	12.96	
32	Indiana	83.92	12.96	
33	Tennessee	83.80	12.95	
34	Mississippi	83.42	12.90	
35	North Carolina	82.60	12.80	
36	Kentucky	82.02	12.73	
37	Arizona	80.69	12.56	
38	New Hampshire	78.69	12.31	
39	Washington	78.02	12.23	Mandatory*
40	Florida	77.98	12.22	
41	Georgia	77.49	12.16	
42	Michigan	76.91	12.09	

TABLE 4.2 (Continued)

Rank	State	Cumulative Increase	Annual Increase
43	Nebraska	74.47	11.77
44	Massachusetts	72.41	11.51 Mandatory*
45	New Jersey	68.22	10.96 Mandatory*
46	Delaware	67.56	10.87
47	Rhode Island	67.42	10.86 Mandatory*
48	Maryland	67.23	10.83 Mandatory*
49	Connecticut	65.51	10.60 Mandatory*
50	Vermont	63.14	10.28
51	New York	51.62	8.68 Mandatory*
	U.S. Average	79.60	12.42
	Mandatory	61.83	10.1
	Nonmandatory	86.59	13.29

SOURCE: U.S. Secretary of Department of Health and Human Services. "Hospital Prospective Payment for Medicare." A Report to Congress Required by the Tax Equity and Fiscal Responsibility Act of 1982, December 1982. Reprinted in *Medicare and Medicaid Guide*. Chicago: Commerce Clearing House, Inc., No. 374 (January 5, 1983).

*Those programs that require hospitals both to participate and to comply.

In late 1982, Secretary Schweiker (U.S. DHHS, 1983) presented the DHHS proposal for prospective Medicare payment methods for hospitals, and this approach was adopted by Congress in the Social Security Amendments of 1983. The new methodology uses case mix to adjust reimbursement to take into account the severity of illness of patients. Categorizing patients on the basis of diagnostically related groups (DRGs), this case mix method is based on work developed at Yale University and used by New Jersey, Maryland, and other states (Fetter et al., 1980, 1982). While this methodology is considered to be valid and reliable, it is extremely complex, using some 467 different group codes. A potential danger in using the complex DRG system is that providers might artificially inflate the DRG level in order to increase their reimbursement. Although DHHS plans to institute a DRG verification system to monitor hospitals (U.S. DHHS, 1983), the ability to carry out the necessary monitoring with such a large, complex system is questionable.

Another problem with the proposed prospective methodology is that capital costs for hospitals, considered to be a major factor in the inflation of hospital costs, will continue to be paid in full (passed through) on a pro rata basis per patient by Medicare, as will medical education costs at teaching hospitals. By paying the costs for construction and medical education, Medicare will encourage growth in these areas.

Even where ceilings are placed on high-cost facilities by reimbursing on the basis of the average rate for hospitals in a given geographic area, overall costs are likely to increase for *all* hospitals so that the overall rates of growth may not be reduced (Feder et al., 1982). Moreover, hospitals may adjust their accounting procedures to maximize their allowable costs and avoid real losses. To the extent that hospitals are able to shift Medicare charges to other payers, average hospital rates will continue to increase, thereby raising the amount that Medicare must pay to meet the test of a reasonable rate.

Various policymakers and groups have advocated mandatory state budget and rate-setting systems for all payers (Medicare, Medicaid, and private) to regulate hospital costs. By utilizing state prospective budgeting systems with annual ceilings for both hospital and nursing homes for all payment sources, Medicare costs could be brought down to the rate of inflation. Prospective budget and rate setting for all basic providers is one method of reducing budgets and preventing cost shifting to private payers (Health Security Action Council, 1982). The extent of reductions in costs would be, of course, dependent on the specific details of the methodologies, as some methods have had greater success than others in reducing costs.

While it is extremely doubtful that a proposal for budget and rate setting over all hospitals for all payers could be implemented on a national basis due to opposition by the powerful hospital industry, states could be encouraged to develop such systems. Twenty-two states now have alternative reimbursement rate methodologies to that of Medicare, and many other states are considering such proposals (National Governors' Association, 1982; La Jolla Management Corporation, 1982; Intergovernmental Health Policy Project, 1982; Harrington et al., 1982). The ability and willingness of states to develop such systems could be enhanced by developing financial incentives and streamlining federal waiver procedures for reimbursements.

MEANS TEST PROPOSAL

Another proposal to reduce the cost of Medicare is to institute means testing for Medicare beneficiaries. Although not a part of the

President's 1984 budget message, this proposal was discussed for 1984. It would allow only those with demonstrated financial need, however defined, to receive benefits or to become eligible for Medicare. Such a means test would dramatically alter the nature of the program, introducing eligibility resembling that for Medicaid, which requires beneficiaries to be indigent. Such a change is strongly opposed by many aged who view means-tested programs as punitive, stigmatizing, and demeaning for clients (see Kutza, 1981, for a discussion of the merits of such a proposal).

Since Medicare Part A is financed by employer and employee contributions, attaching a means test is considered by many to be unfair to those with high incomes who have already paid into the Medicare program. In order to change the approach to benefits, some would argue that the method of financing the system should be changed from payroll taxes to general funds. Another approach would be to continue the existing financing system but to have premiums, copayments, and deductibles paid on a sliding fee basis (Davis, 1975). This type of system could be established with a limited amount of financial reporting and would ensure greater equity for the beneficiaries who are least able to pay for the program.

Any proposals for changing eligibility or benefits through means testing are likely to engender strong opposition by aged advocates. Such advocates argue that the program entitlements have been established historically, and changes would be unfair to those who have paid into the system. Opposition to the stigma of Medicare's becoming a welfare program also is high.

OTHER PROBLEMS: INTEGRATED FINANCING

The greatest problem with the current Medicare program is the need for integration with other financing programs. Medicaid continues to cover primarily hospital and physician services, leaving long term care, drugs, hearing aids, dentures, eyeglasses, and other services uncovered. Those aged eligible for Medicaid may be able to obtain some or all such services, but many other (that is, most) aged are subject to loss of their income and property in order to pay long term care bills before becoming indigent and eligible for Medicare coverage. With the administration of the Medicare program at the federal level and the Medicaid program at the state level, there are many barriers to delivering a coordinated system. Each program has its own distinct and complex federal eligibility, benefits, reimbursement, and program policies. There is additional variation at the state level among Medicaid programs.

Merging the Medicare and Medicaid programs has long been a goal of federal officials, but political and structural problems in accomplishing this goal are extensive. Because the Reagan proposal to transfer the administration of Medicaid to the federal level has raised fears of program reductions and program changes at the state level, supporters are difficult to find. No doubt the proposals will continue to be discussed, but approaches are needed to ensure equity at the state level to existing Medicaid beneficiaries. An effort to expand existing Medicaid benefits to the level offered by the most generous states would, of course, be extremely expensive at a time when the federal government is seeking methods to reduce the budget.

Conclusion

A number of policy options proposed for cost containment in Medicare would affect beneficiaries and providers. The areas discussed include increased copayments and deductibles, catastrophic coverage, vouchers, prospective budget and rate setting systems, means testing, and program integration.

Federal Supplemental Security Income program policies have not been modified since 1981, but low benefit levels, declining state supplementation, and inequities in benefits among states all threaten this basic income support for the aged. The inequities among states remain despite federalization of the program in 1974, and they will continue to be an issue as the number of aged beneficiaries continues to decline. The clear need to raise the SSI levels up to the federal poverty standard contrasts sharply with federal policies for reducing expenditures for income maintenance.

No policy issues have created more concern among the aged as those for restructuring the Social Security system and for reducing Medicare coverage costs. The Social Security proposals offered by a bipartisan compromise of the National Commission on Social Security Reform and adopted by Congress attempt to solve both short-term and, to some degree, long-term financing problems. While there is general opposition to many aspects of the Commission's proposal, the most opposition from low-income aged is to postponement in the cost of living increases. Other inequities in benefits for older women remain unresolved.

Proposed increases in copayments and deductibles are expected to (1) increase the out-of-pocket payments for the aged; (2) increase the number of aged who cannot afford to purchase Part B Medicare coverage of physician services; (3) increase the price of supplemental insurance so that many aged will not able to purchase it; and (4) increase the number of physicians who refuse assignment, thus further increasing costs to the aged. The small increase in coverage for catastrophic insurance is not expected to offset the increased costs to the elderly for Medicare.

Voucher proposals are designed to allow the aged to purchase their choice of health insurance for a limited amount paid by Medicare, the remainder to be paid by the beneficiary. Also designed to increase consumer cost-consciousness, these options have the same inherent disadvantages as other proposals that increase cost sharing. Health maintenance organizations are seen as a major competitive option to controlling costs. Providers are hesitant to market HMO plans to the aged on an extensive basis for fear of potential risks, and aged beneficiaries are cautious about HMO enrollment. For a variety of reasons, the enrollment potential of HMOs continues to appear limited.

Federal efforts are now focusing on a new prospective hospital reimbursement proposal as a means of controlling the fastest-growing component of the Medicare budget. While this system clearly moves in the direction of controlling unnecessary hospital cost inflation, with less detrimental impact on beneficiaries than other types of proposals, there are limits to the amount of savings that can be expected. The new legislation continues to be flawed in that it controls reimbursement rates only for Medicare rather than for all hospital payers. The legislation passes through costs of construction and medical education, both of which contribute substantially to price inflation. The use of DRGs to adjust for case mix provides an opportunity for artificial inflation in case mix reporting and increased costs. Alternative methods of setting prospective rates for all payers have greater potential for substantially controlling costs.

Finally, the need to integrate the Medicare and Medicaid programs is widely recognized. Proposals to federalize the Medicaid program continue to face serious political opposition. States that are less generous in their Medicaid programs could have benefits, eligibility, and reimbursement increased to the level of the most generous states, but the costs are considered prohibitive. States with generous Medicaid programs object to reductions in their programs to the level of less generous states. State officials are afraid the proposal is simply a method of cutting overall Medicaid benefits rather than an approach to integrate and improve the delivery of services.

References

ASN Care Reports. *Aging Services News,* 132 (January 25, 1983).

Ball, R. M. *The Financial Condition of the Social Security Program.* New York: Study Group on Social Security, 1982.

Callahan, J.J., and S.S. Wallace, eds. *Reforming the Long-Term-Care System.* Lexington, MA: D.C. Heath, 1981.

Cantwell, J.R. "Copayments and Consumer Search: Increasing Competition in Medicare and Other Insured Medical Markets." *Health Care Financing Review,* 3, No. 2 (December 1981), 65-76.

Carroll, M.S., and R.H. Arnett. "Private Health Insurance Plans in 1978 and 1979: A Review of Coverage, Enrollment, and Financial Experience." *Health Care Financing Review,* 3, No. 1 (September 1981), 55-87.

Coelen, C., and D. Sullivan. "An Analysis of the Effects of Prospective Reimbursement Programs on Hospital Expenditures." *Health Care Financing Review,* 2, No. 3 (Winter 1981), 1-40.

Commerce Clearing House (CCH) *Medicare and Medicaid Guide.* Chicago: Commerce Clearing House, 1981-1983.

Dallek, G., and M. Parks. "Cost-Sharing Revisited: Limiting Medical Care to the Poor." Unpublished paper. Washington, DC: National Health Law Program, 1981.

Davis, K. "Equal Treatment and Unequal Benefits: The Medicare Program." *Milbank Memorial Fund Quarterly/Health and Society,* 53, No. 4 (1975), 449-488.

———. "Reagan Administration Health Policy." *Journal of Public Health Policy,* 2, No. 4 (December 1981), 313-331.

———, M. Gold, and D. Makuc. "Access to Health Care for the Poor: Does the Gap Remain?" In *Annual Review of Public Health,* Vol. 2. Ed. L. Breslow, J. Fielding, and L. Lave. Palo Alto, CA: Annual Reviews, Inc., 1981.

David, K., and C. Schoen. *Helath and the War on Poverty: A Ten-Year Appraisal.* Washington, DC: Brookings Institution, 1978.

Enthoven, A.C. "Health Care Costs: Why Regulation Fails, Why Competition Works, How to Get There from Here." *National Journal* (May 26, 1979), 885-889.

Estes, C.L. *The Aging Enterprise.* San Francisco: Jossey-Bass, 1980.

———. "Social Security: The Social Construction of the Crisis." Paper submitted to Milbank Memorial Fund Quarterly. San Francisco: Aging Health Policy Center, University of California, 1983.

Feder, J., J. Holahan, R.R. Bovbjerg, and J. Hadley. "Health." In *The Reagan Experiment.* Ed. J.L. Palmer and I.V. Sawhill. Washington, DC: Urban Institute, 1982.

Fetter, R. B., et al. "Case Mix Definition by Diagnosis-Related Groups." *Medical Care Supplement* (February 1980).
————. *Diagnosis Related Groups Classification Scheme*. Final Report. New Haven, CT: Health Systems Management Group, School of Organization and Management, Yale University, 1982.
Fisher, C. R. "Difference by Age Groups in Health Care Spending." *Health Care Financing Review*, 1, No. 4 (Spring 1980), 65-90.
Freeland, M. S., and C. E. Schendler. "National Health Expenditures: Short-Term Outlook and Long-Term Projections." *Health Care Financing Review*, 2, No. 3 (Winter 1981), 97-138.
Glenn, K., and J. F. Brazda, eds. *Washington Report on Medicine & Health Perspectives*. New York: McGraw-Hill, 1982.
Harrington, C., R. J. Newcomer, C. L. Estes, P. R. Lee, J. Swan, L. Paringer, and A. E. Benjamin. *Eight-State Comparative Report on Medicaid Services*. San Francisco: Aging Health Policy Center, University of California 1983.
Harrington, C., R. J. Newcomer, and P. Newacheck. *Prepaid Long-Term Care Health Plans: A Policy for California's Medi-Cal Program*. California Policy Seminar Monograph. Berkeley: Institute of Governmental Studies, University of California, 1983.
Harrington, C., A. Pardini, V. Peguillan-Shea, and G. R. LaLonde-Berg. *Massachusetts State Discretionary Policies and Services in the Medicaid, Social Services, and Supplemental Security Income Programs*. Draft. San Francisco: Aging Health Policy Center, University of California, 1982.
Health Security Action Council. *Health Care Cost Containment – A Constructive Approach*. Washington, DC: Health Security Action Council, 1982.
Health Policy Week (HPW). 12, No. 4 (January 31, 1983).
Hudson, R. B. "The 'Graying' of the Federal Budget and Its Consequences for Old-Age Policy." *Gerontologist*, 18, No. 5 (October 1978), 428-440.
Intergovernmental Health Policy Project (IHHP) and National Governors' Association (NGA) State Medicaid Information Center. *Recent and Proposed Changes in State Medicaid Programs: A Fifty State Survey*. Washington, DC: IHHP, 1982.
Kahne, H. "Aid Old, Poor Women." Editorial. *New York Times*, February 1, 1983.
Kutza, E. A. *The Benefits of Old Age: Social Welfare Policy for the Elderly*. Chicago: University of Chicago Press, 1981.
La Jolla Management Corporation. *Medicaid Program Characteristics: Summary Tables*, Vol. 1. Washington, DC: U.S. Health Care Financing Administration, Office of Research and Demonstrations, 1982.
Long, S. H., and R. F. Settle. "Equity and Medicare: Evidence for Vulnerable Elderly Subpopulations." Paper presented at the American Public Health Association, Montreal, November 17, 1982a.
————. "Medicare Cost Sharing and Private Supplementary Health Insurance: Selected Research Findings." Paper presented at the American Public Health Association, Montreal, November 15, 1982b.
Luft, H. S. *Health Maintenance Organizations: Dimensions of Performance*. New York: John Wiley, 1981.
Merritt, R. E., and D. B. Potemken, eds. *Medigap: Issues and Update*. Washington, DC: Intergovernmental Health Policy Project, George Washington University, 1982.

Muse, D. N., and D. Sawyer. *The Medicare and Medicaid Data Book, 1981.* Washington, DC: U.S. Health Care Financing Administration, Office of Research and Demonstrations, 1982.

Myles, J. "The Trillion Dollar Misunderstanding." *Working Papers* (July/August, 1981), 23-31.

National Governors' Association (NGA), State Medicaid Program Information Center. *A Catalogue of State Medicaid Program Changes.* Washington, DC: Author, 1982.

New York Times. "Lawmakers Assert Pension Proposals Will be Approved." January 17, 1983, sec. A, p. 1.

Olson, L. K. *The Political Economy of Aging: The State, Private Power and Social Welfare.* New York: Columbia University Press, 1982.

Rigby, D. E., and E. Ponce. *The Supplemental Security Income Program for the Aged, Blind and Disabled: Selected Characteristics of State Supplementation Programs as of October, 1979.* Washington, DC: U.S. Social Security Administration, 1980.

Roemer, M. I., et al. "Cost Sharing for Ambulatory Care: Penny-Wise and Pound-Foolish." *Medical Care,* 13, No. 6 (June 1975), 457-466.

Ross, D., and W. Birdsall. *Social Security and Pensions.* Staff Report. Washington, DC: U.S. Special Study on Economic Change, Joint Economic Committee, 1980.

Ruther, M., and A. Dobson. "Equal Treatment and Unequal Benefits: A Reexamination of the Use of Medicare Services by Race, 1967-1976." *Health Care Financing Review,* 2, No. 3 (Winter 1981), 55-83.

Rymer, M., et al. *Comprehensive Review of Medicaid Eligibility.* Washington, DC: U.S. Health Care Financing Administration, 1977.

Sloan, F. A. *Medicaid Voucher: Prospects and Problems.* Prepared for presentation at the 1981 Commonwealth Fund Forum, "Medical Care for the Poor: What Can States Do in the 1980's?" Lake Bluff, Illinois, August 9-12, 1981. (Nashville, TN: Vanderbilt, University, 1981)

U.S. Department of Health and Human Services (DHHS), Office of Health Maintenance Organizations. *1980 Health Maintenance Organizations Census.* Rockville, MD: U.S. Public Health Service, Division of Program Promotion, 1980.

U.S. Department of Health and Human Services (DHH), Office of the Secretary. "Hospital Prospective Payment for Medicare." Report to Congress Required by the Tax Equity and Fiscal Responsibility Act of 1982. *Medicare and Medicaid Guide,* No. 374 (January 4, 1983).

U.S. General Accounting Office (GAO). *Rising Hospital Costs Can Be Restrained by Regulating Payments and Improving Management.* Washington, DC: GAO, 1980.

U.S. House, Select Committee on Aging, Statement by Elizabeth Hanford Dole, Commissioner, Federal Trade Commission. Hearing: *Abuses in the Sale of Health Insurance to the Elderly.* 95th Congress, 2d Session. Washington, DC: U.S. Government Printing Office, 1979.

U.S. House, Committee on the Budget. *First Concurrent Resolution on the Budget-Fiscal Year 1983.* Washington, DC: U.S. Government Printing Office, 1982.

U.S. Office of Management and Budget (OMB). *Budget of the United States Government, Fiscal Year 1984.* 97th Congress, 2d Session. Washington, DC: U.S. Government Printing Office, 1983.

U.S. [President's] National Commission on Social Security Reform. *Report of the National Commission on Social Security Reform.* Washington, DC: U.S. Government Printing Office, January 1983.

U.S. Public Law 97-35. Omnibus Budget Reconciliation Act of 1982 (HR 3982). Amendments to Title XXI — Medicare, Medicaid, Section 2100, passed by Congress, July 31. 1981. Washington, DC: U.S. Government Printing Office, 1981.

U.S. Public Law 97-248. Tax Equity and Fiscal Responsibility Act (HR 4961). Provisions Relating to Saving in Health and Income Security Programs, passed by Congress, July 12. Washington, DC: U.S. Government Printing Office, 1982.

U.S. Public Law 98-21. Social Security Act Amendments of 1983, April 20. Washington, DC: U.S. Government Printing Office, 1983.

U.S. Senate, Special Committee on Aging. *Developments in Aging: 1978,* Vol. 1. Washington, DC: U.S. Government Printing Office, 1979.

U.S. Senate, Committee on Finance. *The Social Security Act and Related Laws,* April. Washington, DC: U.S. Government Printing Office, 1982a.

U.S. Senate, Special Committee on Aging. *Developments in Aging: 1981,* Vol. 1. Washington, DC: U.S. Government Printing Office, 1982b.

U.S. Senate, Special Committee on Aging. "Health Care Expenditures for the Elderly: How Much Protection Does Medicare Provide?" Information Paper. Washington, DC: U.S. Government Printing Office, 1982c.

U.S. Senate, Special Committee on Aging. *Aging Reports,* January. Washington, DC: Author, 1983.

U.S. Social Security Administration (SSA). *Income and Resources of the Aged.* Washington, DC: U.S. Government Printing Office, 1980a.

———. *Social Security Disability. Disability: Past, Present and Future.* Washington, DC: U.S. Government Printing Office, 1980b.

———. *Social Security Bulletin,* 45, No. 9 (September 1982a).

———. *Social Security Bulletin,* 45, No. 10 (October 1982b).

———. *Social Security Handbook.* Washington, DC: U.S. Government Printing Office, 1982c.

———. *Social Security Bulletin,* 46, No. 1 (January 1983).

Vladeck, B. C. *Unloving Care: The Nursing Home Tragedy.* New York: Basic Books, 1980.

Waldo, D. R., and R. M. Gibson. "National Health Expenditures, 1981." *Health Care Financing Review,* 4, No. 1 (Summer 1982), 1-35.

CHAPTER 5

FISCAL CRISIS
Economic and Fiscal Problems of State and Local Governments

James H. Swan
Carroll L. Estes
Juanita B. Wood

State and local governments today are undergoing a period of "fiscal crisis." This generally means that for whatever reason, revenues are not sufficient to meet the expenditure needs of government. Whether with reluctance, resignation, or enthusiasm, state and local government officials are faced with the task of enforcing limits and/or cutbacks in government programs. In this environment, health and social service programs, particularly those for the aged, face cutbacks.

As a consequence of public policy trends established in the mid-1960s and the 1970s, the planning and administration of state-level health and social service programs in general and aging services in particular have generally been based on the assumption of continued growth, or at least of maintenance of effort. Although many programs have been state-administered, basic funding and other policy decisions have been made at the federal level. Moreover, present health and social programs have, over a period of years, evolved largely, but not exclusively, in reaction to initiatives from the federal level. This is

Authors' Note: The authors wish to acknowledge the efforts of Jon Garfield and Mary Kreger, members of the staff of the Fiscal Crisis Project. Both contributed to the conceptual design and data collection efforts. In particular, a literature review by Jon Garfield was invaluable in the preparation of this chapter. The data in this chapter are derived from research supported by the U.S. Administration on Aging Grant No. 90-AR-0016.

particularly the case for Medicare and for the aging services funded under the Older Americans Act (Estes, 1979). It is also true of health and social service programs not designed specifically for the aged but on which the aged are heavily dependent — for example, Medicaid and Title XX Social Services (now a social services block grant).

Many of these assumptions of state health and social service programs are now being seriously challenged: program growth has largely stopped, and in many cases programs are shrinking; greater administrative and programmatic responsibility is being given to states through block grants and other New Federalism initiatives. Further, these major changes in health and social programs have been introduced over a very short period of time, and the future portends still more changes. Finally, these changes come amid a period of economic crisis that has radically cut the revenue base of government, created increased need for particular types of social expenditures, and exacerbated the problems of governments that were already in fiscally weak, or crisis, situations. Thus, state and local governments are faced with increased fiscal and program responsibilities in multiple program areas at a time when many programs are undergoing federal cutbacks and when government resources are dwindling. These fiscal conditions have led to such unprecedented moves as the League of California Cities' informing municipalities how to initiate bankruptcy proceedings (Salzman, 1983).

Until the current period of crisis, the aged have been viewed as the most legitimate or "deserving" among service recipients (Cook, 1979; Klemmack and Roff, 1981). Nevertheless, budgetary constraints and recent federal policy developments make it clear that the services and other hard-won benefits for the aged are not exempt from the consequences of shrinkage in the public service sector. Aging services have already begun to feel the funding crunch in many states and localities. Even if benefits for the aged are the last to be cut, they nevertheless will be cut. Thus, fiscal crisis defines the conditions under which programs for the aged are cut back along with many other services.

This chapter begins with a theoretical overview of fiscal crisis in general followed by an explanation of some of the crucial elements that account for variation in the likelihood of fiscal crisis across (1) different levels of government and (2) different geographic locations. The remainder of the chapter presents data from our recent research on fiscal crisis and its impact on services for the aged. Our data illustrate the specific application of the theoretical framework built in the early part of this chapter.

Fiscal Crisis

"Fiscal crisis" is a term widely applied to the fiscal difficulties of governments in the United States. It generally refers to the inability of government to meet current operating expenses, impending or actual fiscal deficits, defaults on government fiscal obligations, or other general fiscal problems of government. Other uses of the term are more precise or more analytical — fiscal crisis is defined as a tendency for expenditures to rise faster than revenues, a fiscal threat to a government's survival as a relatively autonomous entity, or a declaration of crisis involving government finances (O'Connor, 1973; Mollenkopf, 1975; Schultze et al., 1977).

O'Connor (1973), in his seminal work on the fiscal crisis of the state, spoke of a "structural gap between state expenditures and revenues." This gap consists of simultaneous tendencies toward an increase in demand for expenditures and a limit to the base for revenue. Various aspects of these conflicting tendencies have been explored by the theorists of fiscal crisis (see O'Connor, 1973; Gordon, 1977; Mollenkopf, 1977; Schultze et al., 1977).

The theoretical model of O'Connor (1973) and others proposes a tendency for expenditures to exceed revenues. For this tendency to exist, deficit spending is not necessary. In the United States only the federal government can engage consistently in deficit spending. State governments holding budget surpluses can engage in spending that exceeds revenues until such surpluses are depleted, but few states have budget balances large enough to allow this to be a consistent practice (National Governors' Association [NGA], 1981, 1982). States with biennial budgets may show first-year deficits but must balance the budget by the end of the two-year period. All but one state (Vermont) are prohibited from end-of-budget general fund deficits — that is, expenditures outstripping budget resources (for a discussion, see NGA, 1981, 2-5). City governments generally have much smaller budget reserves and must balance annual budgets. They therefore have less capacity to incur expenditures greater than revenues.

Deficit spending, moreover, is only one possible outcome of a tendency for expenditures to outstrip revenues. Governments often respond with attempts to raise greater revenues, especially through higher taxation. This has led in some cases to the sparking of taxpayer revolt. Of course, another response is to cut expenditures, usually by cutting back on services, on transfer payments, or on transfers to other governments. In fact, one part of the "tax revolt" involved the enacting of spending limits, striking at a government's ability to spend rather than at its ability to collect revenues. In our fiscal crisis study (Swan et al., 1982), states and locales varied in their responses to fiscal constraint. States appeared to use a reduction in expenditures as the first resort and then turned to increasing revenues, while the local level did just the opposite. This difference reinforces the assumption that local governments entered periods of fiscal strain earlier than did state governments, and that they depleted their resource bases earlier. The first response to fiscal strain was to increase revenues, and when that was no longer possible, to reduce expenditures.

An important tenet of this interpretation of fiscal crisis is that the phenomenon is not accidental; rather, it is created by the very structure of government. This "structure" involves functions of governments which by their nature both increase expenditures and limit revenues. For example, governments must stimulate the economy. This involves public expenditure urban renewal, and redevelopment (Keynesian economics at the national level), as well as limits to revenue (particularly tax cuts and tax breaks). Likewise, government must ameliorate social problems and provide for the defense of the system against external and internal threats. The general process noted by O'Connor (1973) is for governments to incur the costs of the expansion of the private sector, while the resulting profits are retained in that sector. The "collectivization of costs" and "privatization of profits" are seen as the primary factors involved in the creation of what O'Connor refers to as a "structural gap" between revenues and expenditures.

Recently, supply-side economists have challenged this dual role of government. Essentially, the government role is defined as ensuring that profits are retained in the private sector, but not as actively ensuring the expansion of that sector: free enterprise can expand itself as long as the government does not tax away the capital needed for this expansion. Thus, the role of ameliorating social problems is specifically denied as appropriate for the government. In practice, however, the proponents of supply-side economics have not eluded the dynamics of the fiscal crisis. First, the reduced expenditures for federal social programs to ameliorate social problems have been more than offset by increases in defense expenditures. Second, the reductions in social expenditures and problems in the economy, at least in large part the result of Reagan administration policy, have apparently generated a level of political opposition that makes it doubtful that the government can fully reduce its role of underwriting costs to the degree argued by the supply-side enthusiasts. Finally, a declining economy (resulting in a declining revenue base), massive tax cuts, and rapid increase in defense spending have resulted in gigantic and growing federal budget deficits: Fiscal crisis has reached the federal government. Nevertheless, the major locus of concern over fiscal crisis is currently at the state and local level, especially as their fiscal problems increase with the decline of funds from the federal government.

This discussion of fiscal crisis has not dealt with another set of meanings — the political usages of the term. The declaration of perceived crisis is conditioned by an actor's political judgment, and crisis may serve political purposes (Edelman, 1964, 1970; Estes, 1979). Thus, it can be assumed neither that the declaration of the existence of a fiscal crisis is purely a response to poor government financial conditions nor that the absence of such a declaration indicates favorable fiscal conditions.[1]

In line with these considerations, it should be noted that some theorists employ the terms "fiscal stress" or "fiscal strain" (Peterson, 1976; Friedland et al., 1977) to denote poor fiscal conditions. Such usages would allow for the use of the term "fiscal crisis" in a political meaning: the *declaration* of threat to government integrity or autonomy on the basis of government fiscal problems. It is sufficient to note here that cuts in government programs may be accompanied or occasioned by political declarations of crisis separable in part from poor fiscal conditions. We argue in this chapter that real government fiscal problems exist, resulting in cutbacks to government programs, particularly those for the aged.

State and Local Fiscal Crisis

Multiple state surveys since 1975 show that many states experienced tax initiatives affecting revenues and/or spending prior to the federal cutbacks initiated in 1981. For example, data collected by the Advisory Committee on Intergovernmental Relations (ACIR in New York Times, 1981) indicate that 64 percent of the states (32 of the 50 states) had enacted reductions in income or sales taxes between 1977 and 1980. Thirty-eight percent of the states (19 of the 50) had enacted spending or taxation limits between 1976 and 1980. More than one-fourth (14 of 50) of the states had both an income or sales tax reduction and a spending or taxing limit prior to 1980. Further, state and local expenditures as a percentage of the federal gross national product (GNP) have been shrinking since 1975. Although spending by state and local government for the development of basic infrastructure and services far outpaced the overall economy for almost twenty-five years, accounting for 15 percent of the GNP in 1975, this trend came to an abrupt halt during the 1974-1975 recession. *Business Week* (1981, p. 155) in a special issue devoted to the economic problems of government, sounded the alarm about state and local capacity to respond to the economic and policy conditions of the 1980s. Of special concern were reduced tax capacity, high interest rates, a reduction in the investor attractiveness of state and local government, and increased pressure for states to pick up social program costs:

> National policy now pits states and municipalities squarely against the economy's most powerful borrowers, the federal government and large business corporations. In this kind of struggle, state and local governments cannot win.

Fiscal crises do not pose the same threat nor take the same form for all governments. Local governments in particular constitute a wide array of types, have varied responsibilities and capacities, and possess different degrees of fiscal strength. There are different patterns of distribution of responsibilities for functions (particularly for health and social services) between city and county governments, and in some cases the county government does not exist or is not relevant. Even an examination confined to city governments must recognize the difference between types of city (Howell and Stamm, 1979; Berry and Smith, 1972). Of importance are variables such as fiscal capacity, degree of fiscal responsibility for health and social service, and type of city (Howell and Stamm, 1979).

Gordon (1977) discusses the differences between "old" and "new" cities in terms of a stage theory. Old cities built to accommodate an industrial system ("industrial cities") find themselves at a disadvantage in the new era of the "corporate city." The age of the city has a bearing on the demand for maintenance and renewal costs as well as on the ability to accommodate corporate needs as opposed to industrial needs (Gordon, 1977). The loss of an industrial base leads to social hardships that generate demands for social spending. Efforts to "modernize" generate demands for urban renewal and redevelopment spending. At the same time, the loss of the industrial base means the loss of a revenue base, through loss of productive property, loss of income, and the necessity of giving "tax breaks" in order to retain or attract industry.

Howell and Stamm (1979) conceptualize differences between old and young cities in terms of a manufacturing growth cycle. They find that old industrialized cities suffer from "an environment which is neither financially sound nor economically sustainable; but argue that "at least some cities can buck the strong trend toward higher taxes, debt, and expenses that accompanies the process of industrial aging" (Howell and Stamm, 1979, pp. 120-121).

In spite of the differences among cities, they experience much in common. Sternlieb and Hughes (1977) emphasize job shifts from cities in some regions to those in others, but find much in common among all of these cities; in particular, all experience industrial and residential suburbanization. Schultze et al. (1977) argue that all large cities will experience fiscal problems because expenditures tend to outstrip the revenue bases. This applies to the governments of large cities with increasing revenue bases as well as to those with declining revenue bases.

Further, in the system of governments making up the public sector in the United States, local governments are in very dependent roles. They have neither the fiscal resources of the federal and state governments nor the same power over their own finances (O'Connor, 1973; U.S. Congress, 1975). Cities in weak fiscal positions are especially dependent on the federal and state governments for aid, but may find these governments assuming less of the burden while pushing more responsibilities to the local level (Silverman, 1977).

Moreover, local governments are particularly likely to have their revenue bases limited by state law or the state constitution. For example, of the 25 states with general fiscal limitation laws in 1979, 23 had laws that applied to local governments, of which 22 had limitations on local property taxation; in only 9 states did these laws apply to the state itself (Ellickson, 1980). Howell and Stamm (1979) note that few city governments are near the theoretical limits of their revenue-generating abilities but that an increasing number are prevented by states from realizing their full revenue-generating capacities.

The fiscal conditions of local governments have varied impacts on health and social services. Much of the health and social service dollar expended at the local level has come from higher levels of government (Howell and Stamm, 1979). However, the shifting of responsibilities for government services means that local government is being left with greater responsibility for human services. An example in California is the shifting of responsibility for medically indigent adults from the state Medicaid program (MediCal) to county government through a block grant and a 20 percent cut in state funding.

State finances are somewhat different from local finances. The Joint Economic Committee of the U.S. Congress (1975, p. 3) stated: "Most states finish their fiscal year with surpluses remaining in their general fund accounts after all revenues have been collected and expenditures made." This is very different from the case for local governments:

> Unencumbered surpluses are much less significant for local government budgets than for state governments. Local governments tend to operate as near to a balanced budget as possible, with surpluses generally returning to citizens through tax reductions or service improvements [U.S. Congress, 1975, p. 10].

The relatively greater strength of states to build up surpluses can be traced to their greater abilities to tax and to broaden revenue bases. For example, California was able to build a large surplus ($5 billion), which it then used to "bail out" local governments after the passage of Proposition 13. Such surpluses are often generated through state income taxes, but California and other energy-producing states also received large infusions of severance and other natural resource taxes (NGA, 1981).

Nevertheless, state governments also face fiscal crises — as illustrated in California's difficulties with its fiscal year (FY) 1983 budget. State budget surpluses are sometimes depleted, especially in times of economic downturn (U.S. Congress, 1975), or the political pendulum may swing toward taxpayer movements that limit the ability to generate or maintain surpluses at the state level. O'Connor (1973) finds much in common between state and local governments, in contrast to the federal government. He notes that state and local governments are more responsive to special interests; are more concerned with economic development and are in fierce competition with one another for industries; have more fragmented budgeting procedures and therefore less control over expenditures; and are much more limited in their abilities to borrow and go into debt. As a result, state and local governments are more dependent on financial institutions, more subject to high interest rates, and more open to influence on the part of financial institutions regarding the ways in which borrowed funds are to be expended.

Prediction of State Fiscal Strength

States differ over time and among themselves in their relative fiscal positions. During the recession of 1974-1975, energy-producing states tended to have large, unencumbered budget surpluses and to suffer little or no depletion of these surpluses. Agriculture-producing states tended to have large surpluses that were, however, subject to depletion. By contrast, "high unemployment" states tended to have very small or nonexistent surpluses (U.S. Congress, 1975).

These data suggest not only that some economic resources improve a state's fiscal strength, but also that some factors (such as energy production) become relatively more important and that others (such as agricultural production) become less important in the process. Data on state budget balances are available by state for the period 1978-1983 (NGA, 1979, 1981, 1982) and make possible a more thorough analysis over time (see Table 5.1).[2] States that are high fuel producers[3] and high agricultural producers fare better than states that are not, but most of the effects are concentrated among the states high on both types of production (see Table 5.1). The difference in fiscal health and viability between these nine states and the others greatly increased for the period 1981-1983 — as the national economic picture worsened. This accords with the findings of the Joint Economic Commission for the 1974-1975 recession (U.S. Congress, 1975), but the important factor is a state's being a high producer of both fuel minerals and agricultural products rather than simply being high in production of energy.

States that rely heavily on manufacturing[4] are much less likely than are other states to have high budget surpluses, especially in the period 1980-1983. Reliance on manufacturing is a structural factor that negatively affects state fiscal conditions. Of the six states high on both fuel and agricultural production and also low on manufacturing production, all have budget surpluses amounting to 5 percent or more of expenditures in fiscal years 1978-1980 and 1983; five of the six have such surpluses in FY 1981 and FY 1982.[5]

Thus far we have considered only the resource side. The arguments regarding fiscal problems have also to do with expenditures.

TABLE 5.1   Prevalence of "Reasonable" Budget Balances by State Characteristics

Type of State	State Fits Type	Nᵃ	Percentages of States of Given Type with Budget Balance 5% or More of Expenditures in Fiscal Year:					
			1978	1979	1980	1981	1982ᵇ	1983ᵇ
Total		50	63	74	62	40	26	30
High fuel	yes	15	87	80	80	67	47	60
Mineral producersᶜ	no	35	53	71	54	29	17	17
High Agricultural	yes	18	83	89	72	56	44	56
Producersᵈ	no	32	52	66	56	31	16	16
Both high fuel and agricultural producers	yes	9	100	100	100	89	78	89
	no	41	55	68	54	29	15	17
High reliance on manufacturingᵉ	yes	34	62	62	50	21	12	15
	no	16	67	88	88	81	56	62
High fuel-high agricultural-low manufacturing	yes	6	100	100	100	83	83	100
	no	44	58	70	57	34	18	20
Low shares for both public welfare and healthᶠ	yes	17	75	88	76	59	41	53
	no	33	58	67	55	30	18	18
"Structural gap": low fuel-low agriculture-high manufacturing-high health or welfare shares	yes	19	47	53	47	11	0	5
	no	31	73	87	71	58	42	45

SOURCES: National Governors' Association, and National Association of State Budget Officers. *Fiscal Survey of the States: 1978-79*, Table A-2; *1979-80*, Table A-2; *1980-81;* Table A-3; *1981-82*, Table A-2; Washington, DC: NGA and NASBO, 1979; 1980; 1981; 1982. U.S. Bureau of the Census. *Statistical Abstract of the United States: 1979*, Table 493; *1981*, Tables 1175, 1307, 1416. Washington, DC: U.S. Department of Commerce, 1979; 1981.

a. Data are missing for Nevada in 1978; total N=49.

b. FY 1983 figures are estimates made during FY 1982; FY 1982 figures are projections to end of fiscal year.

c. "High" fuel mineral-producing states are those with values of production per capita of al least $300 in 1979.

d. "High" agriculture-producing states are those with values of production per capita of at least $600 in 1978.

e. "High" reliance on manufacturing states are those with value added in manufacturing of at least $2000 per capita in 1977.

f. "Low" health and welfare share states are those with both (1) less than 16% of total direct general 1979 expenditures devoted to "public welfare", and (2) 8% or less of total direct general 1977 expenditures devoted to "health and hospitals."

Fiscal crisis results from tendencies involving both revenues and expenditures (O'Connor, 1973). Measures based on the share of public welfare and of health and hospital spending in total state government general expenditures[6] do not predict relative budget surplus; but a measure classifying states as low on both types of expenditure is positively correlated with FY 1981 and FY 1983 budget surpluses. The relationships are not statistically significant, however, when controlled for the resource measures (such as fuel and agricultural measures).

Given the logic of the arguments regarding the "structural gap," our prediction would be that states with limited resources and high expenditures will be at the highest risk of fiscal problems (although all governments theoretically will suffer to some degree from such a structural gap). States with low fuel and low agricultural production, high reliance on manufacturing, and high health or welfare shares of expenditures (19 of 50) were classified as most vulnerable to a structural gap between revenue resources and expenditures. The other states were classified as less vulnerable to such a gap. This measure correlates significantly with the budget surplus measures for fiscal years 1979 and 1981-1983, indicating that the likelihood of a state shortfall is increased under the conditions of high vulnerability to a structural gap. The relationships are as expected — the greater the vulnerability to a structural gap, the lower the probability of state fiscal well-being (Table 5.1). The associations are in general stronger over time, suggesting that the structural gap has a greater negative effect on state fiscal health as economic conditions worsen.

In sum, structural aspects of state economies, and human service generosity in government expenditures, have been linked to the probability of fiscal health in state government. In general, the resource side, based on state economic structure, provides the strongest determinants of fiscal health. There is, however, some evidence to support the arguments regarding a structural gap involving simultaneous resource limits and demand for expenditures. The question remains as to how this affects state and local funding for the aged.

Effects of Fiscal Problems

In the current era of cutbacks, fiscal problems, and economic recession, it is no secret that government expenditures are being controlled or cut in most parts of the nation. The contention that

government expenditures should be cut and many services curtailed
is not new; the view that government has grown too large, or at least
contains too much "fat," has been associated with the tax revolt
starting in the late 1970s. Assessing the effects of government fiscal
crisis on expenditures is more complex, however. It can be argued
that it was the appearance of government fiscal crisis (accompanied,
but not totally determined, by an economic downturn) that made the
cutting of government expenditures not only a winning argument and
campaign for the proponents of such cuts but, at least temporarily, a
political necessity for the former advocates of government programs.

Some light is thrown on this process by examining data from our
fiscal crisis study[7] on the impacts of tax revolt and fiscal crisis on
government services for the aged. Data were collected from a sample
of 791 elite respondents[8] — government officials, institutional leaders
and service advocates, and other opinion leaders — from ten states[9]
(representing eight federal regions) and from thirty-two urban
localities, selected as representing local governments of medium to
large size within the sample states. The sample states appear to be
generally representative of nonsample states in terms of relative
deficit or surplus status (see Table 5.2).[10] These data were collected
prior to the implementation of Reagan's first major cutbacks in the fall
of 1981. Thus, the data reported in this chapter represent governmental reactions to state and local fiscal problems prior to the changes in
federal expenditures and policies contained in the 1981 Omnibus
Budget Reconciliation Act and the Economic Recovery Tax Act.

General Governmental Response
To Fiscal Problems

A variety of data allow us to consider the nature of governmental
response to fiscal problems. Of particular interest are responses to
survey items asked only of respondents who had reported some
degree of fiscal weakness. Public officials in the sample (N=72 at the
state level, 140 at the local level) responded to items regarding the
existence of fiscal shortfalls for FY 1981 and FY 1982.[11] Those responding affirmatively were asked whether the major response of
their government to the shortfall emphasized cutting expenditures or
increasing revenues. They were also asked about the major forms
taken by expenditure cuts (see Table 5.3).

TABLE 5.2   Comparison of Fiscal Crisis Study Sample States with Other States on Percentages Falling in Budget Balance Categories

States	Categories: Budget Balance as Percentage of Expenditures	Percentages of States in Each Category for Fiscal Year:					
		1978	1979	1980	1981	1982[a]	1983[a]
Fiscal crisis sample (N=10)	5% or over surplus	70	80	50	30	30	30
	0=5% surplus	20	20	40	60	50	70
	negative (deficit)	10	0	10	10	20	0
Non sample states (N=40)[b]	5% or over surplus	62	72	65	42	25	30
	0=5% surplus	38	28	35	50	62	65
	negative (deficit)	0	0	0	8	12	5

SOURCES: See Table 5.1.

a. FY 1983 figures are estimates made during FY 1982; FY 1982 figures are projected to end of fiscal year.

b. N=39 for 1978.

Even before federal cuts were implemented, fiscal problems were relatively widespread among state and local governments. Of the state-level public influentials, 42 percent reported fiscal shortfall in FY 1981; this percentage increased to 54 percent in FY 1982.[12] The same pattern occurred at the local level, where 59 percent of the public influentials reported FY 1981 shortfalls, and 67 percent projected FY 1982 shortfalls.

While it is clear that the most common governmental response to fiscal problems in the early 1980s has been to reduce expenditures, efforts to generate more revenues did emerge. Of the state-level public officials reporting shortfall, almost all reported expenditure reductions as a major response (see Table 5.3).[13] Very few reported revenue increases as responses to shortfall. At the local level, the percentages reporting expenditure reductions are similar (and very high), but revenue increases are far more common as a local-level strategy for dealing with fiscal constraint.

Effects of Fiscal Problems on Human Services

Cuts to human services figures prominently in the responses of state governments to fiscal shortfall. Of the state-level respondents

TABLE 5.3   Percentages of Public Influentials Reporting Shortfalls and Governmental Responses to Shortfalls

	State (N=72) 1981	1982	Local (N=140) 1981	1982
Fiscal Shortfall Exists	42%	54%	59%	67%
Important governmental responses reported by those indicating shortfall[a]	(N=30)	(N=36)	(N=82)	(N=89)
Expenditure reductions[b]	83%	86%	76%	83%
Revenue increases[b]	12	25	34	31
Human service cuts[c]	46	50	15	16
Across-the-board cuts[c]	29	34	26	28
Cuts in public employment costs[c]	36	21	61	48

SOURCE: Aging Health Policy Center Fiscal Crisis Elite Survey, Public Influential Instrument.

Items asked: "Approaching fiscal year 1981, did projections show that (STATE/LOCAL) government's estimated revenues would fall short of what would be required to maintain existing levels of expenditures?" " Does (STATE/LOCALITY) face a projected shortfall, for fiscal year 1982?"

"In (STATE/CITY) government's approach to this projected shortfall, which received more emphasis: reducing expenditures or increasing revenues?"

"Briefly, what where the most important things (STATE/CITY) government did to reduce expenditures?"

a. These items were asked only of these indicating shortfall; numbers shown in parentheses to right are bases for percentages.

b. Responses of "both" were coded under both "expenditure reduction" and "revenue increase" categories; "other" responses coded in "other" category; sum of percentages in table may be above or below 100%.

c. Item was open-ended, responses coded into categories, multiple responses allowed; other categories exist but are not reported here; sum of percentages in table may be above or below 100%.

who reported shortfalls, about half reported some form or other of human service cuts as among the "most important" things done to reduce expenditures. About one-third reported that across-the-board cuts had been invoked. In contrast, human service cuts are not as commonly reported as among the primary local-level responses to shortfall. This is not surprising, given the different responsibilities and structures at the local and state levels. However, cuts in the costs of public employment were very commonly reported as local-level shortfall responses. Such reductions may especially affect human service programs through staffing reductions, increased workloads, and turnover of experienced personnel in service agencies.

TABLE 5.4   Percentages of Public Influentials Reporting 1978-1981 Cutbacks in Services

| Services/Benefits | Percentage Reporting Cutbacks[a] by Government at Level: | |
	State (N=72)	Local (N=140)
Aging services	5%	16%
Health services	11	21
Social services	15	29
Income maintenance	8	16

SOURCE: See Table 5.3.

Item asked: "Since 1978, has (STATE/LOCAL) government spending in the following areas been: greatly cutback, cutback, left as same level, increased, or greatly increased?" (Items are as listed in this table.)

a. Percentage responding "greatly cutback" or "cutback."

Cuts to aging services are less commonly reported than are those to human services in general. Public officials were asked specifically about cuts in aging services, health services, social services, and income maintenance during the period 1978-1981 (see Table 5.4). At most, one-sixth of the state and one-third of the local public officials reported cutbacks to any one of these areas. Cuts to aging services were least likely to be reported; however, they were more likely to have occurred at the local than at the state level.

Cuts in services to the aged are more strongly linked to fiscal problems than are more general cuts in human services. To investigate these links, we examined the correlations between reports of cutbacks and the fiscal condition of the states and localities studied (as measured by shortfall in FY 1981), taking positive associations to indicate that these early cutbacks were necessitated by poor fiscal conditions. When state-level and local-level measures were correlated with the percentage reporting cuts in various service areas during the 1978 to 1981 period, cuts in aging services are significantly related to the percentage reporting FY 1981 shortfalls at both state ($r=.65$) and local ($r=.37$) levels (see Table 5.5). At the state level, cuts in income maintenance ($r=.75$), and at the local level, cuts in social services ($r=.40$), are also significantly related to the percentage reporting shortfall. Thus, it may be that the aged are generally spared direct cutbacks until fiscal conditions worsen, but any such exemptions are not likely to hold when governments experience severe fiscal difficulties.

TABLE 5.5   Correlations: Changes in 1978-1981 Service Funding by FY 1981 Fiscal Shortfall

| Public Influential Measures for: | N | Correlations Percentages of Respondents Indicating FY 1981 Shortfall with 1978-1981 Funding Changes[b] in: | | | |
		Aging Services	Health Services	Social Services	Income Maintenance
States	10	.65[a]	.46	—[c]	.75[a]
Localities	32	.37[a]	−.07	.40[a]	—[c]

SOURCE: See Table 5.3. Funding change measures employ 5-point scale.

a. Significant at .05 level.

b. Change scores created by allocating values 1 to 5 to categories listed in Table 5.4. "Greatly cutback" is 1; "greatly increased" is 5.

c. The variation on this item at this level was insufficient to allow for meaningful use of this item in correlational analysis.

Moreover, it should be remembered that the aged are affected as well by other reductions in the human services. In particular, Medicaid cutbacks, especially for institutional services, have an important impact on the aged. Likewise, cuts in public services other than health and social services may especially affect the aged, who are dependent on public transit, consumer protection, police and fire protection, recreation, and libraries. Our data suggest, however, that government fiscal problems of the 1980s may generate direct cuts in programs for the aged, as well as the less direct cuts to programs used by the aged. This is the era in which even Social Security appears to be assailable. Before the current crisis is over, services to the aged may be cut as drastically as those for other age groups.

Class issues are also involved in the cuts at the state and local levels. It is argued in Chapter 1 that the poorest of the aged are most dependent on those services (such as Medicaid) that are most heavily influenced by variable and inequitable state policies and that are wholly or partially supported by state funds. An implication of state fiscal problems, and resulting cuts in funding for social programs, is that these cuts are likely to be concentrated on those services on which the poorest of the aged are most dependent. It is true that some states have attempted to cut life-enhancing programs (such as recreation) before touching life-sustaining programs (for example, income maintenance). Nevertheless, it would appear that programs primarily serving the poorest of the aged are at risk wherever state or local governments face fiscal problems.

Conclusion

Our conclusions are not a surprise to those who have been following the literature on fiscal crisis in recent years. Governments in the United States are undergoing a period of crisis. This crisis is not uniform; it strikes deeper at governments in states that have neither fuel nor agricultural productiioion as revenue bases, in states that are dependent on manufacturing, ánd in those that are more generous with regard to human services funding. There is some support in the observed patterns of variability across states for the argument that there is a structural gap between revenue limits and the demand for expenditures. At the same time, the major determinant of fiscal weakness appears to come from the revenue side — limits on revenue bases. As the general economic crisis deepens, not only will the fiscal positions of all governments weaken, but the differences between the fiscally stronger and weaker governments will widen. If many governments seem to fall into the fiscal abyss, some nevertheless fall first and fall fastest.

The responses of state and local government to fiscal crisis provide no more surprises than do fiscal conditions themselves. Whatever the ideology of those in power, cuts to human services seem inevitable. Attempts may be made to raise revenues, but such attempts are not likely to succeed in eliminating altogether the necessity for cuts. What may be surprising is evidence that links cuts in aging services to fiscal problems — the aged constitute a "truly needy" group whose funding once was thought to be inviolate. The findings reported in this chapter merely underline the relatively favorable position of aging programs vis-à-vis programs for other groups. Other programs were cut first, but with advanced crisis the cuts have reached the aged. Because funding for the aged is no longer inviolate, one of the most dependent of populations faces an austere future.

Notes

1. In our survey research on fiscal crisis, we have included both (1) items regarding judgments of specific fiscal and economic conditions, and (2) items regarding the existence of "fiscal crisis."

2. Data are available for prior years, but FY 1979 is the first year for which there are data for all of the states; data are available for 49 states for FY 1978.

3. Fuel mineral production, rather than energy production, was used for this analysis. On both the fuel mineral and agricultural variables, states were classified on

the value of production per capita (as close as possible to the beginning of the 1978-1983 period) — $300 or higher in 1979 for fuel mineral production, $600 or higher in 1978 for agricultural production.

4. Unemployment is not a good concept to operationalize for our purposes, because it is extremely variable and cyclical and combines factors limiting revenues and increasing demand for expenditures, thus making disaggregation of revenue and expenditure sides difficult. Reliance on manufacturing is used because it (1) is less variable over time, (2) represents a structural feature of state economics, and (3) is conceptually linked to state government resources and more than to demand for expenditures. The manufacturing measure is created by classifying states as "high" or "low" on value added by manufacturing per capita — $2000 or more is high.

5. Because a budget surplus amounting to 5 percent of expenditures is considered to be a "reasonable reserve" (NGA, 1978, 1980), states were classified for each fiscal year as too whether they had a budget surplus of 5 percent or more of expenditures. States with surpluses of 4.9 percent were rounded to 5 percent or more of expenditures. States with surpluses of 4.9 percent were rounded to 5 percent for this purpose.

6. States were classified as "low" on public welfare if 1977 expenditures in this area were less than 16 percent of all direct general expenditures. They were low on health and hospitals if 1977 expenditures in this area amounted to 8 percent or less of direct general expenditures. The 17 states low on both of these measures are the "low generosity" or "low share" states. Measures of per capita spending on public welfare and on health and hospitals did not predict as well as did the share measures.

7. Supported by Administration on Aging Grant No. 90-AR-0016.

8. Data were also gathered from ninety-four respondents in eight rural localities. These data are not reported here.

9. The sample states are California, Florida, Massachusetts, Missouri, Nebraska, Pennsylvania, Texas, Vermont, Washington, and Wisconsin.

10. The 5 percent "reasonable reserve" classification was used; but in addition, those states with budget balances less than 5 percent of expenditures were further classified as to whether they showed a deficit (negative budget balance). Among all states, those with negative balances varied from none in FY 1979 to 7 in FY 1982.

11. See Table 5.3 for the text of fiscal shortfall items asked of respondents. The public influentials consist of elected public officials, city managers, executive and legislative budget analysts, and respondents from the state offices of the political party not in the governor's office. The elected public officials include the governor, state representatives and state senators on budget and aging committees, mayors of cities, city council members, and county commissioners.

12. The percentage of respondents from each state indicating a FY 1982 shortfall correlates −.91 with a measure of fiscal health created from published state budget data (NGA, 1981). The budget measure is created by dividing 1982 state government general fund resources by 1981 expenditures, thus indicating the degree to which 1982 resources could cover 1981 expenditures. The definition of FY 1982 "fiscal shortfall" is the inability of resources to cover the past year's expenditures. Thus, the extremely high magnitude and negative sign of the correlation are taken to validate the survey shortfall responses.

13. Because multiple responses are allowed, and because there are response categories not reported here, the percentages reported here do not necessarily sum to 100 percent.

References

Berry, B.J.L., and K.B. Smith, eds. *City Classification Handbook: Methods and Applications.* New York: John Wiley, 1972.

Business Week. "State and Local Government in Trouble." October 26, 1981.

Cook, F. L. *Who Should Be Helped? Support for Social Services.* Beverly Hills, CA: Sage, 1979.

Craig, J., and M. Koleda. "The Urban Fiscal Crisis in the United States, National Health Insurance, and Municipal Hospitals." *International Journal of Health Services,* 8, No. 2 (1978), 329-349.

Edelman, M. *Political Language: Words That Succeed and Policies That Fail.* New York: Random House, 1970.

———. *The Symbolic Uses of Politics.* Urbana: University of Illinois, 1964.

Ellickson, P.L. *The Fiscal Limitation Movement: Present Context and Outlook.* Santa Monica, CA: Rand Corporation, 1980.

Estes, C.L. *The Aging Enterprise.* San Francisco: Jossey-Bass, 1979.

Friedland, R., F. F. Piven, and R. Alford. "Political Conflict, Urban Structure, and the Fiscal Crisis." *International Journal of Urban and Regional Research,* 1, No. 3 (1977), 447-471.

Gordon, D. "Capitalism and the Roots of Urban Crisis." In *The Fiscal Crisis of American Cities.* Ed. R.E. Alcaly and D. Mermelstein. New York: Vintage, 1977.

Grossman, D.A. *The Future of New York City's Capital Plant.* Washington, DC: Urban Institute, 1979.

Howell, J.M. and C.F. Stamm. *Urban Fiscal Stress.* Lexington, MA: D.C. Heath, 1979.

Klemmack, D.L., and L.L. Roff. "Predicting General Comparative Support for Governments Providing Benefits to Older Persons." *Gerontologist,* 21, No. 6 (December 1981), 592-599.

Mollenkopf, J.H. "The Crisis of the Public Sector in America's Cities." In *The Fiscal Crisis of American Cities.* Ed. R.E. Alcaly and D. Mermelstein. New York: Vintage, 1977.

———. "The Postwar Politics of Urban Development." *Politics and Society,* 5, No. 3 (1975), 247-295.

National Governors' Association (NGA) and National Association of State Budget Officers (NASBO). *Fiscal Survey of the States: 1977.* Washington, DC: NGA and NASBO, 1978.

———. *Fiscal Survey of the States: 1978-1979.* Washington, DC: NGA and NASBO, 1979.

———. *Fiscal Survey of the States: 1979-1980.* Washington, DC: NGA and NASBO, 1980.

———. *Fiscal Survey of the States: 1980-1981.* Washington, DC: NGA and NASBO, 1981.

———. *Fiscal Survey of the States: 1981-1982.* Washington, DC: NGA and NASBO, 1982.

New York Times. "Rating Capabilities of the States." September 27, 1981.

Oakland, W.H. "Proposition 13 — Genesis and Consequences." In *Policy Studies Review Annual,* Vol. 3. Ed. R.H. Haveman and B.B. Zellner. Beverly Hills, CA: Sage, 1979.

O'Connor, J. *The Fiscal Crisis of the State*. New York: St. Martin's Press, 1973.

Peterson, G. E. "Finance." In *The Urban Predicament*. Ed. W. Gorham and N. Glazer. Washington, DC: Urban Institute, 1976.

Peterson, P. E., and S. M. David. *Urban Politics and Public Policy: The City in Crisis*. New York: Praeger, 1976.

Salzman, E. "In Historic Move, Cities Exploring Bankruptcy. *Sacramento Bee*, January 19, 1983.

Schultze, C. L., et al. "Fiscal Problems of Cities." In *The Fiscal Crisis of American Cities*. Ed. R. E. Alcaly and D. Mermelstein. New York: Vintage, 1977.

Silverman, E. B. "New York City Revenues: The Federal and State Role." In *The Fiscal Crisis of American Cities*. Ed. R. E. Alcaly and D. Mermelstein. New York: Vintage, 1977.

Sternlieb, G., and J. W. Hughes. "Metropolitan Decline and Inter-Regional Job Shifts." In *The Fiscal Crisis of American Cities*. Ed. R. E. Alcaly and D. Mermelstein. New York: Vintage, 1977.

Swan, J. H., C. L. Estes, J. B. Wood, M. Kreger, and J. Garfield. *Fiscal Crisis: Impact on Aging Services*. Final Report. Prepared for the U.S. Administration on Aging under Grant No. 90-AR-0016. San Francisco: Aging Health Policy Center, University of California, 1982.

U.S. Bureau of the Census. *Statistical Abstract of the United States: 1979*. Washington, DC: U.S. Government Printing Office, 1979.

————. *Statistical Abstract of the United States: 1981*. Washington, DC: U.S. Government Printing Office, 1981.

U.S. Congress, Joint Economic Committee. *The Current Fiscal Position of State and Local Governments*. Washington, DC: U.S. Government Printing Office, 1975.

CHAPTER 6

SOCIAL SERVICES
The Impact of Fiscal Austerity

David A. Lindeman
Alan Pardini

The needs of the disadvantaged elderly and other at-risk populations may not be met solely by income-maintenance, health, and housing programs. Frequently, the aged are in need of one or more services that have been categorized as general or personal social services. Among the array of services encompassed by this concept are counseling, community centers, congregate and home-delivered meal programs, protective services, day care, respite care, homemaker services, chore services, information and referral, and transportation services. Unlike most welfare programs, receipt of social services is not based solely on income, but frequently considers age and/or other categorical factors as criteria for eligibility. These services are instrumental in helping many elderly individuals maintain their independence and self-sufficiency through the provision of a community-based service system. The current social service system has come to play a major role in the welfare of the elderly by providing necessary linkages among and filling "gaps" within the array of federal, state, and local income-maintenance, health, and housing programs.

Social services in the United States have been provided since the turn of the century through a variety of public and private systems. Starting in the early 1960s, the federal government assumed a progressively more extensive role in the financing of social services. Until

Authors' Note: The authors wish to acknowledge the invaluable contribution of Carroll L. Estes. The data in this chapter are derived from research supported by the U.S. Health Care Financing Administration Grant No. 18-P9762019 and the U.S. National Center for Health Services Research Grant No. H504042.

1980 federal support for social services increased steadily through the enactment of social welfare legislation and increased federal and state appropriations. Since 1980, however, federal financing for social services, particularly those services provided through the Social Services Block Grant, has been significantly reduced. The total amount of federal funding provided under the block grant has decreased from a maximum of $2.9 billion in fiscal year (FY) 1981 to $2.45 billion in FY 1983. The proposed federal budget for FY 1984 indicates that this trend in reduced federal expenditures for social services will likely continue.

These reductions in federal support for social services are occurring at a time of substantial economic difficulty at the state level as well as nationally (Swan et al., 1982). The abrupt reversal of the trend of expanding federal support has placed the states in the position of adjusting their programs to accommodate federal revenue losses or to obtain alternative sources of funding in a time of resource scarcity and pervasive fiscal austerity. For the most part, state and local governments are hard pressed to maintain social service programs at their previous levels. Solutions to federal and state fiscal problems do not appear likely in the short run. It can be reasonably expected, therefore, that prolonged fiscal crises will precipitate continued fiscal austerity that over time will further reduce the availability, accessibility, and effectiveness of social services. These limitations on social services will, in general, have a negative impact on those supportive programs serving the elderly.

The two major federal programs that are the primary sources of social services for the elderly are the Social Services Block Grant (SSBG), formerly Title XX of the Social Security Act, and Title III of the Older Americans Act (OAA). Since the OAA is addressed elsewhere in this text, this chapter will focus on social services provided primarily under the rubric of the former Title XX and the current SSBG. It should be noted, however, that OAA and SSBG funds are frequently linked programmatically.

This chapter first presents a brief review of the historical trends in the delivery and financing of social services. The second section identifies the various administrative options available to states to provide funding for the delivery of social services in this time of diminishing federal support and reviews the policies of eight states whose programs have been affected by federal budget reductions. The third section discusses the impact on the elderly of state responses to budget and regulatory changes. The final section presents a discussion of significant policy issues affecting the elderly that have emerged as a result of recent changes in funding for social services and the general atmosphere of fiscal austerity at both the federal and state levels.

Evolution of Social Services

Social service policy has evolved in the backwater of federal and state social policy, as a second priority to the predominant issues of health care and welfare reform (Benton et al., 1978). Although support for the development of social services was articulated over an extended period of time, public financing and support for social services at the federal, state, and local level were not significant until the 1960s. In the nineteenth century, the provision of social services for the elderly was undertaken primarily by families and charitable organizations and, to a lesser degree, by state and local governments. The first intervention of the federal government in the support of social services in the early part of the twentieth century focused on efforts to enhance child welfare and vocational rehabilitation through the creation of the Children's Bureau and the enactment of the National Civilian Rehabilitation Act of 1920, respectively.

Even though federal income, health, housing, and employment programs proliferated after the enactment of social welfare legislation commencing with the Social Security Act of 1935, there was no concerted effort to expand the role of the federal government in providing for the elderly or for other individuals whose needs for support and independence did not fall neatly within the parameters of the medical or welfare models of care. The provision of social services was tied administratively to eligibility for public assistance until 1956. The Social Security Act amendments of that year gave statutory sanction to social service activities for the aged and other vulnerable groups by authorizing 50 percent federal matching funds (Mott, 1976).

States did not make immediate use of the availability of federal funds for social services. The enactment of several statutes in the 1960s, however, provided the impetus for the expanded involvement of state and local governments in the provision of social services. The Social Security Act amendments of 1962 increased the incentive for state and local provision of social services by providing for a 75 percent federal match to state social services expenditures. The

Older Americans Act of 1965 (U.S. PL 89-73) established a vehicle for the provision, on an initially limited basis, of locally based social and recreational programs for the elderly. It was not until 1972 and 1973 that the Older Americans Act funded social and nutrition services to any significant degree (Estes, 1979). The Social Security Act amendments of 1967 broadened the delivery of social services by expanding the definition of eligibles and extending purchase of service authorization to private as well as public agencies (Mott, 1976).

With these and other statutory changes, the 1960s and the early 1970s witnessed a significant expansion of social service programs and increased the availability of social services to the elderly. With an unlimited federal match for social services that accompanied the 1962 Social Security amendments, states began to expand these services and to shift a significant proportion of their cost to the federal government. Led by California, state demand for federal matching more than doubled federal expenditures for social services from fiscal years 1971 to 1972 (Derthick, 1975; see Table 6.1). Besides the rapid and uncontrolled growth of social service expenditures, critics of the burgeoning personal social service system expressed concern about the lack of a single, equitable social service sytem and the lack of programmatic and fiscal accountability.

Several steps were taken to deal with these problems in the early 1970s. In 1971, Congress and the administration attempted to slow the meteoric rise in social service expenditures by legislating a ceiling of $1.68 billion for federal social service expenditures. This ceiling was raised to $2.5 billion in 1973. Then, in 1975, under the Nixon administration's new federalism initiatives, a comprehensive social service program was enacted through the passage of Title XX of the Social Security Act. Title XX transformed the provision of social services in the United States by creating a rational, consolidated delivery system that emphasizes state and local government discretion in determining the number, type, and content of services, the number of recipients, and the level of expenditure (Gilbert, 1977). The passage of Title XX as a parallel human service system to the nation's health and welfare systems acknowledged that social services represent a necessary human resource in their own right.

Title XX was, in effect, a block grant or special revenue-sharing program that consolidated the social service provisions of Titles I, IVA, VI, X, and XIV of the Social Security Act. Under the provisions of Title XX, state and local governments were allowed

TABLE 6.1   Federal Social Service   Expenditures by Source: Fiscal
            Years 1963-1984

Federal Fiscal Year	Actual Expenditure (in billions)	Certified Limitation (in billions)
Social Security Act Public Assistance Titles I, IV-A, VI, X, and XIV		
1963	.194	
1965	.295	
1967	.281	
1969	.354	
1971	.692	
1972	1.598	
1973[a]		
1974[a]		
1975[a]		
Title XX of the Social Security Act		
1976	2.127	2.432
Transitional Quarter	.573	.649
1977	2.515	2.681
1978	2.620	2.673
1979	2.853	2.878
1980	2.681	2.700
1981	2.864	2.900
Social Services Block Grant		
1982	2.400	2.400
1983		2.450
1984[b]		2.500

SOURCES: Grants Allocation Analysis Branch, OHDS, DHHS. Unpublished data, 1983.
1963-1972 expenditures from Office of Financial Management, Social and Rehabilitation Service, DHEW, reprinted in P. E. Mott, *Meeting Human Needs: The
Social and Political History of Title XX*. Washington, DC: National Conference on
Social Welfare, 1976, p. 9.

a. Data not available.
b. Proposed.

wide discretion in determining the number and scope of services to be
provided. States were required to provide at least one service for each
of the five program goals: economic self-support; personal self-
sufficiency; protection from abuse, neglect, and exploitation; prevention of inappropriate institutionalization; and arrangement for
appropriate institutional care. The existing ceiling of $2.5 billion was

maintained while federal funds were allocated to the states on a per capita basis. States were required to provide a minimum of 25 percent match to federal allocations (except for family planning services, for which the federal/state match was 90/10). States were also required to conduct specific planning and reporting activities, including the development of a Comprehensive Annual Service Program Plan (ensuring public input into the planning process) and the preparation of quarterly and annual reports for the Social Services Reporting Requirements.

Within broad federal guidelines, states were permitted to establish eligibility policies consistent with their assessment of social service needs. States were required to provide 50 percent of the social services supported by Title XX funds to low-income eligibles in the Aid to Families with Dependent Children (AFDC), Supplemental Security Income (SSI), and Medicaid programs.

Between 1975 and 1981, there were few changes in the federal component of the Title XX program. The ceiling on federal Title XX funds was raised from $2.5 to $2.9 billion during this period. The level of state funding for social services during this period also increased (Pardini and Lindeman, 1983). Several states, which had reached the maximum of federal support under Title XX, continued to increase social service expenditures with state revenues. By FY 1981, nearly all states had reached their maximum federal allocations.

The Omnibus Budget Reconciliation Act of 1981 (U.S. PL 97-35) provided for a significant restructuring of the Title XX program, particularly as it related to federal support for social service programs and to the relative roles of the federal and state governments in establishing policies and administering these programs. The act replaced the Title XX program with the new Social Services Block Grant (SSBG), one of the initial decentralization efforts emerging from the new federalism of the Reagan administration.

The primary thrust of the SSBG was to reduce federal regulatory authority and to increase state and local administrative and programmatic discretion. The most significant change created by the block grant, however, was the reduction of federal funds for social services. The $3.0 billion in FY 1982 federal budget authority for social services was reduced to $2.4 billion through the legislation creating the block grant. Thus, while states were permitted increased administrative and programmatic latitude under the block grant, they were also faced with an average reduction of 20 percent in their federal social service allocations.

The reductions in and elimination of federal regulations under the block grant were considerable. The state revenue match is no longer required, thereby permitting states to reduce their allocation to social services while still receiving the maximum allowable federal revenues. States maintain complete discretion in the selection of services and are no longer mandated to provide information and referral or protective services, as was required under Title XX regulations. All federal eligibility and reporting requirements have been eliminated. Only minimal requirements for social service planning and for community involvement in the planning process have been maintained.

Reductions in Federal Expenditures and Regulations for Social Services: An Eight-State Comparison

This section identifies the options that have been available to the states and those that have been utilized to meet the reduction of federal monies and regulations for social services. Prior to the analysis of the social services budget in eight study states, one caveat is in order. Because of the built-in flexibility in the social services program (and historically in the Title XX regulations), both at the federal and the state levels, the definition of a social service "program" is nebulous and unique to each state. This attribute reflects the intent of the Title XX legislation, which encouraged states to develop programs according to their determination of client needs with a minimum of federal regulatory interference. This cross-state program variation in social service definitions and configurations complicates both the descriptive and the analytic research task, particularly in terms of comparative budgetary examination. An analysis of Title XX and/or the SSBG must take into account the uniqueness of each state's social service program, budgeting process, reporting format, planning approach, and documentation.

A survey of eight states — California, Florida, Massachusetts, Missouri, Pennsylvania, Texas, Washington, and Wisconsin — was conducted in 1981 with follow-up in December 1982 to determine the impact of federal funding reductions for FY 1982 and FY 1983. Because the survey addresses the policies of only eight states in responding to federal funding reductions, the following data may not be fully generalizable on the national level, but they do illustrate the range of

TABLE 6.2   State Options in Responding to FY 1981 Federal Social
Service Revenue Reductions

1. Reduce scope of social service program.
2. Maintain social service program at pre-1981 level.
3. Increase scope of social service program in excess of pre-1981 level.

Budgetary Options

- Change state contribution
- Change local contribution
- Utilize block grant transfers
- Utilize Medicaid waivers

Administrative Options

- Hiring freeze/attrition
- Layoffs
- Salary freeze
- Increase service contracting

Programmatic Options

- Increase eligibility stringency
- Change scope of services
- Reduce units of service
- Increase fees and copayments

SOURCE: Pardini, A., and D. L. Lindeman. *Eight-State Comparative Report on Social Services*. Working Paper No. 21. San Francisco: Aging Health Policy Center, University of California, 1983.

basic state and local options and trends. The eight-state sample provides a good indicator of the effects of federal funding reductions on the elderly, since these states include approximately 37 percent of the elderly population in the U.S.

STATE OPTIONS

In response to federal resource reductions, state officials have considered an array of budgetary, administrative, and programmatic adjustments, which have profound implications for state social service programs, for the elderly, and for other constituents they serve. States have three basic options to accommodate the reductions in federal support: to reduce the scope of their programs; to maintain programs at pre-1981 levels; or to increase the scope of their programs above pre-1981 levels (see Table 6.2). The approach utilized by each state in accommodating federal reductions in social service support was influenced by a variety of political and economic considerations, including the magnitude of federal funding cuts; the current fiscal condition of the state; the extent of competition for scarce resources with other state programs, particularly entitlement programs; and the political effectiveness of special interest service recipient groups.

Whether states opted to increase social service support, maintain support at pre-1981 levels, or minimize the magnitude of funding reductions, program administrators had three specific actions available to them: (1) budgetary changes, (2) administrative changes, and/or (3) programmatic changes. A number of budgetary changes were available to program managers. First, state general revenues could be applied to make up all or part of the funding shortfall. Second, costs could be shifted to other federal revenue sources such as Medicaid or the Low-Income Energy Assistance Block Grant. For example, states could apply for Title XIX (Medicaid) waivers to receive reimbursement for the delivery of specific services that prevent institutionalization and that could be used to supplant SSBG expenditures. Similarly, states were able to transfer up to 10 percent of their Low-Income Energy Assistance Block Grant monies to the SSBG. A third method of generating additional funds involved requiring a greater local contribution toward the costs of social service programs and/or increasing private charitable contributions. Finally, states could require recipients to contribute part or all of the service cost through fees or copayments.

A second set of options, often tied to attempts to increase program revenues, was the reduction of program costs through administrative reductions. Administrative economies could be achieved by reducing particular administrative functions and personnel and by identifying more efficient means of delivering services, such as contracting-for-service mechanisms.

When, for a variety of political and economic reasons, states found that increased revenues and administrative savings did not fully accommodate reduced levels of support, program reductions were considered. Reductions could take the form of increasing the stringency of eligibility criteria, reducing the number and/or level of services provided, and limiting the availability of services by closing intake or creating service waiting lists. Cutback strategies in each of these areas could be made either on a targeted or an across-the-board basis.

STATE RESPONSES

Just as there is wide variation in the social service programs in each state, there is also wide variation in the way each state re-

TABLE 6.3   Responses to Reductions in Federal Social Services Funding, Fiscal Years 1981-1983: Eight States

Budgetary Changes	CA	Reduce Program				Maintain Program		Expand Program
		FL	MO	PA	WA	TX	WI	MA
• Increase state contribution							X	X
• Decrease state contribution		X	X	X	X			
• Increase local support						X	X	X
• Utilize block grant transfers					X		X	
• Utilize Medicaid waivers		X		X	X	X		
Administrative Changes								
• Hiring freeze/attrition	X		X	X	X	X	X	X
• Layoffs		X	X	X	X		X	
• Salary freeze	X				X		X	
• Increase service contracting		X						X
Programmatic Changes								
• Increase eligibility stringency					X			
• Reduce number of services	X		X					
• Reduce units of services		X	X		X			
• Increase use of client fees						X		X

SOURCE: Pardini, A., and D. A. Lindeman. *Eight-State Comparative Report on Social Services:* Working Paper No. 21. San Francisco: Aging Health Policy Center, University of California, 1983.

sponded to the enactment of the SSBG and the accompanying reductions in federal expenditures. The primary trends in budgetary, administrative, and programmatic changes in the eight states from 1981 to 1983 are presented in Table 6.3. Although two states have been successful in maintaining their social service programs at pre-1981 funding levels and one state has expanded its program, the majority of the eight states studied have found it necessary to reduce the scope of their programs, in some cases quite significantly. California, Florida, Missouri, Pennsylvania, and Washington made extensive cuts in their social service programs. All five states report a substantial reduction in the number of recipients of social services. Pennsylvania, for example, indicated that the number of social service recipients in FY

1982 dropped by approximately 250,000 individuals from the FY 1981 level of 1,350,000 recipients. In addition to the reductions in federal funds, these five states were forced, as a result of revenue-generating problems, to lower the level of state general revenues appropriated for social services in both FY 1982 and FY 1983. Several of these states made efforts to replace revenues lost due to federal budget cutbacks with other federal funds. Florida supplanted social service funds through a Medicaid waiver; Missouri supplemented social service expenditures with increased Older Americans Act (Title III) and Low-Income Energy Assistance block grant funds; and Washington shifted funds from the Maternal and Child Health and the Low-Income Energy Assistance block grants to social services.

Even with augmentation through other funding sources, the combination of federal and state budget reductions resulted in a net loss of social service expenditures in the five states, forcing them to implement cutback management strategies. The strategy most widely employed in managing program reductions was targeting administrative reductions. Pennsylvania, by implementing across-the-board cuts in staffing, services, and expenditures for state programs, was the only exception. Cost-reduction strategies included the elimination of administrative and service delivery positions as well as salary and benefit freezes. All five states that had reduced their social service programs attempted to absorb the largest share of budget cuts in personnel and administrative overhead as a means of protecting direct service resources, a common priority in all eight study states. During FY 1982 and FY 1983, four of these five reduced staff through a hiring freeze and/or attrition, and four laid off employees. All five states reduced program expenditures by reducing the number of administrative personnel.

Additional cutback management strategies employed by the five states included reducing services, tightening eligibility, and imposing fees. Three of the states elected to eliminate selected services and to consolidate resources in the provision of high-priority services. Similarly, three states initiated policies to limit the amount of particular services that may be provided to individual clients. As a result, waiting lists for some services now exist in all states except California. Service reductions have taken place primarily in nonemergency services considered "optional" by many states. These quality-of-life and prevention-oriented services were seen by program officials as a lower immediate priority than acute or crisis services, such as child and adult protective services. Tightening eligibility criteria may limit program costs by reducing the number of recipients eligible for benefits. Washington was the only study state that imposed stricter eligibility criteria by lowering the income eligibility standard for the state's social service programs.

As previously mentioned, not all states elected to reduce the scope of their social service programs. Texas and Wisconsin have maintained approximately the same level of social service expenditures as prior to the federal budget reductions of 1981. Although Texas maintained the level of state revenues allocated to the social service program, funding was not sufficient to prevent initial program reductions. For FY 1983 the federal shortfall was made up by instituting fees and copayments, increasing local support, and supplementing the social service budget with a Title XIX waiver. Thus, by FY 1983 Texas was serving the same number of social service recipients as in FY 1981. Wisconsin has maintained the same scope of social services by supplementing the reduction in federal social service expenditures with local, state, and other federal revenues. Although both states have maintained their social service programs at fairly constant levels, both have had to impose programmatic restrictions. Texas instituted client fees, waiting lists, and some service limitations, while Wisconsin increased client fees, waiting lists, and administrative staff reductions.

Only one of the eight states surveyed reported expanding its social service program during FY 1982 and FY 1983. Massachusetts not only prevented a reduction in social services, but also added several new services and expanded others with additional state revenues. The Massachusetts success was due primarily to strong legislative and public support resulting in expansion of services for the elderly. For example, home care services have grown from $35 to $75 million between FY 1979 and FY 1983. This expansion of aging services has occurred independently of SSBG dollars. The Massachusetts Department of Elder Affairs, which provides nearly all social services to the state's elderly, no longer uses any SSBG funds. Social services for the elderly have been funded largely out of Older Americans Act and state funds.

REGULATORY CHANGES

Although the majority of the Title XX regulations were eliminated by the Social Services Block Grant, several provisions remain in place. Despite the elimination of the 25 percent state matching requirement, most of the study states have elected to maintain pre-1981 levels of state support for their social service programs. Similarly, even though federal eligibility criteria were completely eliminated as part of the SSBG legislation, five study states have retained these criteria. On the other hand, Missouri changed the eligibility criteria for aging social services to group eligibility; Wisconsin kept only minimal categorical eligibility criteria and expanded local discretion in setting eligibility criteria; and Pennsylvania eliminated all Title XX eligibility criteria in favor of the categorical eligibility criteria utilized by the program area in which a service is provided.

In six of the eight states, program, fiscal, and client data collection efforts have been expanded despite the elimination of the federal Social Services Reporting Requirements. Two other study states have retained existing data systems at their pre-1981 levels. Most states have reduced their social service planning efforts because of fewer federal requirements. Texas and Wisconsin, however, have witnessed a sharp increase in the level of local social service planning. Although support functions such as auditing, contract monitoring, and licensing and certification have remained relatively constant for most states, Florida, Pennsylvania, and Washington reduced the amount of contract monitoring they conduct, and Wisconsin reduced its licensing and certification efforts.

Impact of Reductions in Federal Funding and Regulations on the Elderly

The effect of reduced federal and state social service support has been felt by all population groups, including the elderly. The extent of participation by the elderly in programs funded by Title XX and by the Social Services Block Grant is not specifically known. The Office of Management and Budget estimated that during FY 1981 the elderly were benefited by approximately $575 million in federal Title XX funds, which represents about 21 percent of the total program funds for that year (U.S. Senate, 1982, p. 417). The elimination of federal social service reporting requirements, however, has made it difficult to ascertain program, client, and expenditure data in general, and for the elderly in particular. Social service data are available only from state social service data systems. In the eight states surveyed, empirical data on social services are limited. Further, these data are primarily qualitative; quantitative data on social services are, in general, nonexistent. The following summary of social service program data for the elderly is a compilation of qualitative responses from social service program officials.

The impact of federal funding and regulatory changes on the elderly varies widely. In California and Florida, services for the elderly were reduced proportionate to overall program reductions. In Missouri, elderly services appear to have been reduced more significantly than have services to children and nonelderly adults. In Pennsylvania and Washington, all social services except those primarily for the elderly have absorbed the majority of the benefit reductions. The elderly are generally doing comparatively well in securing service resources in the states where social services programs have been maintained or increased from pre-block grant levels. The impact on the elderly in Wisconsin cannot be determined due to the state's decentralized service system. In Texas the elderly are doing as well as other populations, and in Massachusetts the elderly are doing better than other social service recipients in obtaining service benefits.

There is also wide variation within elderly populations in how specific groups are affected by fiscal and programmatic cutbacks in social services. Missouri and Pennsylvania are targeting services to the frail and at-risk elderly at the expense of the ambulatory and middle-class elderly, whereas in Florida the frail elderly appear to be receiving the majority of service reductions. There is no readily apparent discrepancy in the receipt of services within the elderly populations in the other six states studied.

Federal budget reductions have had an impact on model long-term care efforts in only two states. Although most of the alternative long-term care programs reviewed are not funded by SSBG monies, these programs generally provide social services. In Pennsylvania, substantial cuts have been made in the adult day-care program, whereas in Washington alternative long term care efforts have been enhanced. As a result of continued state and federal support, innovative long term care programs in the six other states studied have not been significantly affected by social service funding reductions.

Policy Issues

The impact of the Social Services Block Grant and its attendant reductions in federal programmatic regulations and support, coupled with a pervasive sense of fiscal austerity in many states, has raised a number of issues related to the provision of social services to the elderly. Particularly significant are concerns relating to intergovernmental relations and decentralization; federal, state, and local fiscal capacity; accessibility to services; effectiveness of services; accountability; and equity.

INTERGOVERNMENTAL RELATIONS AND DECENTRALIZATION

Ensuring state and local autonomy in the determination of social service policy was an early concern in the enactment of social service legislation. It was clear that policymakers felt that federal support of social services should not preclude state and local governments determining the specific needs of their constituents. Nor should federal involvement usurp state and local discretion in designing and administering social service programs to meet those needs.

Title XX was initially conceptualized as a block grant or special revenue-sharing program, which allowed state and local governments discretion in the design and implementation of their programs. Decentralization, when used to define the separation of authority, applies to social services on two organizational levels: relationships between the federal and state levels, and relationships between the state and local levels. Under Title XX, the allocation of responsibility and authority from the federal government to the states has been implemented effectively. Since 1975, states have determined policies relative to services, eligibility criteria, and delivery systems — the very heart of the social service system. The few constraints placed on the states through the Title XX requirements (that is, the federal/state match, 50 percent categorical eligibility, reporting, and planning) were perceived by most states as administrative requirements that did not significantly affect program implementation.

The delineation between state and local program authority has not been as clearly defined. Some states viewed their role in Title XX largely as a pass-through mechanism to the local or county level for implementation, with only limited state policy-setting and oversight functions. Other states utilized federal social service funding as a means of centralizing program authority. Four of the eight states surveyed administered substantially decentralized social service programs. The organizational locus of eligibility determination, service authorization, data collection, and service delivery in these states is primarily at the local level. In the remaining four states, the state social service organizations consolidated or centralized most program implementation activities.

The implementation of the Social Services Block Grant in 1981 resulted in a change in both federal-state and state-local levels of program decentralization. As noted in Chapters 2 and 3, the block grant concept was enacted with the goal of eliminating a large share of federal regulatory control in social service (and other) programs. Although this was accomplished, the concurrent reduction of federal funding constrained states in utilizing the additional flexibility they were given. State social service program offices have, for the most part, used their greater administrative latitude to undertake program retrenchment since 1981. The net effect of the SSBG and the reduction in federal funding in the majority of the study states has been a modest consolidation of state control in policies and functions that had previously been federally or locally implemented.

The relative impact on the elderly of more centralized social service policymaking is difficult to determine. It can by hypothesized that local policy decisions, which may have been the most effective way of addressing the needs of the elderly in a specific community, will now be made at the state level. In contrast, statewide social service policies may ensure that the elderly have better access to social services than through the disconnected actions of local governments. Decentralization between state and local agency levels has been affected in a mixed fashion, but not, for the most part, solely as a response to the SSBG. For example, for political and historical reasons and not as a result of federal policies, Wisconsin has increased the degree of policymaking at the local level. Texas, likewise, has increased the amount of local input in planning and policymaking to improve the appropriateness of social services. Florida, a state that previously delegated considerable program authority to the district level, has substantially centralized some administrative and policymaking functions at the state level. This centralization has not occurred as a result of the regulatory provisions of the block grant, but as a response to fiscal austerity initiated by reductions in federal support.

FISCAL CAPACITY

With the reductions in federal funding for social services, the fiscal capacity of the state has primarily defined its ability to prevent or minimize state social service program reductions. As a result of the condition of the national economy and the increased fiscal burden caused by expansion of various economic and medical entitlement programs, few of the states surveyed have sufficient fiscal capacity or resources to compensate for the loss of federal revenues. California, Florida, and Washington, in particular, are facing significant fiscal crises. Although the social service programs in Texas and Wisconsin have been maintained at pre-1981 levels, state fiscal capacity has not been sufficient to maintain the program without increased revenue from nonstate sources such as fees or copayments. Only Massachusetts has been able to expand its social service program with additional state revenues.

The net effect of the reductions in federal support for social services in most states has been to shift the cost of social services to the state and local levels and to program recipients, as well as to reduce the general availability of benefits. The fiscal capacity of state and local governments is currently insufficient to maintain social services at the levels provided previously under Title XX. If current fiscal and administrative trends continue, the elderly may receive fewer, more crisis-related services at a greater out-of-pocket cost.

ACCESSIBILITY

The retrenchment of state social service programs, as a result of federal funding reductions and a generalized climate of fiscal austerity, has reduced the elderly's accessibility to services. Factors contributing to reduced accessibility include: (1) reprioritization and limitations on the number and type of services, (2) reductions in units of service, (3) stricter eligibility criteria, (4) client copayments and fees, and (5) waiting lists. Since many social service programs cannot maintain the same number of services with reduced funds, social service agencies have had to develop a priority strategy for service provision. Services provided to the elderly and to others, such as transportation, nutrition, and respite care, have received a lower priority than day care, protective, and similar services.

The level of services available to the elderly (for example, the number of allowable hours of homemaker service per month) has been reduced in several states. Some elderly persons may thus be prohibited from obtaining the level of services necessary to maintain full independence. Several state social service programs have tightened certain eligibility requirements. The use of a lower percentage of state median income as the criterion for income eligibility, for example, may keep the near-poor elderly from access to services. Also, many states have imposed copayments or sliding fee scales to compensate for lost revenues. These fees are frequently a deterrent for the aged who need services and who must live on fixed, usually low, incomes. Finally, all eight states surveyed indicate that waiting lists exist for many services, and the elderly, along with others, are being restricted in obtaining immediate access to services. Federal and state austerity, then, has led not only to reduced availability of services for the elderly, but to reduced access to the remaining services as well.

EFFECTIVENESS OF SERVICES

The aggregate effect of reductions in federal and state revenues for social services has been potentially to compromise the overall effectiveness of services for the frail, at-risk, and low-income elderly. First, in having to prioritize the type of services that can be provided with reduced revenues, state and local administrators have made larger reductions in preventive and quality-of-life services, while maintaining acute or crisis-oriented services. The elderly are major beneficiaries of preventive and quality-of-life services such as nutrition, respite care, and transportation. Reductions in these services are likely to reduce the independence of many elderly individuals and could put many at risk of subsequent acute problems and potential institutionalization, thus jeopardizing the overall effectiveness of these interventions.

Second, extensive personnel reductions are occurring at both administrative and service delivery levels. Cutbacks in administration may reduce program efficiency, as staff activities will be directed toward maintaining the basic functioning of the program. Opportunities for planning and program evaluation and improvement are likely to be the principal casualties of administrative reductions. Cuts in direct service staffing are increasing client caseloads and reducing the ability of staff to respond to individual needs. Similarly, staff training has been eliminated in several states, potentially lowering the skill levels of service providers.

ACCOUNTABILITY

Improving social service program accountability was a major goal of the original Title XX legislation and subsequent program regulations. Title XX required several measures of accountability for state and local social service programs. States were required to complete quarterly expenditure and recipient reports as well as annual planning documents. In addition, state and local administrators were responsible for public dissemination of the social service plans and for ensuring community input into the planning process. In actuality, neither the reporting nor the planning activities in many states were more than regulatory exercises. In effect, the Social Services Block Grant deleted what appear to have been largely ineffective regulations.

This is not to say, however, that planning, evaluation, and reporting have little significance for social services. Surprisingly, there is no indication that program-auditing and contract-monitoring activities have been significantly reduced in the states studied since the Social Services Block Grant was initiated. While planning activities have been limited in most states due to a reduction in resources, several states have sharply increased their planning efforts (particularly on the local level) in order to determine the best way to manage program resources. Program evaluation and reporting have received strong emphasis in many states since the initiation of Title XX, and in many cases these activities have continued under the SSBG. Most of the eight states surveyed have allocated resources to upgrading their fiscal and program data systems, and three states consider program evaluation and management their primary social service goal for FY 1983 and beyond.

Despite the commitment of individual states to maintaining or improving reporting and evaluation capacity, there is no mechanism to assure a uniform and comprehensive system of comparable data on a national basis to permit assessment of the performance of the programs supported by the SSBG. The lack of comparable reporting and evaluation data also undermines federal capacity to hold state and federal officials accountable for the effective and efficient delivery of services. The elimination of regulatory controls accompanying the SSBG has effectively curtailed the capacity to monitor this system at the federal level. Although program reporting, evaluation, and management remain high priorities for several states, limited state and local resources, further anticipated reductions in federal support, and continued state fiscal austerity may compromise the ability of the states fully to meet these goals.

EQUITY

A significant factor in the expansion of federal support for social services in the 1960s and early 1970s was the notion of equity. "Government has an obligation to assist society's most vulnerable people to attain the highest possible level of independent living of which they are capable" (Mott, 1976). This normative judgment supported policies toward providing equal access to a minimal level of care across states and communities (Gutowski and Koshel, 1982). Two dimensions of equity are of concern in the delivery of social services. These include equity between population groups and equity within a population.

Because the criteria for determining equity are conceptually problematic and operationally difficult, it is hard to determine whether social service benefits have been (or are) distributed equitably to different population groups. Gilbert and Specht (1982) have argued that on the basis of proportional criteria, the elderly received a "fair share" of Title XX benefits between 1976 and 1980. An analysis of proposed federal and state expenditures for fifty states determined that most states allocated a somewhat higher level of funding to services for the elderly than would be expected strictly on the basis of the proportion of the population represented by the aged. This argument, however, ignores the differential, and some have argued disproportionately higher, level of need (for example, poverty) of the elderly (Estes, 1979).

With the reduction of federal revenues that accompanied the enactment of the SSBG, new factors must be considered in attempting to determine whether the elderly are receiving a "fair share" of social service benefits. For example, as a result of the reduction in social service resources, there is increased competition for services among various client groups in need of benefits.

The elimination of uniform and comprehensive reporting measures precludes an analysis of national social service expenditures and recipients, limiting the development of an accurate measure of equity. The survey of eight states, however, suggests that relative to other constituents, the elderly are faring as well as, and in some cases better than, other population groups in obtaining social service benefits (Pardini and Lindeman, 1983). The study indicates that it is likely that the political power of aging constituencies has enabled the elderly to fare better than other recipient groups in their attempts to secure services, although absolute levels of services for the elderly are lower in most states than they were in 1981. As shown in Chapter 5, however, as fiscal conditions worsen, benefits for the elderly may be no more protected than those of other groups.

The concept of an equitable distribution of resources must also be considered within a specific population. Social services provided under Title XX primarily benefited the middle- and upper-class aged (Nelson, 1982). In contrast, under the SSBG, acute or crisis services affecting the frail elderly, such as day-care and protective services, are being given greater attention by states than preventive services. Thus, the frail, at-risk elderly appear to be receiving resources previously allocated to individuals, primarily the middle-class elderly, with nonacute needs.

Conclusion

At the present time, projections of federal budget levels indicate that federal support for social services for the elderly will continue to decline in FY 1984. Although the proposed federal expenditures for the Social Services Block Grant will increase slightly from $2.4 to $2.45 billion in FY 1984, net social service funding for the elderly will be reduced. The administration has proposed merging the Community Services Block Grant (CSBG) with the SSBG while requesting only $3 million for "close-out costs" for the CSBG. The proposed SSBG funding level is insufficient to compensate either for the loss of the $348 million allotted to the CSBG in fiscal year 1983 or for the increase of program costs due to inflation.

The reduction of federal resources for social services since 1980 reflects a major shift in the social welfare policy of this country. One of the original rationales for the provision of social services was the desire to provide an alternative, community-based service system. This social service system was intended to help maintain individuals at the greatest level of functional independence. Further, this system was designed to complement the array of federal and state income, health, and housing programs that constitute a broad social "safety net." Thus, the decrease in federal expenditures for social services reflects a reduction in the capacity and commitment of federal social welfare policy to support these principles. Significant reductions in federal funding have the potential for quickly unraveling the social safety net and allowing many individuals, both the elderly and others, to suffer severe consequences.

With the enactment of Title III of the Older Americans Act in 1973 and Title XX of the Social Security Act in 1975, social services have become an integral component of the system of services that support the elderly. Title XX and the subsequent Social Services Block Grant have funded the organization of federal, state, and local agencies to provide social services in a widely decentralized manner. The reduction of federal funds for social services through the 1981 budget process sharply reduced the capacity of states to maintain the same level of services previously provided. Although states have been relieved of nearly all regulatory constraints through the SSBG legislation, they must cope with providing services from diminished resources. The elderly, who are doing relatively well in comparison to other recipients, are still adversely affected by retrenchment of social service programs. Since the politics and economics of austerity make it unlikely that retrenchment will abate in the near future, it is important to monitor what may become a significant impact of shifting program priorities on the elderly.

References

Benton, B., T. Feild, and R. Millar. *Social Services: Federal Legislation vs. State Implementation*. Washington, DC: Urban Institute, 1978.

Derthick, M. *Uncontrolled Spending for Social Services Grants*. Washington, DC: Brookings Institution, 1975.

Estes, C.L. "Austerity and Aging in the United States: 1980 and Beyond." In *Old Age and the Welfare State*. London: Sage Publications Ltd, forthcoming.

————. *The Aging Enterprise*. San Francisco: Jossey-Bass, 1979.

Gilbert, N. "The Transformation of Social Services." *Social Service Review,* 51, No. 4 (December 1977), 629-641.

————, and H. Specht. "A 'Fair Share' for the Aged: Title XX Allocation Patterns, 1976-1980." *Research on Aging,* 4, No. 1 (March 1982), 71-86.

Gutowski, M. F., and J.J. Koshel. "Social Services." In *The Reagan Experiment*. Ed. J.L. Palmer and I. V. Sawhill. Washington, DC: Urban Institute, 1982.

Mott, P.E. *Meeting Human Needs: The Social and Political History of Title XX*. Washington, DC: National Conference on Social Welfare, 1976.

Nelson, G. "Social Class and Public Policy for the Elderly." *Social Service Review,* 56, No. 1 (1982), 85-107.

Pardini, A., and D. A. Lindeman. "Eight-State Comparative Report on Social Services." Working Paper No. 21. Prepared for the U.S. Health Care Financing Administration under Grant No. 18-P-99762019. San Francisco: Aging Health Policy Center, University of California, 1983.

Swan, J. H., C.L. Estes, J.B. Wood, M. Kreger, and J. Garfield. *Fiscal Crisis: Impact on Aging Services*. Final Report. Prepared for the U.S. Administration on Aging under Grant No. 90-AR-0016. San Francisco: Aging Health Policy Center, University of California, 1982.

U.S. Public Law 87-73. Older Americans Act of 1965. Washington, DC: U.S. Government Printing Office, 1965.

U.S. Public Law 97-35. Omnibus Budget Reconciliation Act of 1981. Washington, DC: U.S. Government Printing Office, 1981.

U.S. Senate, Special Committee on Aging. *Developments in Aging: 1981,* Part I. Washington, DC: U.S. Government Printing Office, 1982.

Wolff, E. C. *Technical Notes: Summaries and Characteristics of States' Title XX Social Services Plans for Fiscal Year 1978*. Washington, DC: U.S. Office of the Assistant Secretary for Planning and Evaluation, 1978.

CHAPTER 7

STATE MEDICAID EXPENDITURES
Trends and Program Policy Changes

Robert J. Newcomer
Charlene Harrington

One of the most important policy problems facing state and federal government is a lack of consensus about the nature and extent of public responsibility for meeting the health needs of the population in general, and the long term care needs of the elderly in particular. Medicare and private health insurance have been oriented to acute care, particularly hospital and physician services, rather than to a continuum of care encompassing a range of health and social services (such as nursing homes and community-based supports). While Medicaid has emphasized hospital and physician services, it has also included provisions for nursing home care because the very poor had no other way to pay for this care. This pattern of care had its origins in the fact that most people were at risk for both physician and hospital services, while only a small percentage of the population received nursing home care.

Private health insurance arose in the 1930s when acute, infectious disease, trauma, and surgical problems were still predominant. As

Authors' Note: Preparation of this chapter was partially funded by the Administration on Aging under Cooperative Agreement No. 90AP0003. We wish to thank Dr. Lynn Paringer of California State University at Hayward and Dr. Nelda McCall of SRI International for their thoughtful comments on the initial drafts. Compilation of the fifty-state data sources used was funded by and the U.S. National Center for Health Services Research Grant No. 1R01HS04042. Case study analyses of state Medicaid programs was funded by the U.S. Health Care Financing Administration under Grant No. 18P97629/9 and the U.S. National Center for Health Services Research Grant No. 1R01HS04042. Project principal investigators are Carroll L. Estes, Philip R. Lee, and Robert J. Newcomer. Project directors are Robert J. Newcomer and Charlene Harrington.

acute, infectious disease has been controlled and death postponed, chronic disease has emerged as the dominant cause of both illness and disability. According to the National Center for Health Statistics (NCHS), 62 percent of all "restricted activity days" and 54 percent of all "bed disability days" in 1980 were due to chronic conditions (U.S. NCHS, 1982). Among the elderly, chronic conditions cause 83 percent of restricted activity days.

The incongruence between the orientation of the American health care system, with its emphasis on hospital and physician care, and the service needs of the chronically ill and disabled is having serious consequences for the aged and their families, both because many service costs must be borne directly by them and because many services simply are not available. Expansion of the health care financing system to include coverage of treatment for chronic disease and long-term care is generally recognized as necessary. Implementation of appropriate changes, however, has been slow. Fundamental reasons for delay are fear and uncertainty about the cost of service expansion coupled with the already high and rapidly growing costs of the present pattern of care.

Current public health care financing programs involve both federal and state governments (and often local governments, too). State and local government effort is particularly focused on the low-income population. Any changes from the current pattern of care or the population served must of necessity consider the implications of these changes for state and local government. The delegation of increased administrative responsibility, for example, presupposes a capacity and willingness of these levels of government to assume such responsibilities. The delegation of increased financial responsibility or risk assumes a capacity to bear these costs or the discretion to tailor programs within existing resources.

Federal and state governments are in a transitional phase, attempting to find the means to constrain the rapidly rising cost of health care without cuts in eligibility or the scope of benefits. In the effort to find short-term solutions, some states are attempting to formulate longer-range system redesign. This chapter will describe and analyze the actions taken by states in their medical assistance (Medicaid) programs under emerging conditions of fiscal austerity. Are states moving to redistribute health service expenditures across a wider or a more narrow range of services? Are they seeking to control costs in the most expensive programs or cutting back costs in other areas to enable continued funding of the high-cost programs?

Change from the status quo is complex because it involves reallocations of existing funds, generation of new funds, risks of expanded service demand, and/or redefinition of intergovernmental responsibility. The pressure for change is urgently experienced by government because of continued rapid rises in public health care cost.

Medicaid is the major source of public funding for long term care, and an increasing proportion of Medicaid funds are expended for long term care services. In 1981 Medicaid cost a total of $31.3 billion nationally in state and federal funds, and it provided benefits for 22.5 million recipients (Waldo and Gibson, 1982). This program has grown rapidly since its first full year of operation in 1967, when nationwide costs were $2.3 billion. Expenditures are expected to continue their rise to $37.2 billion for fiscal year (FY) 1983 (U.S. Congressional Budget Office [CBO], 1981).

Although federal contributions account for almost half of the nationwide Medicaid expenditures, this program has become a dominant factor in state health service provision and budgeting. Medicaid currently accounts for about one-third of state and local government health care expenditures (U.S. CBO, 1981), and often it is the largest program in a state's budget (Freeland and Schendler, 1981). Since 1975 the role of Medicaid has become increasingly problematic as state fiscal capacity has not kept pace with program growth rate. Almost everywhere, Medicaid increases in expenditures have been one-third to one-half higher than the growth rates of state revenues (Bovbjerg and Holahan, 1982).

In addition to temporal fiscal pressures, more enduring pressure for change comes from basic questions of who should pay and who should derive benefits from the mix of public and private payment for services. There are currently significant inequities between the acute and the chronic care systems. To illustrate, in 1981 government expenditures (primarily Medicare and Medicaid) accounted for 54.3 percent of hospital payments. The balance of payments for hospital care (45.7 percent) was privately assumed, with private insurance accounting for 76 percent and out-of-pocket expenditures accounting for most of the rest.

Nursing homes, splitting public and private dollars in approximately the same proportions as hospitals (56.6 percent public and 43.6 percent private), received virtually no private insurance coverage. Of the private payment for nursing homes, only 1.2 percent was from insurance or other third-party payment (Waldo and Gibson, 1982), and the rest was paid for by individuals and their families. Public funds for nursing homes, in contrast to those for hospital care, have come almost exclusively from Medicaid. Community-based care (such as chore services, meal preparation, and shopping assistance) is financed largely by individuals and their families and provided through local nonprofit agencies. It has been estimated (U.S. General Accounting Office [GAO], 1977) that the proportion of this care provided informally (by family members and friends, for example) rises with the severity of the impairment — ranging from 60 percent of care for the slightly impaired to 80 percent for the extremely impaired.

Table 7.1 summarizes the current distribution of public health expenditures across the major services used by the elderly. Spending patterns reflect a strong bias toward hospital, physician, and nursing home care, raising significant policy issues. Should public policy continue to support acute and institutionally based care services without increasing support to a fuller range of care? Should the burden of private out-of-pocket costs for long term care be continued? Should it be reduced or increased?

The Health Care Financing System

Recent state Medicaid policy changes are best understood from a historical perspective on the structure of the program and its relationship to other programs. The health care financing system for the elderly consists of four basic elements: Medicare, Medicaid, elderly individuals and their families, and private insurance. As described in Chapter 4, Medicare is a national program available to all persons aged 65 and over who receive Social Security benefits, regardless of income. Medicare is administered as a federal program through fiscal intermediaries (Blue Cross and commercial insurance companies) in each state. Medicaid, on the other hand, is a state welfare program jointly funded through federal and state taxes. Eligibility for Medicaid, as for other public assistance programs, is based on income. The private health insurance of older persons usually consists of policies designed to supplement or augment health benefits available under Medicare. About two-thirds of those eligible for Medicare have supplemental insurance (Garfinkel and Terrell, n.d.).

Rather than declining as public financing increased, private out-of-pocket spending on health care for the elderly has grown rapidly in recent years. Per capita out-of-pocket spending by the elderly in-

TABLE 7.1   Personal Health Care Expenditures for Selected Services, 1981

Source of Payment	Total (in billions)	Hospital	Physician	Nursing Home	Drugs	All Others
Total all sources	$255.0	46.3%	21.5%	9.5%	8.4%	14.3%
Patient direct payments	81.7	15.7	25.5	12.6	20.9	25.3
Medicare	43.5	72.2	22.1	0.9	—	4.8
Medicaid[a]	29.7	36.0	9.1	40.4	5.4	9.1
All other sources[b]	100.1	63.0	21.7	1.5	2.7	11.1

SOURCE: Waldo, D. R., and R. M. Gibson "National Health Expenditures, 1981." *Health Care Financing Review*, 4, No. 1 (1982), p. 27.

a. The figure shown does not include administration costs of the program, which total an additional $1.6 billion.

b. This figure includes private insurance ($66.8 billion); philanthropy ($3.5 billion); other federal ($14.7 billion); and other state and local ($15.0 billion).

creased from $503 in 1970 to $1436 in 1980. In 1981 personal out-of-pocket spending on health services consumed 19.1 percent of the average annual income of the elderly (U.S. Senate, 1982b). The changes and reforms beginning to emerge at the state level for the Medicaid program are larely designed to reduce public expenditures. The implication for private out-of-pocket costs has usually been ignored, but an expansion of copayments and deductibles could very likely continue the erosion of disposable income available to older persons.

Of particular importance to the concerns of this chapter are likely changes in federal and state responsibility for long term care services. Under the existing structure, these changes largely involve the Medicaid program. Other program changes likely to affect long term care services for the elderly are reductions in supplementation and/or cost of living increases in Supplemental Security Income (SSI) benefits for the poor elderly, and reductions in social services such as homemaker and home health services under Title XX of the Social Security Act (see Chapter 6).

THE MEDICAID PROGRAM

Medicaid, Title XIX of the Social Security Act, was enacted in 1965 to provide federal matching funds for state programs to pay for medical services to low-income individuals and families. Although many poor people are not covered, Medicaid is the principal payer for

health care for the poor.[1] Individuals or families eligible for Supplemental Security Income (SSI) and Aid to Families with Dependent
Children (AFDC) are automatically eligible for Medicaid. In addition, states can choose to cover several other categories of individuals, designated as "medically needy," such as those whose large
medical expenses have reduced their remaining income and assets to
welfare levels. Twenty-nine states had medically needy programs in
1982 (La Jolla Management Corporation, 1982).

Federal regulations require that state Medicaid programs provide
hospital inpatient care, physician services, skilled nursing facility
care, laboratory and X-ray services, some health services, hospital
outpatient care, family planning, rural health clinics, and early and
periodic screening. In addition, states may provide up to thirty-two
other optional services, including intermediate care, prescription
drugs outside the hospital, dental services, and eyeglasses (Muse and
Sawyer, 1982). The program is financed through a combination of
federal and state (and in some cases local) funds. The federal government contributes between 50 and 77 percent of the Medicaid funds,
based on a state per capita income formula (Muse and Sawyer, 1982).

Generally, Medicaid operates as a third-party insurance coverage
program. The state, in other words, pays bills for services rendered to
individuals eligible for the program. The services received are determined by the provider and patient rather than by Medicaid staff, thus
creating a largely open-ended entitlement program. Once eligible for
Medicaid, the beneficiary is entitled to receive state-covered service
from any qualified provider. Providers participating in the program
must accept the Medicaid reimbursement level as payment in full,
except that states may require copayments on services. States assert
fiscal control over the program mainly by changing program policies
such as those on eligibility standards, scope or duration of services
covered, utilization controls, and reimbursement rates.

State and federal Medicaid policies have changed continually
since the inception of the program. Between 1967 and 1973 most effort
was given to expanding eligibility for and use of the Medicaid program. Between 1973 and 1979 many states expanded their service
coverage and unit prices (Bovbjerg and Holahan, 1982). The total
number of recipients peaked nationally in 1976; there has been about
an 18 percent decline since (U.S. Health Care Financing Administration [HCFA], 1982; Harrington et al., 1983). Program changes have
increasingly taken the form of service coverage reductions, more
stringent program eligibility, and a variety of efforts to reduce the
volume and cost of services. Federal policy changes and the dete-

riorating fiscal condition of many state governments have stimulated consideration of these and other program changes.

The 1981 Omnibus Budget Reconciliation Act (U.S. PL 97-35) included a number of Medicare and Medicaid provisions aimed at reducing federal expenditures for these programs in FY 1982 by $2.5 billion. The 3 percent reduction in the federal share of Medicaid expenses for FY 1982 was only one of these policy changes. Other Medicaid policy changes for 1982 included the following, (1) States have been given greater flexibility with respect to coverage of and services for the medically needy. (2) States no longer need to reimburse hospitals at the Medicare rate. (3) The freedom-of-choice provision of the state Medicaid plan can be waived by the Secretary of Health and Human Services; and (4) participation in health maintenance organizations (HMOs) is encouraged (U.S. PL 97-35; Estes and Lee, 1981).

In 1982 Congress passed the Tax Equity and Fiscal Responsibility Act (U.S. PL 97-248), which incorporated additional changes in the Medicaid program. These provisions allowed copayments for almost all services, rather than for optional services only, and permitted these to be applied to the categorically as well as the medically needy, with certain limited exceptions. States were also permitted to place liens on the homes of nursing home residents, but not until the recipient died or the spouse or minor child was no longer living in the house. Also, disabled children were permitted to receive home care as long as that care was not more expensive than institutional care (U.S. PL 97-248).

Additional changes being discussed nationally involve changes in the Medicare program and a possible federalization of the Medicaid program, in which the federal government would assume the financial liability for all or portions of the program.

The recent changes in budgetary allocations and policies marked a significant turning point in the history of the state Medicaid program. The policy changes have been geared primarily to extending the flexibility of the states to make policies (and to cut costs, if they choose), while at the same time restricting total federal budget allocations to the states.

State Medicaid Expenditures

While federal regulations provide important parameters for state actions with regard to the Medicaid program, another significant influence is the level of expenditures and the rate of change in these

TABLE 7.2   Medicaid Expenditures for Health Services and Other Costs, 1979 and 1981, in Fifty States

	All Groups[a] (in billions)		Aged[b] (in billions)	
	1979	1981	1979	1981
Inpatient hospital	5.62	7.09	.36	.94
Physicians	1.62	2.07	.15	.25
Dentists	.43	.54	.03	.04
Other professional services	.16	.23	.02	.04
Nursing homes (SNF, ICF, ICF-MR)	8.65	11.33	4.06	7.01
Laboratory and X-ray	.18	.15	.02	.02
Home health	.26	.43	.02	.27
Drugs	1.18	1.53	.40	.68
Other (e.g., mental hospitals, clinics)	2.29	3.20	.42	.61
Total federal, state, and local expenditures[c]	20.39	26.83	7.65[d]	9.82

SOURCE: U.S. Health Care Financing Administration, Office of Research and Demonstration. Medicaid Statistics. Unpublished tables.

a. Includes all Medicaid-eligible persons (e.g., aged, blind, disabled, and low-income families).

b. Includes only Medicaid-eligible persons classified as aged 65 or over. Does not usually include persons of this age who were blind or disabled prior to reaching age 65, as they may be counted within these other categorically eligible groups.

c. These figures represent only the service expenditures for fifty states. They do not include administrative costs in these states or any expenditures in the territories. Columns may not equal total due to rounding.

d. Figures in this column do not equal total, as several large states did not disaggregate their expenditures for the aged across services.

expenditures within each state. Table 7.2 lists national Medicaid expenditures in 1979 and 1981 for selected health services. The 1981 figures reflect an increase of 31.6 percent over those of 1979. These expenditures represented 11.7 percent of the total personal health care expenditures in the country (Waldo and Gibson, 1982).

Of all Medicaid services, the four with the highest expenditures are general hospitals, nursing homes (including both skilled and intermediate care), physician services, and prescription drugs. All other services combined account for only about 15 percent of total Medicaid expenditures. Among the aged (that is, those aged 65 and over who are not classified as blind or disabled), general hospitals and nursing homes are the two most imposing expenditure items, with the other services confined to relatively minor expenditure levels.

A comparison of the proportion of total Medicaid expenditures for each service with that for aged recipients provides a striking picture of the service utilization patterns by population groups. The aged account for 61.9 percent of Medicaid nursing home expenditures, 62.8 percent of home care, and 44.4 percent of prescription drugs. Therefore, policy changes in these service areas could be expected to have important implications for the aged. Policy changes in the other services (for example, physician services) affect relatively few of the aged and have primary effects on other Medicaid recipients.

A third item to note in Table 7.2 is the rate of change in expenditures between 1979 and 1981, with hospital and nursing home care increasing particularly rapidly. In general it can be expected that policy changes will occur in response to the rate of change, with efforts designed to slow the increase. The actual form of state action, however, will be influenced by whether the rate of change is a function of increases in service price, quality, or quantity of services, and whether the rate of change is a function of attempts to transfer spending from one service category to another.

As noted above, prior to 1979 sharp increases in spending were tolerated as state programs expanded both eligibility and the benefits available. Since then, attention has switched to cost containment. Between 1979 and 1981, expenditures for almost all services increased at a rate above the national rate of inflation. The increase for all services was 31.6 percent compared to 23.3 percent for the consumer price index over the same period. Among the major Medicaid service expenditures, for which cost containment or rollbacks might be desired, physician and hospital care expenditure changes were just below the average level of change. Drugs and nursing home costs were about equal to it. Among the remaining services, for which expansion of benefits and coverage might be desired, home health and other professional health care services appear to have grown markedly in cost. Only laboratory and X-ray services experienced a notable decrease. When only expenditures for aged recipients are considered, the rates of incease tend to be somewhat higher.

These expenditure patterns by service, particularly comparing all recipients with those aged 65 and over, suggest several likely courses of action for state governments in modifying their Medicaid programs.[2] The balance of this chapter compares these expected directions with the actual changes in state policy to date.

(1) It might be expected that priority will be given to constraining the use of services by the aged, since the rate of change in these expenditures is so high.

(2) On the basis of total costs, hospitals, nursing home care, physicians, and prescription drugs can be expected to be the primary targets of expanded regulatory controls and other cost-containment policy, regardless of the populations affected.

(3) Dental services and other professional services with low levels of expenditures can be expected to have few new policy changes.

(4) Home health care, and other personal health care with low overall expenditures but high rates of expenditure increase, can be expected to be targets of service benefit expansion, but with tighter utilization controls.

Patterns of Change in State Medicaid Policy

The choices a state makes in the administration of the Medicaid program are influenced by its commitment to the purchase of medical care for low-income people and by the state's fiscal resources. The level of spending for this program in a very real sense involves a choice between medical services and other public goods. This decision is reflected in the eligibility criteria used for entry into the program and the benefits provided. Some programs are generous in their coverage of potential eligibles and services, yet restrictive in the amounts paid to providers. Others have the reverse philosophy. States do not have unlimited control over their programs. For example, federal statutes define the Medicaid program be an insurancelike program, reimbursing hospitals on the basis of the cost incurred in providing the services, while greater reimbursement flexibility is allowed for other methods. While the 1981 federal waivers permit some flexibility within these limits, particularly in hospital reimbursement, it should be recognized that room for state action is limited.

Three of the major categories of state influence are eligibility, service coverage or utilization controls, and provider payment or reimbursement levels. These areas represent the components of the expenditures equation — spending equals recipients times utilization times price. In this section we review the pattern of policy changes among the fifty states during the years 1979 and 1982. This information will yield some understanding of state responsiveness to patterns of service expenditure and the likely consequences that policy changes will have for the aged and other population groups.

ELIGIBILITY STANDARDS

Eligibility standards are the most influential means for affecting the number and type of people covered by the Medicaid program. For a state to receive federal funds under this program, it must cover those eligibles called "categorically eligible." People in this group are those who receive welfare cash assistance under the Supplemental Security Income (SSI), the state-financed augmentation of this known as State Supplemental Payment (SSP, see Chapter 4), or Aid to Families with Dependent Children (AFDC) programs.

SSI/SSP programs are for aged, blind, or disabled groups, while AFDC is essentially for low-income families with dependent children. States may also choose to cover additional people who do not receive cash welfare assistance under the "medically needy" program and receive matching federal funds. The medically needy are persons with income or assets that are too high to qualify them for AFDC or SSI eligibility, but considered too low by the state to cover their medical bills. If such a program is available, individuals become eligible after their medical expenses, when subtracted from their income and assets, produce income and assets below state-established needs standards. People must "spend down" their incomes to become eligible. Typically, the medically needy income eligibility levels are equal to or no greater than 133 percent of the AFDC standard (Muse and Sawyer, 1982). Extended placement in a nursing home is the major expense leading to Medicaid eligibility for the elderly.

In addition to the eligibility categories receiving federal matching funds, states have the option of including other groups they wish in their medical assistance programs. Expenses for these general relief or medically indigent groups must be financed totally by state funds. Less than half the states had state-funded medical programs in 1982.

Basically, there are two ways for states to control Medicaid eligibility: (1) by setting income and assets criteria for welfare eligibility, and (2) by restricting groups covered specifically and optionally under Medicaid itself (Bovbjerg and Holahan, 1982). Major emphasis has been on the former approach. Few states have raised welfare income eligibility criteria to keep pace with general inflation. Since fewer persons have become eligible for cash assistance, fewer and fewer working poor have become eligible for Medicaid. As a result, since 1977 the Medicaid population has not increased with the increase in the poverty population. Owing to the wide discretion afforded states

TABLE 7.3   Supplemental Security Income, State Supplemental
             Payment, and AFDC Benefit/Need Levels, 1979 and 1981

	1979	1981
Basic Federal SSI Payments[a,b]		
Individual	$208.20	$264.70
Couple	312.30	397.00
Benefit Policies[c]		
States with SSP benefit for independent living	56%	56%
States with SSP benefit for institutional living or supportive housing	62	70
SSP benefits for either of the above	76	80
AFDC need standard, family of 2	$259.00 (average)	$282.00 (average)
AFDC need standard, family of 4	380.00 (average)	409.00 (average)

SOURCES:

a. U.S. Social Security Administration. *Social Security Bulletin,* 43, No. 6 (June 1980).

b. U.S. Social Security Administration. *Social Security Bulletin,* 44, No. 6 (June 1981).

c. La Jolla Management Corporation. *Medicaid Program Characteristics: Summary Tables.* San Diego, CA: La Jolla Management Corporation.

in determining eligibility, it has been estimated that about one-half of all people with annual incomes below the federal poverty level are ineligible for Medicaid (U.S. CBO, 1981; Muse and Sawyer, 1982).

Table 7.3 indicates the proportion of states offering a medically needy program, the changes in SSI/SSP benefits, and changes in the AFDC need standards. Changes in SSI/SSP eligibility criteria were minor between 1979 and 1981. Four states added SSP to institutionalized persons between 1979 and 1982. Federal SSI benefit levels are indexed to keep pace with the rate of inflation. This has aided the aged, blind, and disabled in all states, since this is a federal program.

SSP eligibility policies for the aged living independently have not changed. About half the states continue not to supplement the federal SSI payments for this population. Even when benefits are available, the supplementation tends to be small (Rigby and Ponce, 1980). In July 1979 the average SSP benefit level for the aged in state-administered programs was $88 compared to $121 in July 1982. These benefit levels on average increased by 37.5 percent since 1979 (U.S. Social Security Administration [SSA], 1980a, 1983).[3] Nationally, the number of aged Medicaid recipients has declined by 14.3 percent since 1976 and 5 percent between 1980 and 1981 (U.S. HCFA, 1982).

The medically needy program was available in twenty-nine states in both 1979 and 1981. An important but subtle change in this program is that the income levels permitting access have been lowered in many states. This has occurred because medically needy eligibility is tied to AFDC need standards, which have not been adjusted with inflation. The AFDC program policies were changed during this period by the 1981 Omnibus Budget Reconciliation Act. One of the most important changes mandated states to limit expenses counted against income in determining eligibility for AFDC grants. This mandated policy change eliminated a significant number of working poor and their children from welfare eligibility and thereby from Medicaid.

A more pervasive change in AFDC eligibility results from the level of need standards, that is, the minimum income that states employ to establish eligibility levels. These have been effectively lowered in constant dollar terms between 1979 and 1981. In half the states there was an increase of only 2 percent or less in the need level over this period. Six states actually lowered their standards (U.S. HCFA, n.d.).

The immediate effect of lowered benefit levels or need standards, whether within AFDC, state supplemental payments, or medically needy programs, is to reduce the number of people eligible for, and the cash benefits paid to, these income supplementation programs. A secondary effect is to reduce the number of people meeting the income criterion for the Medicaid program. In states without a medically needy program, these changes lower the total number of people eligible for the program by permanently shifting the eligibility floor. Where there is a medically needy program, these eligibility changes can be expected to lower the total number of eligible people, but with only a short-term delay in Medicaid eligibility for those with high health care costs. This occurs because of the "spend down" provisions defining the medically needy. In such situations individuals and their families will have to spend more of their total annual resources before they can be accepted into Medicaid. In the 40 percent of the states that do not offer medically needy programs, people losing Medicaid eligibility, particularly those with high health care costs, will likely produce increased cost burdens for local government or defaulted payments to private providers and a consequent cost shift to private payers. In either case, federal matching funds are lost to the state economy.

The strategies adopted by most states between 1979 and 1982 appear directly to reduce the number of AFDC clients while indirectly reducing the medically needy. This approach suggests that priority has been given to lowering the expenditures of the working poor rather than focusing on the aged, blind, or disabled. Immediate across-the-board savings in virtually all Medicaid-funded services can be expected from this, the more enduring effect being in services that are not extensively used by the aged or other SSI eligibles. These state Medicaid payment savings, however, are obtained by shifting cost to low-income persons and/or to local governments. While this may be a fiscal benefit to the state budget, and perhaps even provide an incentive to reduce inappropriate use of health services, there are also risks to the population affected, to local government, and to the state economy.

For example, low-income persons who have lost their Medicaid eligibility because of these eligibility changes may go without needed services and/or shift to low-cost care. For some of the working poor, it means going without needed prenatal care or other services until more costly problems develop and hospital care may be required; or, as is already occurring in some states, infant mortality rates begin to rise. The longer-term consequences of these actions on the health and lifestyle of this population are unknown, but it is likely that changes will occur as these limited incomes are reallocated to finance health care instead of being used for other expenses, such as housing, food, heat, and other necessities. Another example of potential short-sightedness in the state policies reviewed here is the continued reluctance of many states to offer cash supplemental payments to persons living independently, and a somewhat greater readiness to offer these benefits to persons in institutional settings. Such an approach will likely further encourage use of higher-cost services, especially since the Medicare and Medicaid programs already have this bias.

Local government is particularly at risk during this transitional stage because it will often have to assume fiscal responsibility for health care of the poor not covered by Medicaid. This care will generally be financed through local property taxes, placing the fiscal burden on a much more limited revenue base than that available to state government. Moreover, local governments will have to pay the total cost of care, whereas if the population were Medicaid-eligible, the federal government would be covering at least half this cost.

In sum, most states reduced Medicaid eligibility between 1979 and 1982, but usually the cuts have not been drastic. Low-income families have been more affected than have the aged, blind, or disabled. No doubt the uncertainty about the savings to be achieved has contributed, but it appears likely that other constraints continue to apply according to surveys by the Urban Institute (Bovbjerg and Holahan, 1982) and our own studies (Harrington et al., 1983) of eight states — California, Florida, Massachusetts, Missouri, Pennsylvania, Texas, Washington, and Wisconsin. States fear the political consequences of reductions in coverage of the institutionalized. Moreover, the population coverage existent within states has been an outgrowth of a philosophy of welfare generosity. There seems to be a reluctance to depart markedly from these historical commitments.

MEDICAID BENEFITS AND UTILIZATION COSTS

The benefits or services covered by a state Medicaid program fall into two general categories — mandatory and optional. Federal regulations require or mandate the existence of the following services: hospitals, physicians, skilled nursing care, hospital outpatient services, rural health clinics, home health, family planning, and laboratory and X-ray services. Additional services can be provided with the federal government sharing the cost. These optional services include, among others, intermediate care facilities, drugs, dental care, personal care, and optometry. States may cover services not on the federally approved optional services list, but without federal assistance.

Beyond the selection of service coverage, states have discretion in the administration of their programs to specify the scope and duration of any service so long as reasonable access to care is preserved. Moreover, Medicaid service coverage for the medically needy can differ from that for those who are categorically eligible for Medicaid (those on AFDC or SSI/SSP assistance). Prior authorization of services, reauthorization, and utilization review are other forms of service control aimed at limiting service coverage to those in need. The requirements of recipient copayments for services, limits on lengths of stay, or limits on the frequency of service use are other examples of state policy options.

In 1981 states were given more flexibility in service coverage and utilization control. The budget act allowed states selectively to limit services for the medically needy. For example, a state could make dental services available to children but not to adults. States were also permitted to enter into competitive bidding arrangements for buying laboratory services and medical supplies, and to limit freedom of choice for services. In practical terms this meant that they could require recipients who were "overutilizing" services to be "locked in," or limited to specific providers. Similarly, providers who have been found to give too many services or poor-quality care can be "locked out," or not allowed to receive reimbursement under the Medicaid program. Other freedom-of-choice restrictions on either providers or services are possible by federal approval. The last notable change arising from the 1981 budget act is that review of Medicaid services by professional standards review organizations (PSROs) is no longer required. States have the option of contracting with PSROs or performing their own reviews of hospital or long term care patient stays.

Mandatory Services. Most states have had a variety of benefit limitations and utilization controls on their mandatory services for some time. These controls include limits on service days or frequency of visits per year, restrictions on weekend admissions, preoperation day limits, and specific procedure limitations. By 1982 the states remained quite varied in the use of these limitations or utilization controls (La Jolla Management Corporation, 1982).

Table 7.4 indicates the proportion of states with selected utilization controls among four mandatory services. Prior authorization of services was the most common control used in 1979, about half the states using it for hospital, physician, skilled nursing home, and home health services. By 1982 just over one-fourth of the states continued to employ prior authorization for hospital services, while limits on service days or visits, and procedure exclusion became more pervasive. Among long term care services, prior authorization has gained popularity. This change is most evident for skilled nursing homes, where there has been a 40 percent increase in the number of states imposing this control since 1979. There has also been a slight increase in the number of states with prior authorization controls in home health services.

The decline of state prior authorization requirements for Medicaid acute care services is very likely a result of the operational difficulty of its application. Based on our interviews with state officials, it seems that retrospective assessments, utilization reviews, and limits on days or specific procedures are more practical (Harrington et al., 1983). Whether these alternative forms of control can be effectively

TABLE 7.4 Selected Utilization Controls on Selected Mandatory Services in 1979 and 1982

Services	Percentages of States with Controls 1979	1982
General Hospital *Inpatient Services*		
Limits on days per year	50%	50%
Prior authorization for elective or selected procedures	46	28
Weekend admissions/pre-op days limits	2	20
Specific procedure limits	6	40
Skilled Nursing		
Prior authorization	50	70
Other limits[a]		28
Physician		
Frequency of visits limited	42	56
Prior authorization	52	42
Specific services not covered	12	34
Other limits, including specific limits for service patient groups, frequency of injections, or treatment	58	52
Home Health		
Prior authorization	42	46
Services limited[a]		36
Other limits[a]		72

SOURCES: U.S. Health Care Financing Administration. *Data on the Medicaid Program Eligibility, Services and Expenditures*, rev. ed. Baltimore: U.S. Department of Health, Education and Welfare, HCFA, 1979. Data derived from La Jolla Management Corporation. *Medicaid Program Characteristics: Summary Tables*, Vol. 1. San Diego, CA: La Jolla Management Corporation, 1982.

a. Policy information not available for 1979.

and politically used to disallow payments, discourage unnecessary utilization, and save total costs remains to be determined.

Although the use of state prior authorization requirements for Medicaid nursing home and home health services appears to pose fewer operational problems because of the nature and timeliness of service need, other forms of utilization control gained prominence by 1982. One problem with prior authorization is that this restriction usually applies only to Medicaid-eligible persons. It does not affect private pay patients until they become eligible for Medicaid. By that time, individual nursing home patients have often been patients for days and the authorization becomes pro forma.

The limit on hospital days in some states has been described as probably the most important change emerging. Bovbjerg and Holahan (1982) have found that these limits (or their threat) give the state some leverage in negotiating lower payment rates while also inducing shorter lengths of stay. There are risks associated with this strategy, however, since the limits are arbitrary and unrelated to needed lengths of care. If patient care extends beyond the limit, the hospital can meet the cost of this care by passing on its costs to private pay patients. Alternatively, private hospitals may avoid patients likely to have long stays, placing these patients in public facilities and increasing their operational deficits.

From this analysis it appears that states are continuing to exercise their discretion to adopt utilization controls on their most costly mandatory health services. However, the majority of states have not yet adopted an extensive or uniform set of controls. Whether the introduction of new controls by themselves will have an impact on expenditure levels and rates of change has not been tested by this analysis, but it is clear that there are many avenues of state regulatory control yet to be tried.

Optional Benefits. In addition to the federally mandated benefits, states have the option of providing an array of other services. A list of optional services, selected either because of their dollar allocations or their importance to the aged, is shown in Table 7.5. With the exception of intermediate care facilities (ICFs), these services do not typically account for a high percentage of Medicaid expenditures. Well over half of the states offered most of these benefits at the end of 1979. However, personal care and private duty nursing were among those least likely to be available. By 1982 there had been some erosion of benefits. Nine services (chiropractic, dental services, dentures, diagnostic, emergency hospital, eyeglasses, private duty nursing, screening, and rehabilitative services) were less widely available, with one to three states dropping each of these benefits. On the other hand, seven of these services (clinic services, podiatry, occupational therapy, other practitioner services, prosthetic devices, personal care, and speech, hearing, and language therapy) were more available in 1982, in one to four additional states.

When optional benefits are available, states have shown a consistent willingness to impose utilization controls. Prior authorization is

TABLE 7.5   Selected Optional State Medicaid Benefits in 1979 and 1982

Service	*Percentages of States with Benefits* 1979	1982
Chiropractor	54%	52%
Clinic	88	96
Dental	68	62
Dentures	70	66
Diagnostic	46	44
Emergency hospital	92	90
Eyeglasses	76	74
Intermediate care (non-M.R.)	100	100
Occupational therapy	50	52
Optometry	82	82
Other practitioner services	58	60
Personal care	32	36
Physical therapy	72	72
Podiatry	78	80
Prescription drugs	100	100
Preventive services	40	40
Private duty nursing	38	36
Prosthetic division	92	94
Rehabilitation	62	56
Screening	32	30
Speech, hearing, and language therapy	60	62

SOURCE: U.S. Health Care Financing Administration, Office of Research and Demonstrations. Medical Services State by State. Unpublished data, 1979 and 1982.

typically required in at least half of the states that actually provide a given benefit. Other limitations on these benefits, such as restricted procedures or service unit maximums, are even more common. About two-thirds to three-fourths of the states that offer an optional benefit have one or more of these limits (La Jolla Management Corporation, 1982). Copayment, another approach assumed to limit service use, was not widely used by 1982, although three services of import to the elderly had copayments (prescription drugs in eighteen states and dental and eyeglasses in eleven states each). Intermediate care facility (ICF) utilization, a component in nursing home costs, has been most commonly controlled through the use of preauthorization screening — 48 percent of the states had this requirement in 1982.

Personal care and physical therapy, two other optional services of particular interest for the aged, are often advocated as a means of reducing SNF/ICF care, the former by providing community-based supportive care, the latter by offering rehabilitation to increase capability and reduce dependency among institutionalized and noninstitutionalized groups. There has been a tendency for more states to add these benefits since 1979, but neither benefit is available in all states. Personal care, independent from home care, continues to be one of the least available optional benefits in 1982.

Our review of optional benefits availability shows that states have generally endeavored to maintain these benefit programs. Expenditure increases tended to be guarded against by employing a variety of utilization controls, preauthorization being the single most common strategy. Unfortunately, several important services for the aged have not been available in one-third or more of the states. Among these are chiropractic, dental, eyeglasses, personal care, and various rehabilitative therapies. Further complicating access to these important benefits, where they exist, is the frequent use of copayments and other restrictive service limitations by state Medicaid programs. These accessibility problems raise the question of what proportion of the eligible public is going without these services, paying for them out-of-pocket or receiving substitutable (and perhaps more costly) services through hospitals and physicians.

Another issue, about which little is known, is whether funding for existing optional services is adequate to meet the real need. Finally, the interrelationship between optional benefits and mandatory physician services should be considered. Services such as those provided by chiropractors, podiatrists, emergency hospitals, and clinics can, under many circumstances, serve as alternatives to physician services. The availability of such services varies across the states. Only clinic services became more available between 1979 and 1982, suggesting that states are not yet using optional benefits as a strategy for reducing physician expenditures.

PROVIDER PAYMENTS AND REIMBURSEMENT

The choice of how reimbursement rates are set, and their levels, is an important public policy issue because of its direct bearing on the supply of service providers and the unit costs of care. Federal law requires state Medicaid rates to be high enough reasonably to pay for the service provided. Providers must accept Medicaid payments as payment in full (with the exception of any state-established copayments). These payments, however, may not exceed the rates that Medicare and private payers would pay for the same services. Within these general requirements, states have always had discretion in setting payment levels. They have had the least control over hospital rates and somewhat more control over nursing homes and individual providers (such as physicians, druggists, and opticians).

For the present analysis, attention is limited to reimbursement processes used by states in financing their three most expensive Medicaid services: inpatient hospitals, skilled nursing, and intermediate care facilities. Physician reimbursement rates have been excluded because these costs account for less that 3 percent of Medicaid spending nationally, and because of the complexity involved in implementing these rates.[4]

Inpatient Hospitals. Although comprising more than one-quarter of the total Medicaid bill, inpatient hospital costs historically have not been an important target for Medicaid cost containment. Prior to 1981 states were required to pay hospitals on a reasonable cost-reimbursement basis. The most commonly used method was retrospective payment based on the Medicare guidelines. In practice, the reasonable-cost approach has given the states little control over hospital cost increases, as almost all costs actually incurred by hospitals have been reimbursed (Bovbjerg and Holahan, 1982). This has posed a particularly serious problem for Medicaid, since hospital costs have consistently risen at rates two to three times the rate of inflation.

While most states used a retrospective payment system for hospitals, some states have considered alternative financing methods, such as setting rates in advance of the receipt of hospital services (that is, making them prospective). Prospective rate setting has been shown effective in slowing the growth of hospital costs by several percentage points a year in several states (Coelen and Sullivan, 1981). Prospective rate setting takes many forms, including statewide rate-setting commissions and individually negotiated rates with participating hospitals. Although prospective rate approaches have been permissible under federal policy since the early 1970s, only ten Medicaid programs had approved these systems prior to 1981.

The major financing alternative in this regard is the health maintenance organization (HMO). HMOs are medical organizations that contract to deliver all covered services for a fixed, advance payment for each enrollee (Luft, 1981). Usually they are organizations that have their own doctors and hospitals, although a variety of administrative forms exist. Mechanisms such as HMOs with a fixed budget give the state more control over its medical resource allocation, while also presumably imposing an incentive for efficiency by the provider. HMOs currently have one major limitation. They do not provide long term nursing home care, nor do they provide the continuum of social services that forms an alternative to institutionalization.

Other prepaid arrangements are being developed for the elderly (see Callahan and Wallack, 1980). One such arrangement involves making an individual private physician or a care management team responsible for monitoring the provision of a wide range of services to patients. In some forms of this approach, the physician (or care management organization) is at full or partial financial risk if total service costs exceed the prepaid budget. Portions of any savings from spending less than the prepaid fees would be retained by the physician or care management organization.

Federal policy changes in 1981 have tried to stimulate the expanded development of the HMOs and other prepaid delivery mechanisms. The more important changes were to increase the ceiling (from 50 to 75 percent) on the percentage of HMO enrollees who were Medicaid patients. Additionally, waivers on the freedom-of-choice requirement have been made easier to get. This has helped states, if they so desire, to limit Medicaid recipients in the choice of their physicians, so as to channel the patients into an alternative delivery system, or to limit them to a choice among several competing alternatives.

Table 7.6 shows the average payments per patient day and the method of payment used for hospital services in 1979 and 1981. Hospital average payments per patient day are used here as a surrogate for state hospital rates. This has been necessary due to the complexity with which hospital costs are reimbursed. National average payment-per-day figures are an aggregation of the net effect of the constellation of state reviews and ceilings on specific procedures for reimbursement requests or prospective rates. They are not a direct measure of a single state policy. Between 1979 and the end of 1981, the average cost per patient hospital day increased by 40.2 percent, from $164 to $230. This rate not only far exceeds the national rate of inflation, but also masks the fact that many individual states experienced even higher rates of change.

In response to this high and continuing cost escalation and the federal changes in the 1981 and 1982 legislation, states have become more active in seeking negotiated rates from hospitals and have given more emphasis to health maintenance organizations (HMOs). By

TABLE 7.6   Changes in State Medicaid Reimbursement Policy, 1979 and 1981

	1979	*1981*
Inpatient Hospitals		
Basis of payment		
Medicare principle	86% (43)	64% (32)
Average Payment[a]		
per patient day	$164.00	$230.00[b]
Skilled Nursing		
Average rate	33.00	42.00
per patient day	(national average)	(national average)
Average medicaid payment	26.00	32.00
per patient day	(national average)	(national average)
Intermediate Care		
Average Rate	26.00	33.00
per patient day		
Average Medicaid payment	19.00	24.00
per patient day	(national average)	(national average)

SOURCE: Data derived from La Jolla Management Corporation. *Medicaid Program Characteristics: Summary Tables,* Vol. 1. San Diego, CA: La Jolla Management Corporation, 1982.

a. Payment data were compiled from HCFA form 2082 for expenditure days of care by the National Governors' Association survey, and average per day was calculated by La Jolla Management Corporation.

b. Calculated using 21 states with complete information. The 1980 average per day payment was $194.

1982, twenty-two states had established alternative systems, others have revamped theirs, and still others are considering the adoption of alternative systems (Intergovernmental Health Policy Project [IHPP], 1982; National Governors' Association [NGA], 1982). The extent of the savings realized by these changes will depend on the number of states that adopt changes, the rates they set, and whether the reimbursement systems or rates can be upheld in lawsuits.

Expanded state control over hospital rates does not come without risks. First, in those hospitals where Medicaid patients form only a small percentage of all patients, it is likely that unmet costs will be shifted to private payers. Alternatively, these hospitals might refuse or limit their participation in Medicaid. Public facilities and those with a high proportion of Medicaid patients will be unable to shift unmet costs to private payers. Any deficits will likely show up as reduced quality of care, facility closures, or nonfederally matched cash subsidies.

SNF/ICF REIMBURSEMENT

State Medicaid programs have had a major interest in SNF/ICF reimbursement because of the large portion of the program budget that goes to these payments. Almost 40 percent of all Medicaid expenditures were for these services in 1981. Over 70 percent of all the Medicaid spending for the aged goes to these services (U.S. HCFA, n.d.). Historically, states have been given greater flexibility in rate setting for nursing homes than for hospitals by the federal statutes and regulations.

In 1976 federal regulations were changed to require that nursing homes be paid on a "reasonably cost-related basis." In 1980 this requirement was modified to become "reasonable and adequate" in order to meet the necessary costs of "efficiency and economically operated facilities." Not implemented until 1982, the new regulations allow greater state control over nursing home rates.

Most often, states have utilized some form of prospective per diem reimbursement. In 1982 only eleven states reported using retrospective reimbursement, and the remainder used some form of prospective reimbursement (IHPP, 1982; La Jolla Management Corporation, 1982). States vary regarding whether they set individual rates for each facility, set a flat rate for all facilities, have rates that apply to specific classes or types of facilities, or use a combination system. States also vary in the relative proportions of skilled versus intermediate care facilities that they license.

The widespread use of Medicaid prospective rate setting for the SNF/ICF industry has been aided by the nature of the service. The calculations of the cost factors are less technical and complicated than for hospitals. Usually they are based on an aggregation of nursing services, dietary services, housekeeping, linen changes, administration, and social activities. Physician services, drugs, and rehabilitation services are usually billed separately to the patient and are not included in the SNF/ICF per diem rate.

The prospective rate-setting approach has risks associated with the methodology used (Bishop, 1980; Winn, 1975). The per diem rate limits the cost of care, the resources available to the home, and ultimately the availability of beds. Nursing homes attempt to balance these costs by the patients they accept (Scanlon, 1980), in terms of both the level of care needed and public or private pay status. Patients needing less care are less costly than so-called heavy care patients. Private pay patients are usually billed at higher rates than are public pay patients. The supply of nursing home beds has also likely been affected by the rates and controls on bed construction. Currently, nursing homes operate at an average occupancy rate of 90-95 percent. When public pay patients cannot be placed in a nursing home, they likely remain "backed up" in hospitals at much higher per diem costs. This cost (for the aged, blind, and disabled), however, is largely financed by federal Medicare funds, in which case state-matched Medicaid program funds are used only to cover Medicare deductible payments.

In spite of the recent federal regulatory language change, states have made few modifications in the type of nursing home methods — eighteen states had retrospective reimbursement in 1979, compared to twelve in 1982 (NGA, 1982; La Jolla Management Corporation, 1982). States appear reasonably satisfied with prospective procedures for Medicaid. Many states have reported refinements in their existing methods to reduce reimbursement rates (Spitz, 1981b). Common changes involve limiting inflation allowances and altering the cost ceilings for specific nursing home rate cost centers (Bovbjerg and Holahan, 1982; Harrington et al., 1983). Not all changes, however, are designed to reduce costs. Efforts to link the reimbursement rate to patient-related costs (and coordination) are being considered in a few states and tested in demonstration programs (Spitz, 1981a, 1981b).

As seen in Table 7.6, SNF and ICF rates went up with the national rate of inflation between 1979 and 1981, but this cost pattern contrasts sharply with a much higher rate of hospital cost increases. The prospective rate structure for nursing homes has, in part, helped to make this possible.

Summary and Conclusion

Health and human service program expenditures for the aged and other low-income populations have grown rapidly in terms of absolute and relative dollars during the past decade. In fiscal year 1983, Medicare, Medicaid, and social services (Title XX), for example, account for more than 15 percent of the federal budget. The level of these appropriations has increased nearly 40 percent since 1980 to $74 billion. Services to the aged account for about 45 percent of the total health care costs borne by government. A large proportion of the balance of these costs is provided through out-of-pocket direct payments by the aged themselves.

Medicaid represents the primary public program for long term care through its coverage of nursing home costs. While long term care services essentially remain uncovered by Medicare and private insurance programs, Medicaid now covers about half of all costs for these services. Partly because Medicare has always commanded the primary attention of aging interests, given its exclusive focus on older persons, and partly because Medicaid is fragmented within its federal-state structure into fifty or more programs rather than one, the significance of the Medicaid program for the aging has not been sufficiently appreciated. What happens to the Medicaid program at the state level over the next several years may have immense implications for nascent efforts to develop a continuum of care for the frail elderly.

The decline in federal revenues, the advent of fiscal crisis at the state and local levels, the continued rise of health care costs, and the inequitable burden of service availability across the continuum of care have combined to produce an important federal and state public policy dilemma. Can the rapidly rising costs of health care, including long term care, be curtailed and a more equitable distribution of services be fashioned? This chapter has examined policy changes since 1979 among state Medicaid programs, identifying state strategies being adopted and assessing their implications for the elderly. As of FY 1982, four main strategies are being pursued by states seeking to reduce the public cost of providing health care to low-income persons, including the elderly:

- Reductions in eligibility need standards are being made both among the AFDC and low-income aged, blind, and disabled populations. This approach is intended to produce both immediate and long-term expenditure reductions.

- Modifications of reimbursement methods are being made, away from the present retrospective cost-based system for hospital services and toward varying forms of prospective rates. This structural change relies on constrained budgets to encourage greater provider efficiency, potentially producing longer-term cost savings.

- Incremental adjustments have been made in utilization controls for both mandatory and optional services, but no significant expansion or contraction of benefits has occurred. This approach is largely oriented toward monitoring the appropriateness and duration of service provision, with the intention of reducing service cost per recipient.

- The introduction of copayments for mandatory and optional benefits has occurred, but on a limited basis. These payments are expected to discourage unnecessary utilization and may allow slower vendor rate increases where the providers receive some of the fees from service recipients.

States have been faced with significant political pressures to control the costs of government, and the Medicaid program has been a primary target of cost-containment efforts in most states. Changes in reimbursement methods and the contraction of eligibility standards appear to be the major approaches being utilized. Efforts by the states to modify reimbursement to hospitals represent a significant new direction in state policy. Recent state attempts to reduce nursing home costs further are also likely to have an impact in the future. The potential overall impact of cost control efforts by use of reimbursement policies will, no doubt, be considerable over time. The impact of such policy changes and budget reductions on the elderly, who are high utilizers of these services (Fisher, 1980) is also likely to be great.

Other state strategies may be widespread, but their impact on costs and service utilization thus far seems modest. Utilization controls and copayments represent administrative responses to calls for efficiency in government and are significant to the extent that they symbolize public sector commitment to containing costs. Their effects, however, are difficult to evaluate for the present. In terms of the elderly, many of whom have very modest incomes at best, we should be particularly sensitive to the impact of copayments (see also Chapter 4). Some state officials clearly believe that Medicaid copayments will reduce utilization of services. If this is so, their dampening effect on utilization of even much-needed health services may be particularly hard on low-income older persons, who are likely to be more sensitive to cost increases than other groups because their income potential declines with age.

For the aged, major problems emerging from state policy shifts are further limits on access to hospitals of their "choice" and, more important, increased private payments for SNF/ICF care and for community-based care. This will occur primarily because the patient and family financial obligations of older persons are being increased, and their eligibility for Medicaid to cover nursing home care is being diminished through more stringent requirements of medically needy programs in the states. At the same time, public payments are continuing to fall behind private payment rates for all health services.

Significantly, there are few signs of a fundamental shift in service provision that many had hoped for — the substitution of lower-cost (community-based) services for other, high-cost hospital and nursing home services. The priority on cost savings rather than system reform is perhaps best understood in light of the current fiscal crisis of state government and the uncertainty regarding future federal and state roles in health care for the poor. Nevertheless, a more agressive public policy response is needed if the existing inequitable distribution of resources for acute and institutional care is to be addressed and if the financial burden that this approach places on the elderly and their families is to be resolved.

Notes

1. In broad terms, hospitals bill Medicaid, Medicare, and other third-party payers for the services performed. These claims are then reviewed for their appropriateness for individual patients and whether they are within allowable cost limits. Claims meeting these and other criteria are paid. The state may have more control over these costs by using a prospective payment system (a system in which per patient day cost and/or other costs have been established in advance).

2. In considering this list or other possible state responses, it is important to keep in mind that reductions in a service may result in a shift of patients or service costs to other services. In other words, simple cost reductions in one or more areas may not affect total expenditures because of service substitution. Further analysis will be needed to assess whether the changes reported in this chapter are, in form or substance, for the population served and achieve overall cost savings.

3. SSP data are extremely complex, since standards vary by individuals and couples and have minimum and maximum rates based on a wide variety of living arrangements. As a consequence, group aggregations, like average or median benefits across states, are poorly reflective of the phenomena being studied. For a state-by-state listing of these benefit levels, see U.S. SSA, 1982.

4. Physician payments are typically established by relying on the prevailing or usual and customary rate (UCR) received from private patients and charged to Medicare. States then use the UCR as a ceiling and establish the Medicaid reimbursement rate as a percentage of UCR. This practice follows procedures used by Medicare and, in most respects, private insurance. The logic underlying this approach includes an assumption that market forces establish these rates and that being responsive to this mechanism helps assure Medicaid patients freedom of choice in selecting their providers. See Holahan (1982) and Holahan et al. (1981) for a discussion of physician rate setting.

References

Bishop, C.E. Cost-Related Reimbursement. Waltham, MA: University Health Policy Consortium, 1980.

Bovbjerg, R.R., and J. Holahan. *Medicaid in the Reagan Era: Federal Policy and State Choices.* Washington, DC: Urban Institute, 1982.

Callahan, J., and S. Wallack, eds. *Reforming the Long-Term-Care System.* Lexington, MA: D.C. Heath, 1980.

Coelen, C., and D. Sullivan. "An Analysis of the Effects of Prospective Reimbursement Programs on Hospital Expenditures." *Health Care Financing Review,* 2, No. 3 (Winter 1981), 1-40.

Estes, C.L., and P.R. Lee. "Policy Shifts and Their Impact on Health Care for Elderly Persons." *Western Journal of Medicine,* 135, No. 6 (1981), 511-517.

Fisher, C.R. "Differences in Age Groups in Health Care Spending." *Health Care Financing Review* (Spring 1980).

Freeland, M.S., and C.E. Schendler. "National Health Expenditures: Short-Term Outlook and Long-Term Projections." *Health Care Financing Review,* 2, No. 3 (Winter 1981), 97-138.

Garfinkel, S., and S. Terrell. *The Use of Private Insurance Plans for the Aged Medicare Population.* Baltimore, U.S. Health Care Financing Administration, n.d.

Harrington, C., R. Newcomer, J. Swan, L. Paringer, C. Estes, and P. Lee. *Eight-State Comparative Report on Medicaid Services.* San Francisco: Aging Health Policy Center, University of California, 1983.

Holahan, J. "A Comparison of Medicaid and Medicare Physician Reimbursement Rates." Working Paper No. 1306-02-04. Washington, DC: Urban Institute, 1982.

————, J. Gornick, and D. Nichols. "Physicians' Fees in State Medicaid Programs." Working Paper No. 1298-9 (rev.). Washington, DC: Urban Institute, 1981.

Intergovernmental Health Policy Project (IHPP). *Recent and Proposed Changes in State Medicaid Programs, A Fifty State Survey.* Washington, DC: George Washington University, 1982.

La Jolla Management Corporation. *Medicaid Program Characteristics: Summary Tables,* Vol. 1. Washington, DC: U.S. Health Care Financing Administration, 1982.

Luft, H. *Health Maintenance Organizations: Dimensions of Performance.* New York: John Wiley, 1981.

Muse, D., and D. Sawyer. *The Medicare and Medicaid Data Book, 1981.* Baltimore: U.S. Health Care Financing Administration, 1982.

National Governors' Association (NGA). *Medicaid Program Changes: State by State Profiles.* Washington, DC: NGA, 1982.

Rigby, D., and E. Ponce. *The Supplemental Security Income Program for the Aged, Blind and Disabled: Selected Characteristics of State Supplementation Programs as of October, 1979.* Washington, DC: U.S. Government Printing Office, 1980.

Scanlon, W.J. "A Theory of the Nursing Home Market." *Inquiry,* 17, No. 2 (1980), 25-41.

Spitz, B. *Medicaid Nursing Home Reimbursement: New York, Illinois, California Case Studies.* Baltimore: U.S. Health Care Financing Administration, 1981a.
———. *State Guide to Medicaid Cost Containment.* Washington, DC: Intergovernmental Health Policy Project, Center for Policy Research, National Governors' Association, 1981b.
U.S. Congressional Budget Office (CBO). *Medicaid: Choices for 1982 and Beyond.* Washington, DC: CBO, 1981.
U.S. General Accounting Office (GAO). *Home Health – The Need for a National Policy to Better Provide for the Elderly: Report to the Congress by the Comptroller General of the United States.* Washington, DC: GAO, 1977.
U.S. Health Care Financing Administration (HCFA). "National Medicaid Statistics: Fiscal Year 1979." Unpublished tables. Washington, DC: HCFA, n.d.
———. *Data on the Medicaid Program: Eligibility, Services, Expenditures* (rev.). Baltimore: HCFA, 1979.
———. *Long Term Care: Background and Future Directions.* Baltimore, HCFA, 1981.
———. "Medicaid Statistics: Fiscal Year 1981." Unpublished tables. Washington, DC: HCFA, 1982.
U.S. National Center for Health Statistics (NCHS). Unpublished data. Washington, DC: NCHS, 1982.
U.S. Public Law 97-35. Omnibus Budget Reconciliation Act of 1982 (HR 3982). Amendments to Title XXI — Medicare, Medicaid, Section 2100, passed by Congress, July 31. Washington, DC: Government Printing Office, 1981.
U.S. Public Law 97-248. Tax Equity and Fiscal Responsibility Act (HR 4961). Provisions Relating to Savings in Health and Income Security Programs, passed by Congress, July 12. Washington, DC: U.S. Government Printing Office, 1982.
U.S. Senate, Special Committee on Aging. *Developments in Aging: 1981,* Vol. 1. Washington, DC: U.S. Government Printing Office, 1982a.
———. *Health Care Expenditures for the Elderly: How Much Protection Does Medicare Provide?* Washington, DC: U.S. Government Printing Office, 1982b.
U.S. Social Security Administration (SSA). *Social Security Bulletin,* 43, No. 1 (January 1980a).
———. *Social Security Bulletin,* 43, No. 6 (June 1980b).
———. *Social Security Bulletin,* 44, No. 6 (June 1981).
———. *Social SecurityBulletin,* 46, No. 1 (January 1983).
Vladeck, B. "The Design of Failure: Health Policy and the Structure of Federalism." *Journal of Health Politics, Policy and Law,* 4, No. 3 (Fall 1979), 522-535.
Waldo, D.R., and R.M. Gibson. "National Health Expenditures, 1981." *Health Care Financing Review,* 4, No. 1 (Summer 1982), 1-35.
Winn, S. "Assessments of Cost Related Characteristics and Conditions of Long-Term Care Patients." *Inquiry,* 12 (1975), 344-351.

CHAPTER 8

THE OLDER AMERICANS ACT

Robert J. Newcomer
A. E. Benjamin
Carroll L. Estes

The strategies represented by the Older Americans Act of 1965, the general and special revenue-sharing legislation of the 1970s, and the health and social services block grant enactments of the early 1980s share a common emphasis on decentralized authority for resource allocation and program priority setting. With this legislation Congress has transferred decision-making authority from the national to state and local governments. Primary among reasons underlying this transfer is a desire to enhance the ability of government to plan responsively for and to meet the needs of the nation's diverse population. An additional and perhaps more consequential rationale for this legislation is the transfer of fiscal responsibility and the political pressure associated with program provision from the federal level to other levels of government.

A range of questions remain unanswered regarding the consequences of increased decentralization of federal programs. While answers to normative questions about what is best for the political system and its constituencies remain in the realm of politics, many descriptive questions concerning the nature of the performance of given levels of government under various federalistic arrangements can be addressed by policy research. Amendments to the Older Americans Act in the last decade have created and shaped a system of state and local agencies that are expected both to carry out federal

Authors' Note: The authors wish to acknowledge the invaluable contributions of Victoria Peguillan-Shea and James H. Swan. The data in this chapter are derived from the research supported by U.S. Administration on Aging Grant No. 90-A-979.

mandates and to be responsive to varied regional conditions. An examination of the experiences of these agencies may cast some light on three important descriptive questions of consequence for debates about federalism.

First, to what extent do those priorities established in federal legislation and regulation in fact guide agency behavior at the state and local levels? In other words, what is the relative efficacy of a three-tiered system in which the highest (federal) level establishes certain priorities, the middle (state) level interprets and monitors the operationalization of these priorities, and the lower (local) level implements them? To the extent that compliance with federal goals is observed at the middle and lower levels, we can conclude that this specific version of federal relations is effective in translating national priorities into local action. While decisions about the desirability of federal goals are essentially political, knowledge about relative success in carrying them out is important to the policy debate.

Second, to what extent do state aging agencies operating within a federal structure (that is, with directives from above and responsibilities below) establish strong policy and administrative roles for themselves in addition to their more specified "federal" roles? Policy roles in representing the interests of the elderly are especially important at the state level, where a bureaucratic locus of aging interests is essential. Administrative roles in establishing state-specific priorities for local aging agencies and providing various forms of assistance to these relatively young organizations also seem significant. More broadly, we are interested in learning something about the initiative and activism of state agencies within a federal structure.

Third, what has been the experience of local agencies operating under federal and state directives? To what extent have they mirrored the priorities of higher levels of government? Have they established distinctive roles or responses for themselves in view of widely heralded differences in local conditions? If so, has this activity increased their effectiveness as local advocates of aging interests?

Currently, a number of alternative directions in public policy are being discussed at the national level. Among these are whether the Older Americans Act should be reauthorized, the future role of state and area agencies, and the role of the aging network in long term care service planning and delivery. These issues have implications beyond the Older Americans Act and touch on federal, state, and local roles in future planning and delivery across the continuum of care for the aged.

Legislative History

The Older Americans Act, originally enacted in 1965 (U.S. PL 89-73), is the single federal social service statute designed specifically for the aged. Initially funded at $6.5 million dollars, the act established the Administration on Aging (AoA) within the federal government, required states to establish state units on aging, and authorized state and community social service programs, as well as research, demonstration, and training projects. It also established a set of objectives aimed at improving the lives of older Americans in the areas of income, health, housing, employment, retirement, cultural and recreational opportunities, restorative services, community services, and gerontological research (U.S. Senate, 1982).[1]

The Older Americans Act funds a broad array of services for persons over age 60 under its several titles. Title III-A provides funds for community service projects to develop coordinated and comprehensive service systems. Title III-B funds various social services such as information, referral, homemaker, and transportation. Title III-C supports congregate meals, nutrition education, and counseling. Title IV provides funds for research and demonstration projects; Title V, for training (U.S. House, 1978). A range of social and health services are provided to older persons in all states under Title III, and there is a significant overlap in goals and provisions with the Social Services Block Grant (SSBG) program.

When the act was initially passed, it was implemented through small social service grants and research projects. By 1971 the total appropriation under this act had grown to $27.3 million. About one-third of the appropriation was for area planning and social services, while another 40 percent was for the foster grandparent and retired senior volunteer programs. Major amendments to the act occurred in 1972 (U.S. PL 92-258) and 1973 (U.S. PL 93-29). The 1972 amendments created the national nutrition program and authorized grants to public and nonprofit sponsors for the development of congregate meal services. Appropriations for the act had expanded to $101 million by this time.

The 1973 amendments significantly revised and expanded the scope of the Older Americans Act by creating area agencies on aging (AAAs). These organizations were given responsibility for planning, coordinating, and advocating programs that would benefit older persons, and for funding most of the services financed under the act. Area agencies were to be designated by state units on aging (SUAs) to operate within defined planning and service areas (PSAs). The 1973 amendments also explicitly delegated program priority setting and implementation decisions to state and substate areas. This change was significant for several reasons that went beyond the expanded, but still very limited, resources appropriated under the act ($253 million in 1973). First, decentralization created a focal point for aging within local communities. At this level of government, as at other levels, aging services traditionally had been accorded low priority, and providers and advocates associated with aging were accorded low status (Morris and Binstock, 1966). The new agency "focal points" were expected to be in a position to build a political constituency, legitimize themselves, and ultimately raise the visibility and viability of the aged and their services (Estes, 1976).

Subsequent amendments to the Older Americans Act in 1975 (U.S. PL 94-135), 1978 (U.S. PL 95-478), and 1981 (U.S. PL 97-115) extended the authority for continued program operation and the basic strategy enunciated in 1973 (Coombs et al., 1982). The principal changes were to give area agencies broader programmatic responsibility for Older Americans Act funds under their jurisdiction and a review and comment authority on all programs and policies affecting older people in the geographic area served by the area agency. The number of federally mandated services and other federally established priorities (such as specific coordination agreements) generally has been reduced since 1978 (Newcomer et al., 1981). Area agencies are currently required to allocate "an adequate portion" of their social service funds to one or more of the national priority services. Currently, these include information and referral, transportation, in-home assistance, and legal services. In addition, there are separate authorizations for home-delivered and congregate meals, and a requirement that states operate a nursing home ombudsman program (U.S. Senate, 1982).

Appropriations under the Older Americans Act rose from a 1973 level of $253 million to $1054 million in 1983, but they are expected to decline (with a proposed 1984 appropriation of $998 million). Although these appropriations grew substantially in the last decade, they nevertheless represent a relatively minor national social service expenditure when distributed among 57 states and territories and over 600 area agencies to serve more than 23 million older persons. Available funds are even more limited if actual funds for social services are considered separately. Funds for "area planning and social services" account for only about 26 percent of the total Older Americans Act appropriation. This compares with shares of 36 percent for the nutrition program and 29 percent for the community service employment program for older workers. Various other activities, including research and training, account for the remaining funds. In effect, the potential importance of the Older Americans Act arises not from the volume of funding for its social programs, but from its definition of national goals for the aged and creation of a state and local network for planning, advocacy, and delivery.

Federal Directives and State and Area Agency Behavior[2]

A major question regarding federalism and the Older Americans Act is the extent to which federal legislation and regulation guide and limit agency behavior at the state and local level. One aspect of this issue is conformance to federal requirements, or accountability. A second aspect deals with state autonomy and initiative, or the will and/or capacity of state and area agencies to establish policies and directions in their own right.

Two issues to be examined are the proportion of federal directives that are reflected in state and local statements of goals and the proportion of state and local goals that reflect federal mandates. As part of our research on state and area agencies on aging,[3] all federal (AoA) directives for the period 1974 to 1979 were catalogued, with state (SUA) and area agency (AAA) plans and other documents examined and coded. Federal directives were grouped into two categories: those that were formally required and those that were encouraged but not required. An assessment was made of the extent to which state units and area agencies on aging were responsive to these types of federal direction in two broad areas: (1) specification of the services to be delivered and (2) agencies with whom coordination was desirable (see Tables 8.1 and 8.2). The former concerns the funding and advocacy emphasis to be placed on specified services, while the latter concerns the specification of the agencies and organizations with which the SUA or AAA should coordinate.

Our analysis suggests that aging agencies respond to federal directives regarding service emphasis more readily than to those regarding coordination. Probably the major reason for this difference is the lack of clarity and specificity of the federal directives on coordination, in

TABLE 8.1   AoA Required/Encouraged Service Emphasis, 1974-1979

Service	Status	Effective Date for Area Agencies	Effective Date for State Units
Education	Encouraged	1978	1976-1978
Employment	Encouraged	1975, 1976, 1979	1976-1979
Energy	Encouraged	1977, 1978	1975-1978
Financial assistance	Encouraged	1975, 1977	1974-1975, 1977
Home health/homemaker[a]	Required	1976-1979	1976-1979
Home repairs/renovation[a]	Required	1976-1979	1976-1979
Housing	Encouraged	1978	1976-1978
Information and referral[b]	Required	1974-1979	1974, 1975-1979
Legal[a]	Encouraged	1974, 1975	
	Required	1976-1979	1976-1979
Medical services	Encouraged	1976, 1978	1977-1978
Mental health	Encouraged		1977
Nursing home ombudsman[c]	Encouraged	1975, 1977	1975-1978, 1979
Nutrition[a,c]	Encouraged	1974-1979	
	Required		1974-1979
Outreach[b]	Required	1974	
Rehabilitation services	Encouraged	1977, 1978	1976
Senior centers	Encouraged	1976	1978-1979
Transportation/escort[a]	Required	1974-1979	1976-1979
Volunteer services	Encouraged	1975-1979	1974-1978

SOURCE: AoA policy is derived from Federal Policies and Procedures Manual for the Older Americans Act, Titles III and VII (AoA, 1977) and Information Memoranda, Technical Memoranda, Program Instructions, AoA quarterly reports and assessment guidelines. "Encouraged" refers to policy which is officially encouraged within AoA procedure manuals, program instructions, or federal regulations. "Required" refers to policy which is officially required within AoA procedure manuals, program instructions, or federal regulations. The policies considered apply only to the Older Americans Act, Title III, area planning and Social Services program.

a. Mandated national priority service in 1975 Older Americans Act amendments.

b. Originally required in FY 1974; later waived until 1975.

c. Required of state units only.

contrast to those for service emphasis. The service priorities designated by federal law or language represent the most important subset of federal policy directives given to state and agea agencies on aging under the Older Americans Act. AoA directives have instructed these agencies regarding the service areas (for example, information and referral, transportation) that are considered most significant for agency funding, coordination, and advocacy attention. State units on aging have been devoting almost three-fourths of their planned service objectives to federal priorities, including both required and encouraged services. Local-level agencies (AAAs) appear to have been

TABLE 8.2   AoA Required/Encouraged Interorganizational Partners,
1974-1978

Agency/Department	Status	Effective Date For Area Agencies	Effective Date For State Units
ACTION	Required	1974/1979	
	Encouraged	1976	
Agriculture (food stamps)	Required	1975	1975
	Encouraged	1976	
Adult Social Services (Title XX)	Required	1975	1975
Economic Opportunity/Community Service Administration	Encouraged	1976	1976
Education (re: school lunch/ school bus)	Encouraged	1976	1976
Energy	Encouraged	1978	
Employment/volunteer services	Encouraged	1975	
Federal Disaster Assistance Administration	Required	1976	1976
Federal Executive Board (re: I&R)	Required	1975	
Federal Highway Administration	Encouraged	1977	1977
Health Planning and Resource Development	Required	1979	
	Encouraged	1977	1977
Housing and Community Development	Required	1979	
	Encouraged	1977	1976
Law Enforcement Assistance Administration	Encouraged		1976
Legal Services Corporation	Encouraged	1977	1977
Labor (manpower & CETA)	Required	1979	
	Encouraged	1976	1976
Public health	Encouraged	1976	1976
Social Security Administration (re: I&R)	Required	1974	
	Encouraged		1976
Social Security Administration (re: Medicaid)	Required	1979	
	Encouraged	1976	
Transportation	Required	1979	
	Encouraged	1976	1976
Treasury	Encouraged	1977	1977
Vocational rehabilitation	Encouraged	1976	1976

SOURCE: AoA Policy is derived from Federal Policies and Procedures Manual for the Older
Americans Act, Titles III and VII (AoA, 1977) and Information Memoranda,
Technical Memoranda, Program Instructions, AoA quarterly reports and assessment guidelines. "Encouraged" refers to policy which is officially encouraged
within AoA procedure manuals, program instructions, or federal regulations. "Required" refers to policy which is officially required within AoA procedure manuals,
program instructions, or federal regulations.

somewhat less locked into federal priorities, devoting slightly more than half of their objectives to the federally specified priority services.

Regarding the presence and influence of federal priorities, our research reveals that, in general, (1) SUAs and AAAs are highly variable in their responses, (2) these agencies conform with around two-thirds of the directives, (3) conformance is greater when federal priorities are required than when they are only encouraged; and (4) conformance levels have shifted (that is, declined) over time, with federal influence being highest early in the history of these agencies (1974-1975). As SUAs and AAAs developed and adapted to their respective policy environments, their dependence on federal direction from the AoA declined. Federal requirements are still compelling, but not strictly so, while less stringent (or encouraged) policy demands are perceived as opportunities from which direction and discretion may be derived selectively.

Although SUAs and AAAs must devote attention to federal directives, they do not totally circumscribe state and local efforts. Older Americans Act federal priorities have, nevertheless, provided the structure and coherence that permits us to label a set of agencies a "system" or "network." Within this structure, SUAs and AAAs have taken the opportunity to exercise substantial discretion in establishing their priorities. It appears that state units on aging have been more reluctant to set their own directions than have area agencies.

State Roles

One of the challenges of research on federalized programs is to assess the degree of state initiative and innovation within the context of federal direction. SUAs that do not comply with some proportion of federal directives and add their own goals to federally specified ones are exercising discretion and initiative. It is easy to argue that under conditions of less federal direction, these state agencies will assume increased discretion, shaping state policy in ways that are consistent at least partially with the directions they have already taken. By contrast, SUAs that have been highly compliant with federal directives and have done little to supplement them with state-derived goals are not innovators; they do not exercise the discretion available to them.

Based on the findings of our own research in ten large states representing various regions of the nation (Newcomer et al., 1981), there is reason to believe that most state units on aging are relatively high in federal compliance and relatively low in state initiative. A major question, then, is how such SUAs will behave in the absence of the federal directives that historically have closely directed and framed their activities.

In considering the response to this question, another dimension of state policy discretion should be examined — the nature and extent of SUA guidance to AAAs, as evidenced in their policies and procedures. Again, our research is informative. Both the AoA and the SUAs provide policy direction to AAAs, with some federal directives channeled through state offices and others communicated directly to local agencies. The extent to which state agencies have added their own priorities to federal directives for local agency priorities provides another measure of SUA leadership and exercise of discretion. For the 1974-1978 period, five of the ten SUA studied added no state priorities to the federal set of required services that they passed on to the local AAAs; and only one state added as many as three. (The average set of priorities numbered ten.) SUA policy regarding agencies with which the AAAs were expected to coordinate revealed a similar pattern. There was little evidence of effort to extend state influence beyond federal-level AoA requirements.

Policy directives are not the only means by which state units may attempt to influence area agencies. Other important potential mechanisms for state leadership involve monitoring and technical assistance (O'Brien et al., 1976). Here state units appear to have devoted more attention to developing leadership roles. However, our ten-state study reveals that SUAs generally used the technical assistance mechanism to respond to area agency needs, rather than as a vehicle for initiating new directions. In terms of monitoring, all sample SUAs implemented the AoA minimum requirements for tracking area agency expenditures, budget obligations, program matching funds, and client and service characteristics.[4] The major differences among state units occurred with respect to monitoring the characteristics of clients served (that is, targeting). All sample SUAs monitored low-income status and race, but only two disaggregated the population above age 65; none required indicators of population frailty. In short, state units helped to put a federally required basic reporting and accountability system into place, but they did little to develop additional data, some of which could have been of great assistance in setting their own priorities and increasing their planning and monitoring capability.

In summary, the general picture that emerges of state units on aging is that they primarily act as conduits for federal policy and only in limited ways choose to establish priorities extending beyond those defined by federal activities. At least three interpretations of the SUA context may account for this portrait. First, it may be that federal priorities are so numerous and/or comprehensive as to leave no "policy room" for state discretionary activity. An examination of Tables 8.1 and 8.2 suggests that there may be some basis for this explanation. The range of service areas covered, in particular, is quite broad and would require significant state agency resources and energy. Consequently, the exercise of discretion by SUAs regarding service emphasis more often takes the form of selecting from a large federal menu, rather than going beyond federal priorities.

Second, although SUAs seem compliant in terms of their attention to federal directives, compliance may be only formal, while operationally the SUAs ignore federal policy. Other phases of our research examining agency budgets and activities suggest that generally this is not the case.

Third, it could be that state leadership and initiative have no effect because local agencies are not responsive to these priorities. However, we know this is not so for two reasons already discussed. Area agencies are relatively responsive to both federal and state priorities, both in planning and operational terms. They are especially responsive, moreover, when technical assistance by the state accompanies federal or state directives. In all cases, state priorities are important when they are supported by state agency behavior and are consonant with local capacity and need.

Local Roles

SERVICE EMPHASIS

While the federal Administration on Aging and state units on aging have among their primary roles the establishment of priorities for area agencies on aging, the local agencies make the most direct decisions regarding the allocation of Older Americans Act service funds through local grants. In other words, whatever impact federal and state policy may have on local planning and decision making, local decisions in turn shape federal policy, given the federalistic structure of the Older Americans Act. Our recent study of policies and performance under the Older Americans Act gives particular attention to "area planning and social services" under Title III and provides some interesting insights into patterns of AAA choice.

Analysis of local service spending for 1974-1978 was based on annual area plans, audit reports, and agency summary budget data that reflect actual allocations. (For a more detailed description of methods and findings, see Newcomer et al., 1981.) Two broad questions were asked: (1) On what services do AAAs spend their funds? (2) What seems to account for differences among agencies as well as shifts in patterns over time? In response to the initial question, it was found that spending for national priority services represented about half (49 percent) of the allocations made by the average AAA in 1978. The variation among area agencies was significant, as was the relative allocation to given services. Indeed, it was found that federal and state directives were much more likely to affect which services received funding than how much they received.

Patterns of local spending also shifted between 1974 and 1978, the greatest changes occurring in those services defined as national priorities. The largest decreases in funding emphasis occurred in information and referral, outreach, and transportation — areas that received federal emphasis in the early years of agency network development but declined as attention was given to other services. Service categories with the greatest increases were home care and legal services, which received federal emphasis in the middle and later years of our research. Area agencies varied in terms of the extent to which their service priorities were changed over time. In fact, two subsets of AAAs were identified: (1) agencies that selected certain services for funding priority early in their history and made few subsequent changes in them, and (2) agencies that altered either their service emphasis or the share of funds allocated in particular service areas.

In the attempt to understand why some agencies established certain service patterns and continued with these commitments, while others altered them in significant ways over a five-year span, two important structural factors emerge. The first concerns the number of counties included in the planning and service area (PSA) of the AAA. Agencies with multicounty PSAs tended generally to be more stable over time in their service priorities. The most likely explanation for this stability involves the role of local politics as a force in AAA decision making. It can be argued that area agencies that must deal with county politics across several counties generally are confronted with a more complex political environment than are agencies with responsibility for only one or two counties. Early choices regarding services in multicounty PSAs are often made of necessity in light of the need of any new agency to balance the political demands made on it. In other words, new agencies in a turbulent political environment find it necessary to allocate funds in ways that keep varied interests content or indifferent. If these early commitments reflect hard choices made in response to complex political demands, it is likely that these commitments will not change rapidly, inasmuch as they are fairly stable responses to relatively stable conditions. In effect, where local political circumstances are complex, AAA discretion to respond to changing federal and state priorities or to the needs assessments of planners is probably more constrained than it is in less complex political environments.

A second factor with an impact on the extent of changes in local priorities involves the presence of non-Older Americans Act funds in state and local aging budgets. In states where such funds (primarily from Social Security Act Title XX sources) were available to AAAs because of SUA "pooling" efforts, two patterns were evident. First, AAA service priorities across the state tended to be more uniform than in states where only Title III funds were involved. Second, AAAs in these states were less likely to alter appreciably their service priorities over time. The primary explanation for both patterns probably lies in the increased authority that outside resources yield to the SUA and the central role of the SUA in securing administrative control over Title XX social service dollars. The result is greater uniformity and stability in local service patterns.

TARGETING

The Older Americans Act is universal its commitment to services for all persons over sixty years of age. Its framers were committed to avoiding means tests and the welfare stigma yet have also included in the legislation, with its various amendments and related regulations, specific language calling for attention to those subpopulations of the elderly most in need of services: the low-income, minority, and frail elderly. Federal mandates have been suffciently general, however, that the actual decisions regarding population priorities have been left to state and (especially) local agencies. The nature and extent of targeting by AAAs was examined in our research on the Older Americans Act, and several findings are relevant to this discussion.

An analysis of local plans and local service contracts revealed wide variation in area agency targeting by income, race, and physical disability. Agencies varied from 15 to 100 percent in the proportion of service funds targeted to groups other than those identified only by age (that is, 60 years of age and older). State policy was not, with one significant exception, an important factor in explaining these variations. While a majority of sample states encouraged targeting by income, only one state strongly emphasized targeting and required local compliance. That one state emerged as the only state in which all three of the sample AAAs ranked high in targeting for the low-income elderly, suggesting that stringent state policy can be effective in producing local compliance.

In arguing for a strong local role, supporters of federalism base many of their arguments on the importance of enhanced local responsiveness to varying local needs. Indeed, if responsiveness to local conditions occurred, it would be expected that variations in AAA service targeting might be explained, at least in part, by differences in the socioeconomic circumstances of elderly populations across planning areas. Among area agencies grouped as highest and lowest on targeting by income for one study year (FY 1977), we found that the high-targeting agencies have service populations that are lower in median income, higher in percentage of low-income elderly, and higher in percentage of minority elderly. The differences between the two agency groups were substantial — for example, 24.3 percent of the elderly were poor in the high-targeting group versus 19.8 percent for the lower group. These patterns suggest that where there is local discretion, as is the case of targeting under the Older Americans Act, local need is a factor in shaping AAA behavior. The normative issue unanswered by these findings, of course, is whether a low level of income targeting is a desirable agency response in communities where 19.8 percent of the elderly are poor.

Conclusion

Like much of the federal legislation that emerged from the "creative" federalism" and "new federalism" politics of the late 1960s and early 1970s, the Older Americans Act established a three-tiered arrangement in which authority and funding were distributed among federal, state, and local agencies. A number of broad federal program goals, including service provision to those in need, coordination with other service programs, pooling of aging resources, and advocacy for aging interests, were to be implemented through a system of state and local organizations created by federal law.

This chapter has examined some basic questions regarding how the organizational components of this aging "network" have responded to the opportunities and constraints presented by the Older Americans Act. Larger issues regarding the impact of the program on the elderly have not been raised here. (For more on issues of impact and performance, see Newcomer et al., 1981; Westat, Inc., 1978; Estes, 1979). Instead, we have addressed important prior questions about the infrastructure of the system and relationships among agencies within it. Still, to the extent that answers to these questions indicate that this particular federalistic arrangement has achieved some level of stability, coherence, and innovation, it would seem to create those conditions under which enhanced program impact on the elderly is likely.

The portrait suggested by the data examined in our national study of Older Americans Act agencies is one of growing stability and coherence, with innovation apparent in some places. Our initial question concerned the extent to which federal priorities guide state and local aging agencies and the extent to which these agencies go beyond the federal minimum in imposing state and locally determined priorities. It was found that state and local conformance with federal directives is relatively high and that conformance (in contrast to agency initiative) generally is higher at the state level than at the local level. Not surprisingly, conformance is higher when federal policy directives are stringent (that is, when compliance is demanded and sanctions are suggested). We also discovered that conformance levels vary with policy type — for example, it is easier for federal agencies to specify and influence which service areas should receive state and local attention than which organizational partners should be the objects of coordination efforts.

The opposite of conformance to federal directives is the exercise of state and local discretion. In examining the discretionary performance of state and area agencies, we found that state units on aging have been relatively cautious about establishing new (nonfederal) policy directions or new priorities and standards for themselves or their area agencies on aging. While our research provides ample evidence that state agencies can have significant impact on the policy direction of local agencies, what is in short supply is evidence of state efforts to provide such direction. Many state agencies have relied primarily on federal leadership for policy direction and on local agencies for implementation.

The picture at the local level suggests conformance with federal and state directives but variation in exercising the discretion that is available to area agencies on aging in defining other goals and strategies. Variations emerge for a variety of reasons, including differences among the local political environments with which agencies must contend. A state agency that succeeds in securing administrative control of non-Older Americans Act funds such as those in the Social Services Block Grant (formerly Title XX) is likely to have an enhanced influence over local AAAs in the state. Somewhat paradoxically, it appears to be the infusion of outside funds that contributes most to making state and local Older American Act agencies into a coherent "state system."

As was suggested early in this chapter, an analysis of administrative agencies under one set of federal arrangements (more federal direction and structure) does not necessarily reveal a great deal about how those same agencies would behave under a different set of arrangements (less federal direction and structure). Throughout this book we have noted that the policy context within which public agencies are operating has changed significantly in the past several years, due primarily to increasing decentralization of authority and the growing fiscal crisis confronting many governments. For aging agencies, as for others, these changes can be expected to mean growing responsibility for service allocations and greater limits on resources available to allocate. One purpose of the research described briefly in this chapter has been to determine the extent to which the experience of agencies under the Older Americans Act has prepared them for the greater demands certain to accompany new federalism under conditions of fiscal crisis.

Several observations are warranted in considering the implications of recent experience for the near future. First, state units on aging may not be any more willing to exercise authority and discretion with respect to area agencies next year than they were last year. If SUAs have been cautious about establishing priorities and providing direction to AAAs under conditions of relative budgetary prosperity, there is little reason to believe that they will want to be more involved with local decision making at a time when those decisions may involve budgetary cutbacks. It seems axiomatic that where they have a choice, state agencies will avoid sharing responsibility for local decisions that deprive recipients of services. If federal policy constraints are reduced, many SUAs are likely to exercise their choice by passing through to the AAAs whatever increased authority they receive.

The exceptions here are at least as important as the rule. It has been noted that SUAs can have substantial influence on local decisions — that is, that authority, when exercised, can be efficacious. A notable minority of state agencies have provided significant leadership to their area agencies, both in enforcing new commitments (for example, funding and planning for alternatives to institutionalization) and in devising various options for enhancing local agency effectiveness in making and implementing policy decisions. Growing state and local authority will represent new problems for aging agencies in these states, but for these SUAs, assuming that authority will not be one of them.

Since AAAs are the objects of influence attempts from several sources, including the federal AoA, the SUA, local aging interests, other agencies, and local government, predictions based on adjustments in the roles of one or two sources are necessarily tentative. Still, we know that most allocation decisions are local ones and that cuts in available resources will make these decisions more politicized than in the past. It is also apparent that federal (and in some cases state) priorities have provided area agencies with a policy shield to use in dealing with competing local demands. AAAs have not completely despaired in saying, "AoA made us do it," since federal constraints permit local agencies to sidestep difficult political choices (for a related argument, see Hudson, 1982). Even in states where the SUA has not played a strong role, federal directives have continued to ease the burden of local choice for many AAAs. The reduction of the federal role in these same states, combined with the anticipated reluctance of many SUAs to take up the policy reins, will leave AAAs to face local cutback politics alone. While many AAAs may be prepared to deal with such changes, local agencies in states where SUAs eschew a strong policy role are likely to devote more energy to managing political bargaining and less to program management and implementation.

As the pool of resources available to local agencies for aging services shrinks, decisions regarding the targeting of these resources are likely to become more difficult. Pressures to target resources are certain to grow, even as increases occur in the numbers of those elderly with serious needs for service, and thus in the number falling outside any feasible current target. We saw that targeting of resources varies considerably across local planning areas and that state policy has generally permitted such variation. To the extent that this variability involves responsiveness to divergent local conditions, it is generally valued in our political system. It was observed, for example, that where poverty levels are higher, more targeting is likely to occur. But it was also noted that substantial numbers of poor persons reside in areas where poverty levels are relatively low (but not absolutely so) and where targeting effort is low. To the extent that this version of local responsiveness reduces the probability that low-income elderly in these areas will receive aging services, the results are inequitable. Equity issues pervade Older Americans Act programs, and rather than addressing them, new federalism reforms simply shift the responsibility to other levels of government.

Viewed from another perspective, state and area agencies on aging were designed to advocate as well as to plan, coordinate, and channel service dollars to the community delivery system for the elderly. Although severely limited by recent administration policies, the advocacy role of these agencies has been shown to be important in this era of fiscal austerity. Our research on the activities of state and area agencies during the first wave of cutbacks in late 1981 (Swan et al., 1982) shows that these agencies, particularly AAAs, were extremely likely to engage in efforts to stem the effects of cutbacks, but only where these were clearly and directly targeted to the aged — ignoring across-the-board cutbacks where the aged were as likely to be affected. Moreover, less severe cutbacks appeared to follow in those urban localities where SUAs and AAAs were judged to be influential in aging. Further, the elderly were reported as more vulnerable in states and localities where the SUAs and other aging interest groups are perceived as weaker. Thus, the influence and advocacy of state and area agencies on aging appears to be a very important function, if limiting the vulnerability of the elderly is a goal of the Older Americans Act.

Notes

1. Additional reviews of the act and its origins can be found in U.S. Senate (1982); Coombs et al. (1982); Gelfand and Olsen (1980), Estes (1979); and Fritz (1979).

2. A number of other studies have been conducted evaluating various aspects of SUA and AAA operations and performance. Among the more important of these are

those by Applied Management Services, 1975; Binstock, 1975; Greenblatt et al., 1978; Howenstein et al., 1975; Marmor and Kutza, 1975; Steinberg and Childs, 1976; U.S. General Accounting Office, 1977a, 1977b, 1981a; U.S. House, 1978; and Westat, Inc., 1978.

3. This research was conducted during 1976 and 1981. It involved extensive document analyses, site visits to all ten AoA regional offices, and in-depth case studies of ten SUAs and twenty-four AAAs selected from within the states (California, Florida, Massachusetts, Missouri, Nebraska, Pennsylvania, Texas, Vermont, Washington, and Wisconsin). The primary source used for compiling federal regulations was the Federal Policies and Procedures Manual for the Older Americans Act, Titles III and VII (U.S. AoA, 1977). This was augmented by reviews of all AoA information memoranda and program instructions during the study period.

4. The U.S. General Accounting Office (1981b) has looked much more closely at AAA contract monitoring procedures and recommended further guidance by state units.

References

Applied Management Sciences. *A Study of State Agencies on Aging.* Silver Spring, MD: Applied Management Sciences, 1975.

Binstock, R. H. *The Roles and Functions of State Planning Systems: Preliminary Report on a Nationwide Survey of State Units on Aging.* Washington, DC: U.S. Administration on Aging, 1975.

Coombs, S., T. Lambert, and D. Quirk, eds. *An Orientation to the Older Americans Act.* Washington, DC: National Association of State Units, 1982.

Estes, C. L. "Goal Displacement in Community Planning for the Elderly: Implications for National Policy." In *Community Planning for an Aging Society.* Ed. P. Lawton, R. Newcomer, and T. Byerts. Stroudsberg, PA: Hutchinson Ross, 1976.

————. *The Aging Enterprise.* San Francisco: Jossey-Bass, 1979.

Fritz, D. "The Administration on Aging as an Advocate: Progress, Problems and Prospects." *Gerontologist,* 19, No. 2 (1979), 141-150.

Gelfand, D. E., and J. K. Olsen. *The Aging Network: Programs and Services.* New York: Springer, 1980.

Greenblatt, B., et al. *Attitudes of Aging, Intergovernmental Relations and Grants Management in the Title III Program: Evidence and Policy Implications.* Buffalo, NY: School of Social Policy and Community Services, State University of New York at Buffalo, 1978.

Howenstine, R. A., J. Miller, and R. C. Tucker. *Research on Social Systems and Interagency Relations: A Study of the Area Agencies on Aging.* New Haven: Gerontology Study Unit, Training and Consultation Division, Connecticut Mental Health Center, School of Medicine, Yale University, 1975.

Hudson, R. B. "A Block Grant to the States for Long-Term Care." *Journal of Health Politics, Policy and Law,* 6, No. 1 (Spring 1981), 9-28.

Marmor, T. R., and E. A. Kutza. *Analysis of Federal Regulations Related to Aging: Administration on Aging Legislative Barriers to Coordination Under Title III.* Report submitted to U.S. DHEW under Grant No. DHEW (SRS) 90-A-364-01. Chicago: School of Social Service Administration, University of Chicago, 1975.

Morris, R., and R. H. Binstock. *Feasible Planning for Social Change.* New York: Columbia University Press, 1966.

Newcomer, R. J., C. L. Estes, A. E. Benjamin, J. Swan, and V. Peguillan. *Funding Practices, Politics, and Performance of State and Area Agencies: Final Report.* Vols. 1 and II. Prepared for the U.S. Administration on Aging under Grant No. 90-A-979. San Francisco: Aging Health Policy Center, University of California, 1981.

O'Brien, J. E., T. Wetle, and D. G. Montgomery. *Closing the Gaps: Strategies for Technical Assistance; State Agencies Strengthening the Capacities of Areas Agencies on Aging to Help Service Providers Reach Older Americans.* Portland, OR: Portland State University, 1976.

Steinberg, R. M., and N. M. Childs. *A Study of Funding Regulations, Program Agreements and Monitoring Procedures Affecting the Implementation of Title III of the Older Americans Act.* Los Angeles: Social Policy Laboratory, Andrus Gerontology Center, University of Southern California, 1976.

Swan, J. H., C. L. Estes, J. B. Wood, M. Kreger, and J. Garfield. *Fiscal Crisis: Impact on Aging Services.* Final Report. Prepared for the U.S. Administration on Aging under Grant No. 90AR0016. San Francisco: Aging Health Policy Center, University of California, 1982.

U.S. Administration on Aging (AoA). *Federal Policies and Procedures Manual for the Older Americans Act, Titles III and VII.* Washington, DC: U.S. Department of Health, Education and Welfare, 1977.

U.S. Code of Federal Regulations, 45: 903.

U.S. General Accounting Office (GAO). *Local Area Agencies Help the Aging but Problems Need Correcting: Report of the Comptroller General of the United States to Administration on Aging, U.S. Department of Health, Education, and Welfare, August 2, 1977.* Washington, DC: GAO, 1977a.

————. *Report of the General Accounting Office's Survey of Area Agencies on Aging.* Washington, DC: GAO, 1977b.

————. *Scope, Objectives, and Methodologies Used for GAO's Ongoing Review of Area Agencies on Aging: Statement of Morton E. Henig.* Washington, DC: GAO, 1981a.

————. *More Specific Guidance and Closer Monitoring Needed to Get More from Funds Spent on Social Services for the Elderly: Report by the Comptroller General of the United States.* Washington, DC: GAO, 1981b.

U.S. House, Committee on Education and Labor, Subcommittee on Select Education. Hearings: *Reauthorization of the Older Americans Act.* Washington, DC: U.S. Government Printing Office, 1978.

U.S. Public Law 89-73. Older American Act of 1965 (as Amended by U.S. PL 90-42, 1967; 91-69, 1969; 92-258, 1972; 93-29, 1973; 93-351, 1974; 94-135, 1975; 96-65, 1977; 95-478, 1978; 97-115, 1981). Washington, DC: U.S. Government Printing Office.

U.S. Public Law 97-35. Omnibus Budget Reconciliation Act of 1981. Washington, DC: U.S. Government Printing Office, 1981.

U.S. Senate, Special Committee on Aging. *Developments in Aging: 1981.* Report 97-314. Washington, DC: U.S. Government Printing Office, 1982.

Westat, Inc. *Evaluation of the Area Planning and Social Services Program (July 1974-June 1976),* Vol. 1: *Focus on Changes in Services to Older Persons: The Area Agency Role;* Vol. 2: *Program Description.* Rockville, MD: Westat, 1978.

CHAPTER 9

HEALTH PLANNING AND LONG TERM CARE

A. E. Benjamin
David A. Lindeman

That the policy attention of aging advocates increasingly has been directed to the health care needs of the elderly in recent years is no surprise. Both awareness of the health problems faced by the elderly and recognition of the size and cost of public programs related to at least some of these needs have grown steadily in the last decade. It also is no surprise that among the various programmatic priorities embraced by aging advocates, health planning has been of relatively little significance. The American system of health planning as it has evolved since 1966 has remained modest in funding, narrow in scope, and limited in its concern with specific population groups. In addition to continuing problems in demonstrating their impact on the health care system, health planning agencies have suffered from the lack of constituencies with a defined interest in their continued operation. While other health programs with substantial funding levels to underwrite the provision of services (such as Medicare) have powerful constituency support from hospitals, physicians, and elderly interest groups, similar support for health planning has not emerged.

This chapter describes the health planning system established by major federal legislation in 1966 and 1974 and summarizes issues attending its development. We describe why and how health planning

Authors' Note: The authors wish to acknowledge the many contributions of the faculty and staff of the Institute for Health Policy Studies, University of California, San Francisco. Special appreciation is due to Dr. Peter Budetti, co-principal investigator of the project with Dr. Benjamin, and to Paul Newacheck and Peggy McManus, whose energy and commitment were essential to designing and implementing the research. The data in this chapter are derived from research supported by the U.S. Administration on Aging Grant No. 90-AR-0028.

activities are important to the elderly and their advocates. Data from a national study of health planning and the health care needs of the elderly are utilized to illustrate the range of these activities. The relationships between health planning and aging agencies are described, and the extent to which aging interests have a stake in the health planning reforms now being considered is discussed.

The Context of Health Planning

Long term care has emerged as one of the foremost policy problems currently facing the U.S. human services system. The uncertain development of health planning is important to understanding the health policy context in which recent long term care issues have emerged. Certainly in this country it is not easily argued that a strong planning system would have altered significantly the character of this policy context, particularly since public planning has rarely been prominent or effective in American government (Benveniste, 1977). It is relatively easy, however, to demonstrate that various decisions about the scope and intent of health planning have been important in limiting the policy options now available to those interested in long term care reform.

While the American health care system has been shaped by a variety of forces over a period of many years, its fundamental character has been defined largely by decisions in four areas: facilities, personnel,[1] financing, and the policy process.[2] Decisions about the nature and scope of health care facilities establish the institutional basis for the supply of services. Choices regarding the character and numbers of personnel help determine which professions will provide their brand of health care. The nature and scope of the financing system establishes incentives for certain categories of providers to provide specified services to selected users. Finally, in its broadest sense, the policy process establishes the framework for making decisions regarding facilities, personnel, and reimbursement.

The relationship of health planning to decisions taken in these four areas of health policy has evolved slowly and unevenly since World War II. While in some areas (such as facilities) an apparatus for state and local planning has existed for several decades, in other areas (such as personnel) no such efforts have been made, and the general pattern has been one of expansion of the resources devoted to health care in a fashion shaped primarily by provider groups. The result has been a health care system characterized by acute care provided in institutional settings at high costs. The many implications of this pattern for long-term care have been elaborated in earlier chapters of this book.

FACILITIES

The Hospital Survey and Construction Act of 1946 (U.S. PL 79-725), known as Hill-Burton, provided funds for hospital construction in underserved areas and established a planning process for allocation of these funds. The $4.4 billion provided under the act between 1947 and 1975 funded the construction of close to one-half million inpatient hospital beds (National Academy of Sciences, 1980). Planning was organized by the states and essentially involved the application of simple formulas based on population levels and optimum occupancy rates. Other factors, such as the size and needs of the elderly population, were rarely considered within this context. Until 1964, when amendments to the act authorized local planning boards to complement state planning activities, little attention was given to intrastate variations in need or demand. When local planning was introduced, moreover, the emphasis at all levels of government continued to be on the development and expansion of facilities rather than on planning for health care. The expansion of medical care facilities, especially hospitals, fueled by Hill-Burton has generated an excess of acute care beds and represents one important component of the dramatic rise in the costs of medical care (U.S. Congressional Budget Office [CBO], 1982).

PERSONNEL

The passage of the Health Professions Educational Assistance Act of 1963 (U.S. PL 88-129) marked the beginning of a federal role in providing direct support for the education of health professionals. The act was a response to a series of "manpower" reports that argued that improvement in the society's health was dependent on rapid increases in the supply of physicians. This repeated call for expansion was rationalized largely in terms of population growth; that is, the number of physicians was not keeping pace with the growth in population (Bloom and Peterson, 1979). The Comprehensive Health Manpower Training Act of 1971 (U.S. PL 92-157) extended federal financing to the regular operational support of schools for the health professions. While both the 1963 and 1974 legislation provided the basis for increases in the supply of nurses, dentists, technicians, and others, the most dramatic impact of the acts has been on the number of physicians, which increased by 55 percent between 1965 and 1980.

Although state government continues to play a substantial role in the financing of medical education, at neither the state nor the federal level is the supply of health personnel linked to health planning. Indeed, it can be argued that with respect to the numerous federal and foundation "manpower" reports that presented information on which the calls for expansion were based, little of the data utilized were obtained in any well-designed or systematic manner (Bloom and Peterson, 1979). The resulting growth in physician supply has been a major factor in the growth of the costs of medical care.

FINANCING

If the expansion of medical facilities and personnel has only loosely been tied to mechanisms for planning, the dramatic shift in patterns of public financing has proceeded until recently with little or no attention to planned allocations. As with facilities and personnel, the federal government was prodded into playing a more substantial role in underwriting the provision of services. Unlike the circumstances surrounding policy initiation in other areas, major provider groups did not provide the early impetus for an expanded federal role in financing medical care. Whatever the interest group scenario, it appears that decisions regarding public financing were made separately from those about facilities and personnel. Planning in its most general sense was confined to marshaling data that revealed differences among income, ethnic, and age groups in access to health care and variations among states in participation in programs for financing health services. Rather than planning determining desired patterns of health expenditures, the system of financing greatly limited the scope of planning.

The landmark Social Security Act of 1935 (U.S. PL 74-241) established public assistance categories for low-income persons, including the aged, and provided for federal matching of payments for medical care expenses made directly to welfare recipients. It excluded direct payment to providers. The 1950 amendments to the act removed this restriction, permitting federal matching to states for payment of medical services directly to physicians, hospitals, and clinics.

From the 1930s until the middle 1960s, regular and unsuccessful attempts were made to persuade Congress to approve some form of national health insurance. The passage of the Kerr-Mills Act of 1960 (U.S. PL 86-778) represented a successful effort to deflect one such reform measure (Holahan, 1975). While essentially an expansion of the medical vendor-payment program established by the 1950 amendments, under Old Age Assistance (OAA), Kerr-Mills was important for at least three reasons: It allowed states to define as "medically indigent" those not poor enough to receive OAA; it placed no ceiling on federal matching for "medical assistance for the aged" (as the program was known); and it was widely perceived to be a failure (Vladeck, 1980). While most states adopted programs, very few established comprehensive ones. At least in part, the passage of Medicare (Title XVIII) and Medicaid (Title XIX) in the Social Security Amendments of 1965 (U.S. PL 89-97) resulted from the failure of Kerr-Mills to provide incentives sufficient to move states to provide medical care for the elderly.

The legislative process surrounding passage of Medicare and Medicaid has been described elsewhere (Marmor, 1973; Vladeck, 1980). These programs established separate but related systems for financing medical care. One (Medicare) was the result of three decades of political drama, yet the most significant decisions about its character were left to the administering agency (Feder, 1977). The other (Medicaid) was viewed as a modest extension of the Kerr-Mills principles and was the object of almost no congressional debate. While Medicare was a medical insurance program for the elderly and Medicaid was a means-tested program for the poor, they shared at least two characteristics that have contributed to the dramatic rise in medical care costs in the last fifteen years.

First, both programs were open-ended reimbursement schemes designed to pay bills in response to services provided. Decisions about how many of which services were left to those health professionals providing care. Second, reimbursement was to be retrospective and on the basis of cost. Whatever a provider (minimally) could demonstrate to have spent was to be reimbursable; not surprisingly, the more services that were provided, the more money a provider received (Vladeck, 1981). This Medicare-defined system of reimbursement for hospitals and physicians was extended to Medicaid, and states joined the federal government in unlimited (open-ended) spending for medical care.

The scope of Medicaid also was significant because it provided the basis for the rapid expansion of the nursing home industry and in a fashion even more dramatic than Hill-Burton had been for hospitals. The public provision of long term care services, before Medicaid a phenomenon barely known outside social services circles in a few states, now became defined as public reimbursement for nursing home care. That public payments were structured to be open-ended and only marginally controlled made meaningful health planning of any sort extremely problematic.

THE POLICY PROCESS

As suggested above, federal policy initiatives in health in recent decades have been significant in terms of their impact on health care delivery and the constraints they have placed on health planning. Decisions regarding hospital construction have been important in generating an excessive number of acute care, institutional beds. Decisions regarding the supply of personnel have contributed directly to what is now widely viewed as a physician surplus (U.S. Health Resources Administration [HRA], 1981). Both of these sets of policy choices, plus federal decisions to finance medical care for the elderly and poor in an open-ended, cost-based manner, have created a fiscal crisis in health care. The implications of this changing context of health care delivery for health planning and long term care will be apparent shortly.

Policymaking in health is fragmented across program areas and agencies as well as across levels of government. The process of policy reform is essentially incremental, government proceeding in small, measured steps with current policy as its base (Banta, 1981). The process also is highly vulnerable to organized, well-financed interest groups (often provider groups) that are more adept at containing reform than at initiating it. Since it is fundamentally and necessarily political, the policy process is more successful in meeting the political needs of its participants — that is, accommodating those competing interests that succeed in entering the fray — than in responding to the substantive health care needs of its constituents (Alford, 1975).

Political sentiment has long existed for addressing the limits of the policy process by introducing a system of health planning. As described earlier, the Hill-Burton program set up a state (and later a local) planning process that was supposed to rationalize the allocation of funds, but very little data or planning activity was involved. The

Comprehensive Planning Act of 1966 (U.S. PL 89-749) strengthened voluntary local planning with formula grants to states and localities and a broader planning mandate. Planning councils were directed to plan for health personnel as well as health facilities, and to assess health needs and define appropriate services and facilities. Comprehensive health planning agencies had no authority, however, to translate their recommendations into actual changes. They received limited funding, moreover, and little federal direction regarding program priorities. Further federal legislative action in 1974 established what many hoped would be a broadened and strengthened program of state and local planning for health (U.S. CBO, 1982).

The Current Structure of Planning

The current federal health planning program was authorized by the National Health Planning and Resources Development Act of 1974 (U.S. PL 93-641). Under the act, the Department of Health and Human Services provides funding for state and local planning agencies to assess area health needs, set priorities, target health care resources to populations and localities most in need, and control health costs. These agencies are also authorized to conduct certificate of need (CON) review of proposed health facility construction projects and purchases of major medical equipment. State and local health planning agencies address a variety of problems associated with the allocation of health services — excess capacity, unnecessary duplication of services, rising health care costs, and maldistributed health services. The authorizing act requires that health care consumers as well as providers and insurers be participants in this process. Access to care, costs, and quality are all to be considered by state and local agencies in developing health plans and regulations.

Funding for health planning grew from $91 million in fiscal year (FY) 1976 to $158 million in 1980, but severe reductions were imposed by the new administration in 1981. Appropriations were cut to $116 million in FY 1981 and then further reduced to $58 million in FY 1982 (a net loss over the two-year period of 63 percent). Authorization for the program expires at the end of FY 1983, and the administration has proposed its termination despite a pending reauthorization bill in the House of Representatives.

The act (U.S. PL 93-641) and amendments added in 1979 established a lengthy set of national health priorities, encompassing a broad range of health issues. It was the intent of Congress that health planning agencies promote cost-containment efforts, provide care to the underserved, encourage institutions to coordinate service provision, develop alternative systems of care, promote quality care, encourage programs of preventive care and health education, and assure the availability and access to appropriate mental health services.

Since 1974 a primary responsibility of local health system agencies (HSAs) has been to gather and analyze data regarding health status, health needs, available resources, and utilization of health services. Using this information, HSAs are responsible for designing comprehensive health plans that outline a strategy to improve the cost-effectiveness, quality, and distribution of health care. The plans, which cover a five-year period and are updated every three years, must meet the requirements of the 1974 act to address a broad range of national health priorities and to provide detailed goals and objectives for a range of health services. In addition, an annual plan detailing strategies for implementation of the health plans has been required. Besides preparing health plans and making recommendations to state planning agencies for CON applications, the local health planning bodies engage in a variety of additional activities, including development of programs to educate the public about health care costs and proper use of health services, recruitment of health professionals in underserved areas, assistance in developing alternative health care delivery mechanisms (such as health maintenance organizations, or HMOs), and improvement of service delivery by publishing reports on the availability and prices of local health care services (U.S. CBO, 1982).

Unlike HSAs, which usually are independent organizations, state health planning and development agencies (SHPDAs) are state government agencies, designated by the governors to develop and implement state health plans based on the local HSA plans and to make final CON review decisions after considering recommendations of the HSAs. In most states, the governor has chosen the state health department to fulfill this role. These agencies also prepare an annual inventory of state medical facilities and administer federal loans for health facilities development under the former Hill-Burton program. The other statewide planning agency required by the 1974 act is the statewide health coordinating council (SHCC), with members appointed by the governor. These councils both review HSA health plans and have final approval of state health plans proposed by the

SHPDA. The councils also review HSA budgets and state applications for federal health grant money.

Federal law has established broad policies and called for creation of the health planning network but has relied on states to establish and enforce regulatory laws and direct planning efforts. Consequently, there is great discretion within state and local health planning agencies with regard to the content and emphasis of their efforts. Very little federal direction has been given to health planning agencies concerning the health care needs of the elderly. The national guidelines for health planning, the national priorities of the planning law, and the various sources of policy guidance from the federal Bureau of Health Planning (BHP) have not dealt at length with the needs of the elderly.

Health Planning and Long Term Care

Much of the debate about the effectiveness of health planning agencies has concerned their impact on the cost of hospital care (Sloan, 1981; Policy Analysis, Inc., 1980; U.S. CBO, 1982). This emphasis is appropriate since hospitals are the primary source of cost inflation in medical care. As a consequence of the preoccupation of planning agencies with issues of hospital cost containment, relatively little attention has been devoted to a host of other issues related to the ends and means of health planning. These concern the appropriate relationships between cost containment and other goals defined for health planning by Congress, such as improving access to and quality of care; connections, and divisions of authority, between planning and regulatory bodies at the state level; definition and assessment of those technologies generally referred to as "planning" (Benjamin and Downs, 1982); and the relationship of health planning to the elderly and long term care. The latter relationship is the subject of the remainder of this chapter. Health planning is relevant to long term care in at least two ways, one that is obvious and one that is not so obvious.

CERTIFICATE OF NEED (CON) REVIEW

Certificate of need (CON) review of proposed facility construction and major equipment purchases has been the principal cost-containment mechanism available to health planning agencies. CON review has been applied not only to hospitals but also to the institutional sector in long term care (nursing homes). To the extent that CON review has succeeded in controlling the expansion of nursing homes, it is important in the debate regarding public spending for institutional versus noninstitutional services for long-term care. In many states the relationship between these two sets of services is framed as a tradeoff, with the level of resources available for noninstitutional care greatly constrained by the level of institutional care (hospitals and nursing homes). In this context many state officials argue that no serious commitment to noninstitutional alternatives can occur until the growth of institutional spending is slowed.

It is difficult to assess the precise role of health planning in constraining spending for nursing home facilities in various states. Part of the difficulty lies in the more general problem of separating the impact of health planning from the impact of numerous other political and economic factors that may affect nursing home construction, such as the rise in interest rates for construction loans (Benjamin and Downs, 1982). While research on the effects of CON review on nursing home supply is relatively scarce, available evidence suggests that a number of states have used this tool to limit the rate of growth in the supply of nursing home beds.

Feder and Scanlon (1980) have raised some important questions regarding consequences for the elderly of state use of CON review. They argue that the market for nursing home care differs from that for hospital care, and that CON review may be more appropriate for the second than for the first. They point to research indicating that the number of persons who demand nursing home care is larger than the number who receive it and argue that where nursing home beds are not sufficient to meet demand, "the people most in need of the service have the greatest difficulty finding it" (Feder and Scanlon, 1980, p. 58). Only when CON review is linked to other policy mechanisms, particularly reimbursement reforms, can it be expected to benefit recipients as much as it currently benefits nursing home operators.

CON review for nursing homes has been adopted in forty-eight states because (1) adoption has been linked to federal incentives, (2) it provides state officials with some form of budgetary control, and (3) it is widely viewed by the nursing home industry as a means to control competition. Discussions with state officials suggest that aging interests are of two minds regarding the future of CON review. First (as suggested earlier), some argue that without strict limitations on the growth of the nursing home industry, there is little prospect of increased state investment in noninstitutional care for the elderly. Where this argument has been most persuasive, several states have effectively overridden the CON process by placing a moratorium on nursing home expansion. Others argue, as do Feder and Scanlon (1980), that while controlling nursing home bed supply may have some longer-run rewards, it certainly has few in the short run. Taken alone, limiting supply may keep those poorest and most in need of care out of nursing homes. While keeping people out of nursing homes probably is a good thing (Vladeck, 1979), it ceases to be so if other care is not available.

Further investigation is needed into the consequences of limitations on nursing home bed supply (including CON), as is far more systematic analysis and debate on these issues among aging interests. Without both, federal and state policy in a period of austerity is likely to move in directions that have important implications for the elderly, while aging interests remain uneasy spectators.

OTHER LONG TERM CARE ACTIVITIES

A second area of health planning activity relevant to the elderly and to long term care, and one that has received much less attention from supporters and critics alike, involves a range of activities conducted by planning agencies outside those directed at the review of institutional facilities. Health planning agencies necessarily have devoted a great deal of attention to CON review and to developing health plans as required under federal law. But within otherwise broad federal mandates, these agencies have had considerable autonomy with regard to the content and emphasis of their efforts. In our recent research (Benjamin et al., 1982), we have examined the extent to which these planning agencies have been involved in activities related to the health care needs of the elderly, particularly in long-term care.

Central to the study was a mail survey of all state health planning and development agencies (SHPDAs) and regional health system agencies (HSAs) in the country. As a prologue to specific questions about agency activities, directors were asked to rate long term care (LTC) as a priority or goal in relation to other priorities of their agencies.[3] In response, a majority of both state and local planning agencies accorded LTC a relatively high priority, as indicated in Table 9.1. By contrast, about four of ten agencies rated LTC as something other than a high priority, including a small percentage (8-9 percent) who reported it as low among their priorities. In general terms and by

TABLE 9.1   Relative Priority Given to LTC in the Past Year (percentages)
            by State (SHPDA) and Local (HSA) Health Planning
            Agencies[a]

LTC Priority	SHPDAs	HSAs
Relatively high	60.9	53.6
Moderate	30.4	38.0
Relatively low	8.7	8.4
	(N=46)	(N=166)

SOURCE: Aging Health Policy Center. "Mail Survey Questionnaire" (HSA, Q. 35; SHPDA, Q. 32).

a. Response rates were exceptional: 47 of 51 SHPDAs responded (92 percent), while 167 of 209 HSAs returned the questionnaire (80 percent).

their own account, many (but not all) health planning agencies acknowledge the importance of LTC as part of their mission.

With respect to specific activities related to long term care, a substantial majority of SHPDAs and HSAs reported conducting needs assessments or establishing task forces or committees related to LTC issues (see Table 9.2). Given the relative paucity of federal efforts either to plan for LTC or to mobilize groups and agencies with an interest in these issues, such state and local efforts are important initial steps toward systematically addressing long term care (Spivack and Brody, 1981). Health planning efforts also have extended to attempts to influence state and local legislation in LTC. A substantial number of those agencies reported working with governors, legislatures, and local governments regarding LTC issues.

Interestingly, these various LTC-related activities have not yielded political rewards for health planning agencies. The reasons are numerous. Most of these activities are only vaguely tied to the primary goals established for health planning by federal legislation, and more important, they are not closely related to the cost-containment objectives that dominate the program. The difficulties involved in evaluating the cost-effectiveness of CON review have been enormous, but it has proven even more difficult to assess the impact on costs of other health planning activities, especially given their vague and episodic nature. Political benefits also have been limited, because LTC-related activities have not been part of any concerted health planning agency strategy to carve out for themselves an LTC role or to generate constituency support among the elderly.

TABLE 9.2   Health Planning Agency Involvement in Various LTC
             Activities in the Last Two Years (percentages)

LTC Activities	SHPDAs	HSAs
LTC special needs assessment	65.2	73.7
LTC committees and task forces	69.6	71.9
LTC grant applications	17.4	18.0
Work with legislature on LTC	52.2	36.5
Work with governors on LTC	34.8	16.8
Work with local government on LTC	19.6	43.1
Other LTC activities	34.8	23.4
	(N=46)	(N=166)

SOURCE: Aging Health Policy Center. "Mail Survey Questionnaire" (HSA, Q. 33; SHPDA, Q. 30).

That many health planning agencies have been involved in important work related to LTC has not been apparent to aging interests, with the result that most have stayed at the legislative sidelines on the federal and state levels during the recent (and generally successful) efforts to dismantle the program.

COLLABORATION AND LONG TERM CARE

While Tables 9.1 and 9.2 show that many health planning agencies view long-term care as a high priority, there is also considerable variation across agencies in relative commitment to this policy area. In order to understand why some agencies rate LTC highly and others do not, we looked at a number of characteristics of the agency and its environment that might be important (Butler et al., 1977). We found that several factors were associated with higher agency commitments to LTC. Large agencies, agencies with authority centralized in the director, and agencies with strong support from consumer groups, for example, were more likely to give LTC a high priority than were smaller agencies, less centralized agencies, and those with less consumer support. Interestingly, the analysis also revealed an association between LTC priority and the nature and extent to the relationships between health planning agencies and their counterpart Older Americans Act (OAA) agencies.

Before describing these relationships in more detail, it is worth considering at least three reasons why these interagency ties would be expected to be relatively weak and unimportant. First, collaboration

TABLE 9.3   Nature of Relationship with the Counterpart Aging Agency
             Reported by the Health Planning Agency (percentages)

Nature of Relationship	SHPDAs	HSAs
Little contact	39.5	26.8
Regular contact, little collaboration	32.6	47.1
Regular contact, substantial collaboration	27.9 (N=43)[a]	26.1 (N=153)[a]

SOURCE: Aging Health Policy Center. "Mail Survey Questionnaire" (HSA, Q. 39; SHPDA, Q. 36).

a. A total of 11 HSAs and 2 SHPDAs specified "other" in describing their aging relationships.

among organizations can be costly in terms of the resources required to make the process fruitful (Thompson, 1967; Haas and Drabeck, 1973). Interagency relationships often develop because the exigencies of politics or regulations require the appearance of cooperation, rather than because mutual substantive interests draw organizations together. Second, while both health planning and OAA agencies (state and area agencies on aging) share an interest in planning and a concern with access and quality of care, they are more different than they are alike. They have differing mandates, are traditionally involved with different sets of services (health versus social), are responsible for different target populations (the entire population versus the elderly), and at the local level often have disparate geographic service areas. Third, agencies on aging generally have not distinguished themselves as activists in LTC (Newcomer et al., 1981) and thus would not be expected to be a major factor influencing the LTC priorities of other agencies. Despite the weight of these three arguments, the evidence suggests that while collaboration has not been widespread, it has been more fruitful than expected.

In our national survey, health planning agencies were asked to characterize their relationships with counterpart state and area agencies on aging in terms of the extent of their contact and the substance of their collaboration (see Table 9.3). While a majority of the relationships reflect little contact and/or little collaboration, about one-fourth of the agencies (both state and local) have shown regular contact and substantial collaboration. Joint activities reported include LTC plan development, LTC task forces and committees, LTC needs assess-

TABLE 9.4   SHPDA Priority Regarding LTC by SHPDA Assessment of
             Nature of SUA Relationship (percentages)

Nature of Relationship with SUA	LTC Priority by SHPDA		
	Low	Moderate	High
Little	5.5	55.5	38.9 (N=18)
Moderate	21.4	21.4	57.1 (N=14)
Substantial	0.0	7.7	92.3 (N=13)
			(N=45)

SOURCE: Aging Health Policy Center. "Mail Survey Questionnaire" (SHPDA, Q. 36, 32).

ments, LTC demonstration projects, and community education in LTC.

Collaborative activities may be important in themselves, but more important, they may have implications for the mission and priorities of the participating organizations. In particular, we examined the extent to which levels of interagency collaboration were associated with the priority that health planning agencies accorded LTC. Table 9.4 presents one example of the patterns that emerged; as relationships between state health planning and development agencies (SHPDAs) and state units on aging (SUAs) become more substantial, the SHPDA commitment to LTC becomes more substantial. Similar patterns emerge for local agencies, although not quite as emphatically.

For anyone with a commitment to Older Americans Act programs, including the authors of this book, it is tempting to argue that involvement with aging agencies "causes" increased health planning attention to LTC. To do this convincingly requires elimination of alternative, competing explanations for the relationships observed in the data, and this is not entirely possible. It is conceivable, for example, that health planning agencies already interested in LTC seek out collaboration with aging agencies or are among those most receptive to initiatives coming from OAA agencies. If this is so, then attention levels "cause" collaboration and not the reverse.

However the data are interpreted, our findings regarding the connections between joint activity and agency attention to LTC are relatively solid and suggestive. If attention to LTC is the source from which collaboration arises, then in many settings state and area agencies are considered sufficiently important actors in LTC for joint action with them to be valued by health planning agencies. If aging agency cooperative initiatives are the catalyst, then these seem to increase the probabilities that health planning agencies will give higher levels of attention to LTC issues.

Finally, it should be noted that both sets of agencies function within a larger political environment containing dozens of agencies, organizations, and groups. Considering the amount of organizational "noise" produced by the inevitably complex environment of health planning agencies, the presence of a relatively clear association between one partner (such as aging agencies) and one set of priorities (such as LTC) is not to be treated lightly. While substantial collaboration between aging and health agencies is not very widespread, where it occurs it seems to have some important consequences for long term care.

Conclusion

Any analysis of health planning in the 1980s is likely to have an unhappy ending. What began as a grand experiment in state and local planning has fallen victim to excessive expectations, inadequate authority, the intractability of medical care costs, and finally to a substantial decline in federal funding. Under provisions (known as Section 1536) of the health planning law, states are now able to absorb local planning functions into the state agency and thus to eliminate local agencies; five states had done this by late 1982, and at least six more had applied for federal approval. Because of Section 1536 designations, severe funding cuts, and loss of other support, 44 of the 204 HSAs had ceased operation by early 1983.

The decline of health planning is in large part the result of a persistent federal unwillingness to take planning seriously and to provide the mandates and resources necessary to be effective (Brown, 1982). That the withdrawal of federal support comes at a time when many health planning agencies have begun to give attention to long term care and to the elderly seems especially unfortunate. Very little planning for LTC has been done at the federal level, and much of what little has occurred at the state and local levels has involved health planning agencies and (in some cases) state and area agencies on aging.

As new federalism policies reduce the incentives for state and local planning and the resources to support it, the future of planning for LTC seems especially problematic. Health planning agencies that have survived the drastic reduction in federal support have been forced to reduce their levels of effort, and they have begun to eliminate (among others) those activities adopted most recently, like LTC planning (Lindeman and Benjamin, 1982).

In states and communities where LTC has been adopted as a priority by other established agencies and where a system of planning for LTC is being developed with a broad base of support, the decline of the health planning agency may have little effect on the level of LTC planning efforts. In other areas, however, where the HSA has taken the lead or been the only source of planning for LTC, the decline of health planning (however limited its efforts have been) may mean that LTC issues will slip from the public agenda (Downs, 1972). In this context, our analysis of interagency collaboration assumes additional significance. State and area agencies on aging funded under the Older Americans Act have some capacity for planning and some commitment to LTC, although the extent of both remains uncertain. Local models of health planning for LTC have been developed (Brody and Masciocchi, 1980) and are slowly being disseminated. What remains to be seen is whether OAA agencies, and particularly local area agencies on aging (AAAs), are capable of becoming planning agencies for LTC in communities where health planning otherwise no longer exists.

The health planning program under PL 93-641 was in political difficulty in Congress before the 1980 elections and the advent of severe budget cutbacks; therefore, its decline cannot be attributed solely to fiscal crisis. Rather, its fate has been determined by two related political forces. The first involves the intractability of the medical care system and thus the enormous problems faced in trying to contain its costs. The second involves federalism politics and has as much to do with the federalism of the 1970s as with that of the 1980s. The decision to create a network of state and local planning agencies only loosely connected by federal mandates produced a fragmented program highly vulnerable to provider domination. When a period of budgetary cutbacks arrived in 1980, health planning agencies found themselves with no political constituencies on whom they could depend for support and with little evidence to indicate that they had accomplished much.

Despite these formidable constraints, health planning agencies have begun to emerge as serious participants in state and local arenas for LTC policy. If they do not survive the current budget struggle, OAA agencies may have to fill the planning void that is certain to emerge. But state and local aging agencies share many of the same constraints that have fostered the problems encountered by health planning agencies, including uncertain priorities and inadequate authority. Whether aging agencies can play substantial roles in planning for long term care is a matter of capacity and of will, neither of which is a certainty.

Notes

1. "Personnel" is used here in place of the commonly used term, "manpower." The authors are uncomfortable with the use of the latter term, despite its wide usage.
2. Medical technology is another important area of policy decision and one that has received considerable (perhaps excessive) attention from health planners.
3. Health planning agency directors were asked the following: "In considering the various activities and goals of your agency, rank LTC in terms of the priority it has been given in the last year by your agency" (relatively low, moderate, relatively high).

References

Alford, R. R. *Health Care Politics*. Chicago: University of Chicago Press, 1975.
Banta, D. "The Federal Legislative Process and Health Care." In *Health Care Delivery in the United States* (2nd ed.). Ed. S. Jonas. New York: Springer, 1981.
Benjamin, A. E., P. B. Budetti, D. A. Lindeman, P. McManus, and P. W. Newacheck. *Health Planning Agencies and the Health Care Needs of the Elderly*. Final Report. Prepared for the U.S. Administration on Aging under Grant No. 90-AR-0028. San Francisco: Aging Health Policy Center and Institute of Health Policy Studies, University of California, 1982.
Benjamin, A. E., and G. W. Downs. "Evaluating the National Health Planning and Resources Development Act: Learning from Experience?" *Journal of Health Politics, Policy and Law,* 7, No. 3 (Fall 1982), 707-722.
Benveniste, G. *The Politics of Expertise*. San Francisco: Boyd & Fraser, 1977.
Bloom, B. S., and O. L. Peterson. "Physician Manpower Expansionism: A Policy Review." *Annals of Internal Medicine,* 90 (February 1979), 249-256.
Brody, S. J., and C. Masciocchi. "Data for Long-Term Care Planning by Health Systems Agencies." *American Journal of Public Health,* 70, No. 11 (November 1980), 1194-1198.
Brown, L. B. *The Political Structure of the Federal Health Planning Program*. Washington, DC: Brookings Institution, 1982.
Butler, L. H., et al. *Cooperation Between Health Systems Agencies and Professional Standards Review Organizations*. San Francisco: Institute for Health Policy Studies, University of California, 1977.
Downs, A. "Up and Down with Ecology — The 'Issue-Attention Cycle.'" *Public Interest,* 28 (Summer 1972), 38-50.

Feder, J. M. "Medicare Implementation and the Policy Process." *Journal of Health Politics, Policy and Law,* 2 (Summer 1977), 173-189.

————, and W. Scanlon. "Regulating the Bed Supply in Nursing Homes." *Milbank Memorial Fund Quarterly/Health and Society,* 58 (1980), 54-87.

Haas, J. E., and T. E. Drabek. *Complex Organizations: A Sociological Perspective.* New York: Macmillan, 1973.

Holahan, J. *Financing Health Care for the Poor.* Lexington, MA: D. C. Heath, 1975.

Lindeman, D. A., and A. E. Benjamin. "The Effects of Federal Budget Cutbacks on Health Planning Initiatives in Long Term Care." Paper presented at the American Public Health Association, Montreal, November 1982.

Marmor, T. R. *The Politics of Medicare.* Chicago: Aldine, 1973.

National Academy of Sciences. *Health Planning in the U.S.: Issues in Guideline Development.* Washington, DC: The Academy, 1980.

Newcomer, R. J., C. L. Estes, A. E. Benjamin, J. H. Swan, and V. Peguillan. *Funding Practices, Policies, and Performance of State and Area Agencies on Aging: Final Report.* Prepared for the U.S. Administration on Aging under Grant No. 90-A-979. San Francisco: Aging Health Policy Center, University of California, 1981.

Policy Analysis, Inc., and Urban Systems Research and Engineering, Inc. *Evaluation of the Effects of Certificate of Need Programs.* Washington, DC: Policy Analysis, 1980.

Sloan, F. A. "Regulation and the Rising Cost of Hospital Care." *Review of Economics and Statistics,* 63 (November 1981), 479-487.

Spivack, S., and S. J. Brody. "Comprehensive Long-Term Care Planning: Old Wine in New Bottles?" Paper presented at the Gerontological Society of America, Toronto, November 1981.

Thompson, J. D. *Organizations in Action.* New York: McGraw-Hill, 1967.

U.S. Congressional Budget Office (CBO). *Health Planning: Issues for Reauthorization.* Washington, DC: CBO, 1982.

U.S. Health Resources Administration (HRA). *Summary Report of the Graduate Medical Education National Advisory Committee to the Secretary, DHHS,* Vol. 1. DHHS Publication No. (HRA)81-651. Washington, DC: U.S. Department of Health and Human Services, 1981.

U.S. Public Law 74-241. Social Security Act of 1936. Washington, DC: U.S. Government Printing Office, 1936.

U.S. Public Law 79-725. Hospital Survey and Construction Act of 1946 (Hill-Burton). Washington, DC: U.S. Government Printing Office, 1946.

U.S. Public Law 86-778. Kerr-Mills Act of 1960. Washington, DC: U.S. Government Printing Office, 1960.

U.S. Public Law 88-129. Health Professions Educational Assistance Act of 1963. Washington, DC: U.S. Government Printing Office, 1963.

U.S. Public Law 89-97. Social Security Amendments of 1965 (established Medicare and Medicaid). Washington, DC: U.S. Government Printing Office, 1965.

U.S. Public Law 89-749. Comprehensive Health Planning and Public Health Service Amendments of 1966. Washington, DC: U.S. Government Printing Office, 1966.

U.S. Public Law 92-157. Comprehensive Health Manpower Training Act of 1971. Washington, DC: U.S. Government Printing Office, 1971.

U.S. Public Law 93-641. National Health Planning and Resources Development Act of 1974. Washington, DC: U.S. Government Printing Office, 1974.

Vladeck, B.C. "The Design of Failure: Health Policy and the Structure of
    Federalism". *Journal of Health Politics, Policy and Law,* 4, No. 3 (Fall 1979),
    522-535.
————. *Unloving Care: The Nursing Home Tragedy.* New York: Basic Books, 1980.
————. "Equity, Access and the Costs of Health Services." *Medical Care,* 19
    (December 1981), 69-80.

CHAPTER 10

THE PRIVATE NONPROFIT SECTOR AND AGING SERVICES

Juanita B. Wood
Carroll L. Estes

To understand conditions faced by older Americans, we must consider an important sector of society that falls between the public and the private realms, the private nonprofit sector. Also referred to as the independent sector, the third sector, and the voluntary sector, it is important to the elderly because one of its major functions is service delivery and because it includes charitable funding organizations, which, along with other private sector organizations, are being called upon to fund needed programs and services. The nonprofit sector has become prominent in the discussion of the impact of federal funding reductions as several observers have drawn attention to the possibility that this segment will suffer most from reductions (Sternberg, 1981; Salamon and Abramson, 1981, 1982; Pifer, 1981).

The pressure on the nonprofit sector comes not only from reduced funds and increased demands, but also from the federal policy of transferring categorical grant programs into block grants to be administered by the states. The latter policy shift is expected to result in the competition of private organizations with other service providers as well as municipalities for shares of the reduced funds in block grants (Hansmann, 1980; Pifer, 1981; Berger, 1982). Increased fiscal pressures on the states will, because of their own pressing demands,

Authors' Note: The authors wish to acknowledge the invaluable contribution of Ruth Chance. The data in this chapter are derived from research supported by the Pew Memorial Trust for the study "Public Policy, the Private Nonprofit Sector and the Delivery of Community Based Long Term Care Services for the Elderly."

make them more likely to address state-level funding needs before passing funds on to municipal governments or to nonprofit agencies. This has been reported already by some local governments. For example, in a national survey of city officials conducted by the U.S. Conference of City Human Services Officials (1982), two-thirds of the fifty-five cities studied reported that the conversion to block grants in fiscal year (FY) 1982 had "adversely affected their local human service programs." Of those respondents, 70 percent felt the states had either allocated resources unfairly or had not adequately represented cities in the planning process. Additional fiscal threats to the private nonprofit sector come from a prolonged recession, increasing service and funding demands made on this sector, and a reduction in the availability of funding from both public and private funding agencies (Smith and Rosenbaum, 1982; Lipscomb, 1981).

This chapter begins with a brief description of the private nonprofit sector, followed by a discussion of the current issues facing these organizations, and concludes with some implications for both the funders and the service deliverers, with particular attention to community-based, noninstitutional long-term care services for the aged.

The Private Nonprofit Sector

In the most general terms, the private nonprofit sector includes a wide range of approximately 800,000 private organizations that do not incur a profit, are ruled by a board of directors, and are organizations that do not, in the manner of businesses, make more money than they spend providing their services (Milofsky, 1979). This designation also includes charitable foundations that are required to pay out interest earned each year. The focus of this chapter is on both charitable foundations and private nonprofit organizations that provide human services.

While it is generally acknowledged that very little is known about the specifics of the private nonprofit sector (Douglas, 1980; Magat, 1981), how it operates, the extent to which it is involved in various aspects of the social system, and the exact breakdown on sources of funding, there is an increasing interest in this sector as the promotion of public-private partnerships receives increasing media attention. Many have struggled with the ill-defined nature of this sector, but Salamon and Abramson (1981) have estimated its involvement in the

TABLE 10.1   The Charitable Nonprofit Sector in the United States, 1977

Type of Organization	Number	Percentage of Total	Expenditures (in billions)	Percentage of Total	Paid Employees Number
Social services	40,983	38	$ 8.3	11	676,473
Legal aid services	1,101	1	0.3	—	12,440
Civic, social, and fraternal organizations	34,121	32	3.6	5	255,924
Education and research	11,074	10	15.5	21	980,116
Health	12,307	12	44.0	59	2,431,015
Arts and culture	3,480	3	1.1	2	59,761
Other	3,725	4	1.1	2	44,231
Total	106,791	100	$73.8	100	4,459,960

SOURCE: Adapted from U.S. Bureau of the Census. *1977 Census of Service Industries,* SC 77-A-53. Washington, DC: U.S. Government Printing Office, 1981, p. 3. Reprinted in Palmer, J. L., and I. V. Sawhill, eds. *The Reagan Experiment.* Washington, DC: Urban Institute, 1982, p. 222.

provision of services as shown in Table 10.1. While, of the 106,791 organizations, there are more social service agencies than any other type, the preponderance of both expenditures and paid employees falls within the health care area.

Social service agencies, which comprise the largest proportion (38 percent) of service agencies in the nonprofit sector, are also the most vulnerable, since social services are receiving the major portion of federal cutbacks. Salamon and Abramson (1982) estimated that federal spending in this area would be cut in half in constant dollar terms between FY 1981 and FY 1985. Even this dour prediction may be optimistic, according to Lipscomb (1981), who notes that their analysis is based only on federal cuts and does not attempt to measure the effects of the cuts that are being made simultaneously by state and local governments in addition to (and in response to) the federal cuts. In addition, there are state and local fiscal conditions resulting from unemployment, lost taxes, and increased service needs that affect the ability of state and local governments either to fund social services directly or to pass funds on to private nonprofit service agencies.

Personnel is another area of concern for the nonprofit organizations because of the large involvement of volunteers in these organizations. For example, a recent study on volunteerism reported in 1981 that 47 percent of American adults volunteered time in a structured situation. The dollar value assigned to all volunteer activity for 1981 was estimated at $64.5 billion (Independent Sector, 1981). In addition, a large proportion of the service agencies also used workers funded by the federal Comprehensive Employment Training Act (CETA) to supplement their staffs. According to preliminary data now being collected by the Aging Health Policy Center, the defunding of the CETA program will have a significant and negative impact on the nonprofit sector. While the CETA impact has not been fully documented, it is another element in the retrenchment that is affecting nonprofits. Not only are dollars being lost, but personnel may be lost as well.

Current Issues Facing the
Private Nonprofit Sector

The following discussion does not cover all of the current issues; rather, it focuses on those issues that have received most attention and attempts to provide insight into some of the effects on this sector of new federalism shifts in governmental responsibility combined with economic downturns.

(1) Does, or can, the private nonprofit service delivery sector exist without government support?

It is not often recognized that the private nonprofit sector is heavily subsidized by government funds and that it has expanded in direct response to (and in partnership with) federal government expansion of publicly funded programs in the 1960s and 1970s. The growth of public-private partnerships in which government has underwritten nonprofit organizations in the delivery of services has been particularly notable in education, health, and social services. This sector grew faster than the economy as a whole between 1975 and 1980 (Smith and Rosenbaum, 1982), and it has become increasingly dependent on the government for funding. The government, in turn, grew increasingly dependent on the private nonprofit sector to deliver public services. In this sense, the concept of public-private partnerships is not innovative but has been going on for at least two decades.

In 1979 Nielsen reported that government provided at least one-third, and more likely one-half, of all funds used by the institutions of the nonprofit sector (other than churches). In 1982 Smith and Rosenbaum noted that the dependence of voluntary organizations on government funding for health and human services had reached the stage

TABLE 10.2   Sources of Voluntary Sector Receipts, 1980

	Private Giving Amount (billions)	% of Total	Governmental Support Amount (billions)	% of Total	Service fees and Other Income Amount (billions)	% of Total	Total Amount (billions)	% of Total
Health services	$6.5	9	$29.0	43	$33.0	48	$68.5	100
Human services	4.75	25	8.0	43	6.0	32	18.75	100

SOURCE: U.S. Senate, Committee on Labor and Human Resources, Subcommittee on Aging, Family and Human Services. Hearing: *Voluntarism in America: Promoting Individual Corporate Responsibility,* April 22. Washington, DC: U.S. Government Printing Office, 1982, p. 119.

at which government income accounted for 43 percent of both the health and human services budget (see Table 10.2). The dependence of human (or social) service organizations on federal funding has serious implications for the elderly, since most of those services that constitute the noninstitutional community-based long term care system are financed through social service programs (U.S. Congressional Budget Office [CBO], 1977; Minkler and Blum, 1981) rather than through health care programs (see Table 10.3). Again, it is the social service area that has experienced the heaviest federal cutbacks and is projected to continue receiving proportionately the largest reductions.

Because government funding of private nonprofit organizations now exceeds the portion received by private funding, and in health and social services, by two to three times (Salamon and Abramson in Palmer and Sawhill, 1982), perhaps the leading question is how the nonprofit service sector will survive the major losses of government funds. In a study commissioned by Independent Sector, a national association of voluntary organizations, total income for voluntary organizations in 1981 was calculated at $192.2 billion. Of that, $80 billion came from user fees, government grants and miscellaneous income; only $47.7 billion came from contributions. The balance was the dollar value assigned to contributed time (Independent Sector, 1981). What, then is the future of this system under the joint conditions of a faltering economy and massive federal defunding? The president of Independent Sector (O'Connell, 1982) has estimated that approximately one dollar out of every five of the planned federal reductions would have an impact on the budgets of voluntary institutions, and

TABLE 10.3   Major Federal Programs Funding Community Services for the Elderly

| Service Areas | Federal Funding Source | | | | | | |
| | Social Security Act | | | | | | |
	Medicaid	Medicare	Social Services	SSI	AOA	VA	HUD
Medical services	X	X				X	
Home nursing services	X	X					
Home health aide	X	X	X		X	X	
Homemaker services			X		X		
Personal care	X		X			X	
Chore/home repair			X		X	X	
Home-delivered meals			X		X		
Shopping assistance			X		X		
Transportation			X				
Adult day care			X				
Housing assistance							X
Congregate housing, domiciliary homes, adult foster care			X	X			
Respite care			X				
Congregate meals			X		X		
Day hospital services	X						
Social/recreational					X		
Legal/financial counseling			X		X		
Mental health		X	X				
Information and referral			X		X	X	X

SOURCE: Adapted from U.S. General Accounting Office. *Entering a Nursing Home – Costly Implications for Medicaid and the Elderly.* Comptroller General Report to the Congress, PAD-80-12. Washington, DC: GAO, 1979, p. 74.

that the organizations that would be most affected include those most dependent on government funds and those least able to compete for block grants and other government funding.

Castelli (1982, p. 5) recently remarked on this lack of public awareness of the intertwining of the public and private sectors:

> Much of the Reagan economic program is based on the myth that the voluntary sector is separate from the public sector and has not been involved in public service. But that is not the case, largely because the voluntary sector as we know it today grew up hand-in-hand with "the welfare state."

This view fosters the perception that nonprofit organizations are largely independent of the government, and lays the groundwork for the questionable assumption that the private nonprofit sector can exist in the same form when government withdraws (Castelli, 1982).

(2) Can the private sector compensate for the withdrawal of federal funds from human services?

As soon as the Reagan administration proposed both reductions in and eventual federal withdrawal from the funding of human services, and an intensification of private involvement, the private sector was quick to respond that such an exchange was not possible; others were quick to agree. While there has been general acknowledgment that the "gap" left by government defunding is too large for the private sector to fill, less attention is paid to an equally important factor: what the private sector has traditionally funded. There are two areas to be considered, then. One is the amount of money required for the private sector to replace reduced federal funds on a strict dollar-exchange basis. O'Connell of Independent Sector, for example, noted that private giving would have to increase 140 percent between 1981 and 1984 to make up for the federal cuts (reported in Lipscomb, 1981).

The other issue is where that private sector money, if forthcoming, should go. The private sector has not traditionally been a heavy funder of what has been conceived of as areas covering the "public good." For the private sector to step in where government has withdrawn would then require a reorganization of normal private funding patterns. The arguments evident at this point in time have more to do with responsibility than with money.

The logical question is, Who has responsibility for the "public good"? One argument, classic in the debate over American federalism (see Chapter 3), is that the government is the only body that has the taxing capacity to raise the amount of money required for human services. A counterargument states that, in spite of government resources, these services are delivered at subfederal levels, limiting federal ability to exercise the accountability necessary to ensure that service needs are met. This second, private sector, argument also contends that the private sector can be more accountable than government and should deliver services, although funding of services should remain a public (government) responsibility. The private sector continues to argue for "finding a balance between accountability for the use of government funds and flexibility for independent organizations accepting such funds" (Goddard, 1982, p. 7).

TABLE 10.4   Distribution of Private Sector Contributions, 1980

Organization Type	Amount Contributed in 1980 (in billions)	Percentage of Total
Religion	$22.1	46.0
Educational institutions	6.68	14.0
Health and hospitals	6.49	13.6
Social welfare	4.73	10.6
Arts and humanities	2.96	6.2
Civic and public institutions	1.36	2.9
"Other"	3.37	7.0
Total	47.69	99.7

SOURCE: Data derived from American Association of Fund-Raising Counsel, Inc. *Giving USA: 1981 Annual Report.* New York: AAF-RC, 1981, p. 6.

As mentioned earlier, historical funding patterns in the private sector have been different from government funding patterns. Traditionally, in the private sector, the major portion of charitable giving has been assumed by individuals who account for approximately 90 percent of all private giving. Corporations and foundations generally split the remainder, at 5 percent each. In 1980 corporate contributions totaled $2.5 billion, foundations $2.4 billion, and individual contributions $48 billion (Lyman, 1982). These contributions are not, however, equally distributed among different types of service organizations. In 1980, for example, private giving was reported by the American Association of Fund-Raising Counsel (AAF-RC, 1981, p. 6) to be distributed as indicated in Table 10.4. Religion enjoys the largest proportion of private giving because most individual contributions are made to that category. Within this overall picture in private giving there are, of course, variations among individual, foundation, and corporate giving patterns. Private foundation giving patterns in 1980, for example, were reported by the Foundation Center Grants Index to be distributed as shown in Table 10.5.

These figures represent a sample of private foundations that have awarded grants of $5000 or more. The giving patterns for private foundations are similar to the overall private sector giving picture when religion is excluded. Education and health are the largest recipients, social welfare receiving a smaller proportion of contributions. Within the 5 percent of private giving representing corporate givers, this pattern is repeated (Figure 10.1 and Table 10.6).

TABLE 10.5   Distribution of Private Foundation Contributions, 1980

Organization Type	Amount Contributed in 1980 (in millions)	Percentage of Total
Higher education	198.3	16.7
Medical care and treatment	146.6	12.3
Community activities	67.8	5.7
General welfare	55.3	4.6
Religion	28.7	2.4

SOURCE: Data derived from the Foundation Center. *The Foundation Directory* (8th ed.). New York: The Center, 1981, p. xx.

The withdrawal of federal support, again, is heaviest in the social service and community service areas, which account for a smaller proportion of private giving. In order to fill in these areas, the private sector would have to begin contributing in areas not emphasized in the past (in addition to their normal areas of contribution) or to shift funds from religion, education, and health (thereby creating other funding gaps). The point to emphasize here is that private contributions traditionally have not been concentrated on social services and that it is therefore not reasonable to assume that increased giving would automatically flow into the areas where the severest federal cutbacks are occurring.

(3) Are current fiscal problems the result of current federal policy?

The call for significantly increased resources from the private sector comes at a time when other factors, such as a generally depressed economy, make this a particularly troublesome issue. Fiscal conditions have been characterized in several ways: Richard W. Rehn, vice-president and chief economist for the U.S. Chamber of Commerce, in his address before the Senate, observed that "these are not budget cuts, but reductions in dollar volume growth"; similarly, Jack Moskowitz, director of government relations for United Way (quoted in Lipscomb, 1981, p. 21), noted, "What nonprofits are facing is not an actual dollar decline, but shortfalls in increases." However these fiscal conditions are characterized, cutbacks are only part of a more complex process that has been occurring in the economy and in public policy since the early 1970s (Estes, 1979). This process has affected the public as well as the private sector. The tax revolts and

TABLE 10.6   The Health and Welfare Contribution Dollar, 1979 and 1980

	1980 732 Companies		1979 786 Companies	
	Thousands of dollars	% of Total	Thousands of dollars	% of Total
Health and Welfare				
Federated drives (e.g., United Way)	$170,652	17.1		
National health agencies	11,362	1.1		
National welfare agencies	5,434	0.5		
Hospitals				
Capital grants	29,848	3.0		
Operating grants	11,063	1.1		
Employee matching gifts for hospitals	749	0.1		
Youth agencies (e.g., Boys Clubs, Boy and Girl Scouts, YMCA)	29,710	3.0		
Agencies for senior citizens and elderly	3,467	0.3		
Other local health and welfare agencies	41,724	4.2		
Capital grants excluding hospitals	—	—		
Subcategory not identifiable	33,857	3.4		
Total health and welfare	337,866	34.0	292,641	35.0

SOURCE: Troy, K. *Annual Survey of Corporate Contributions* 1982 Edition. New York: The Conference Board, 1982, p. 30.

fiscal constraints that surfaced at the local level and became nationally prominent in the mid-1970s were caused not only by the increasing share of personal taxes involved in the financing of state and local governments (see Figure 10.2), but also by a disaffection for the ways government was spending that money (Menchik and Pascal, 1980). This disaffection and the imposition in approximately half of the states of fiscal limitation laws (see Table 10.7), most of which were adopted between 1974 and 1980, have increased fiscal problems at the state and local levels.

In our fiscal crisis study (Swan et al., 1982; see also Chapter 5), involving a sample of ten states and forty communities, 65 percent of the mayors and 70 percent of the governors projected fiscal shortfalls for their governments for 1981-1982, and the number of jurisdictions reporting revenue shortfalls increased significantly between 1978 and 1981, indicating a worsening of their fiscal conditions. States and communities, then, were already experiencing fiscal difficulty prior to

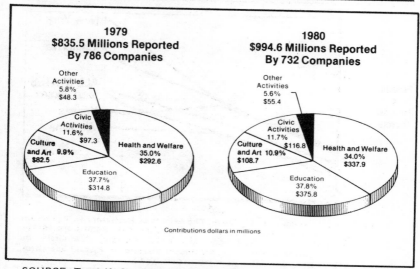

1979
$835.5 Millions Reported
By 786 Companies

Other Activities 5.8% $48.3

Civic Activities 11.6% $97.3

Culture and Art 9.9% $82.5

Health and Welfare 35.0% $292.6

Education 37.7% $314.8

1980
$994.6 Millions Reported
By 732 Companies

Other Activities 5.6% $55.4

Civic Activities 11.7% $116.8

Culture and Art 10.9% $108.7

Health and Welfare 34.0% $337.9

Education 37.8% $375.8

Contributions dollars in millions

SOURCE: Troy, K. Annual Survey of Corporate Contributions, 1982 Edition. York: The Conference Board, 1982, p. 12.

Figure 10.1 Distribution of the Corporate Contribution Dollar, 1979 and 1980

the Reagan administration federal policy shifts, but the current federal policy has increased the degree of state and local fiscal difficulty. This has been due in part to the growing reliance on government grants to supplement state and local revenues (see Figure 10.3). The combination of (1) reductions in federal funds to the states and cities and (2) limitations on spending and taxes creates significant problems in financing both administrative and service delivery functions.

Private sector resources also began diminishing prior to the current policies of new federalism. Magat (1981) notes that the nonprofits were experiencing in the mid-1970s a "fiscal crunch" caused by an increasing demand for services and a leveling off of government support that previously had been increasing. Nielsen (1979) extends the explanation for the difficulty by noting that the 1950s and 1960s saw an increase in government outlays for educational and social programs and that the securities markets increased the value of endowments and portfolios. During the same period, giving by individuals, corporations, and foundations increased. However, "by the

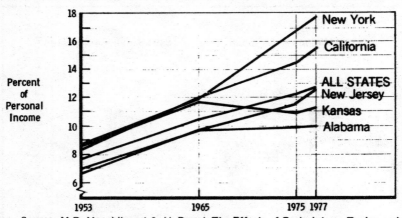

Source: M.D. Menchik and A. H. Pascal. **The Effects of Restraints on Taxing and Spending.** Rand Papers Series. Santa Monica, CA: Rand Corporation, May 1980, p. 7, derived from data in U.S. Advisory Commission on Intergovernmental Relations. **Significant Features of Fiscal Federalism, 1978-79 Edition.** Washington, DC: ACIR, 1979.

Figure 10.2   Percentages of Personal Income Absorbed by State and Local Taxes

early 1970's the bust had come. Double digit inflation, falling security markets, and cutbacks of government spending struck Third Sector agencies with damaging force, both in their expenses and their income" (Nielsen, 1979, p. 9).

As a further indication that foundation assets are diminishing, a Council on Foundations survey of 800 foundations showed a 13 percent decline in total assets between 1977 and 1979 (AAF-RC, 1981). Individual giving has also declined. As a percentage of personal income, individual giving declined from 1.99 percent in 1970 to 1.84 percent of personal income in 1980. This was the lowest proportion of personal giving since 1956 (AAF-RC, 1981).

On the corporate foundation side, the latest Conference Board (1982) survey of corporate contributions indicates that respondents for company foundations indicated that they had paid out $50 million more than they received from their corporate sponsors, resulting in a drawing down of their reserves. Actual giving by corporations increased last year, but the question remains of whether increases can realistically be expected to continue with the strain of a flagging economy, a policy of new federalism, and changes in the 1981 tax laws that have provided significant tax advantages for activities other than

TABLE 10.7 States with General Fiscal Limitation Laws

State	Local Level Affects: Year	Prop. Tax	Other	Type: Growth	Type: Cutback	State Level Year	Affects: Revenues	Affects: Expenditures	Type: Fixed %	Type: Variable[a]
AK	1976	x		x						
AZ	1921	x		x		1978		x		x
CA	1974, 78	x			x					
CO	1955, 71, 76	x		x		1977		x	x	
FL	1971	x		x						
HI	1976	x		x		1978		x		x
ID	1978	x			x					
IN	1973	x		x						
IA	1976	x		x						
KS	1970	x		x						
MI	1978	x		x		1978	x			x
MN	1971	x		x						
MT	1974	x		x						
NE	1978	x		x						
NJ	1976		x	x		1976		x		x
NM	1977	x								
OR	1916	x		x						
RI						1977		x		x
SD	1978	x		x		1978	x		x	
TN						1978		x		x
TX	1978	x		x		1978		x		x
UT	1969	x		x						
VA	1975	x		x						
WA	1973	x		x						
WI	1973	x		x						

SOURCE: May 1979 Rand Survey from Ellickson, "The Fiscal Limitation Movement: Present Context and Outlook." Reprinted in M. D. Menchik and A. H. Pascal, *The Equity Effects of Restraint on Taxing and Spending*. Rand Paper Series, May. Santa Monica, CA: Rand Corporation, 1980, p. 13.

a. As a function, for example, of growth in population, price level, or personal income; or subject to subsequent referendum.

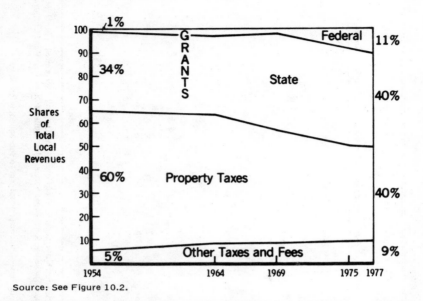

Source: See Figure 10.2.

Figure 10.3 Increase in Proportion of Government Support for Local Revenues, 1954-1977

philanthropy (such as Individual Retirement Accounts and increased depreciation write-offs).

The implications of the current situation go beyond the obvious discussion of decreased resources and increased demand and warrant a closer look into some of the specific consequences for the nonprofit service providers and the charitable foundations.

Implications for the Funding Side

Since all indications are that demand for both services and funding will continue to grow, private funders are now finding themselves in a position of having to weigh not only more requests for services but also different types of requests. Foundations are being approached for help in broad, general categories such as "poverty" and "hunger," which demand both short- and long-term considerations. These "public good" issues are becoming increasingly prominent as federal government cutbacks result in a shift to private funders for solutions to problems that have traditionally been considered part of the public domain. Fund raising has become a major concern in both the public and private sectors. There has been an increase in the number of agencies hiring professional fund raisers to conduct fund drives. Thomas G. Sanberg, of the National Society of Fund Raising Executives, estimates that approximately one-third more professional soliciting is now occurring than eighteen months ago (Teltsch, 1982). There is the perception that this type of activity will continue to increase and thus intensify the competition for the charitable dollar.

One of the potential effects of the current situation is that community and independent foundations, as well as service providers, will be looking for more money and will be finding themselves in increased competition with each other. Also, they may search for an investment plan that yields higher returns or count on an increase in individual giving as they search for new donors. These latter strategies appear unlikely in a depressed economy. Clotfelter and Salamon (1981), in an analysis of the effect of the Economic Recovery Tax Act of 1981, predict that individual giving will actually decline through 1984. Corporate foundations do not, at this point, appear inclined to be responsive to assuming more of the funding burden than in the past. The Conference Board study (Troy, 1982) noted that of the 60 percent of the corporate foundation planning to increase their budgets, only a few were doing so in response to federal cutbacks.

Corporations tend to give the largest percentage of their charitable dollar to agencies of the United Way. (The Conference Board reports 17 percent of total giving in 1980 went to such organizations, comprising the largest single donation made by the corporations studied; see Troy, 1982). However, criticisms have been leveled against United Way organizations as monopolistic, conservative, and inflexible about the agencies they fund as well as minimally involved in their respective communities (Wexler, 1980; Smith, 1978; Rose-Ackerman, 1980). This may have a bearing on the services that will receive corporate foundation support in a community and, depending on the particular United Way organization, is likely to do little to solve the problems of agencies that are not under the umbrella of United Way.

Some attention has been given to forming public-private consortia at the community level to begin to address human service needs. Foundations are somewhat vulnerable to persuasion because of the suddenness with which they have been called upon to become the problem solvers. They are not, by and large, equipped to evaluate all the proposals that they receive, nor are they able, under the immediate pressure they are now experiencing, to sit back and ponder in a long-range manner the issue of what they would like to fund as opposed to what needs to be funded now. Under current conditions they are being forced to react in much the same way cities and states have had to react under the new austerity format. Emergency relief, particularly in food and housing, has become a primary area of concern, but how consistent or how involved the private sector is likely to remain in this area is uncertain.

What seems most likely to occur is that traditional patterns of funding will continue and that the private sector will be staunch in its refusal to "let government off the hook." As many have noted (see Nathan et al. in Ellwood, 1982), the programs serving the lower-income population have been hit the hardest in federal cuts. Since they comprise only a small proportion (about one-fourth) of the federal budget, the cuts in means-tested programs can have only a marginal impact on reducing large federal budget deficits. These programs are not likely to be heavily subsidized by the private sector, which jeopardizes both the service area and the private nonprofit agencies active in that area.

Implications for the Service Provision Side

As a consequence of the situation described in this chapter, there is a significant likelihood that service cuts and eliminations will affect recipient populations inequitably. As noted previously, traditional private sector funding patterns have left primary responsibility for programs that serve the most underprivileged and disabled populations to the public sector. Private sector funders have, by and large, moved more into the area of funding programs that lead to some kind of independence or to some kind of product (Sternberg, 1981).

Of particular concern is the lack of private, nongovernment funding that has traditionally gone to support aging programs. The explanation for this may lie in the ideology that supporting social welfare programs for the elderly and the disabled will not result in either a socially valued product or a member of the workforce. A study of foundation grants reported to the Foundation Center in 1976 and 1977 concluded that outlays in aging amounted to about 5 percent of expenditures reported to the Center (Florence V. Burden Foundation, 1980). Of the money spent, 80 percent of all expenditures went to maintaining existing services. Institutional care programs received about 30 percent of the expenditures, while noninstitutional health care received about 10.6 percent. Such a pattern of funding raises questions about the potential willingness of foundations to fund community-based, noninstitutional long term care services for the elderly. This is of concern when we report that even services for the aged, which, as a group, have been considered morally deserving (Klemmack and Roff, 1981), have also experienced government cutbacks as fiscal conditions worsen (Swan et al., 1982). Funds are decreasing as the aging population increases along with a need for more long term care services.

Long term care is frequently thought of in terms of institutionalization, primarily in nursing homes. The propensity of federal requirements to favor institutionalization over community-based care has, of course, influenced this conception. This situation is likely to be exacerbated with reduced funding and is one of the key funding tradeoffs likely to occur. Our research on fiscal crisis indicates that there is the tradeoff between health and social services in general, with social services being more severely affected than health services. For long term care alternatives to institutionalization for a growing elderly population, this tradeoff poses especially grim consequences when many of these community-based long term care services have been funded (and now essentially defunded) by federal funds for social services.

There are also some institutional tradeoffs occurring in terms of which types of organizations will be offering which types of long term care services. There is growing competition among hospitals, private for-profit providers, and private nonprofit home health agencies for home health care. Private providers have also made inroads into other services generally dominated by nonprofits (Upjohn, for example, in chore services; the nursing home industry in adult day care). If the shift in service provision occurs so that the for-profits have an edge on the market, there is the concern that service quality may be sacrificed to ensure the production of profits. In addition, this shift also brings closer the elimination of a portion of the nonprofit service delivery sector. The rapidly expanding elderly population requiring long term care services cannot afford this loss.

There are some indications that states are addressing the community-based long term care issue. This is, however, again in response to the federal government and its Medicaid regulation changes permitting states to apply for waivers to offer community-based long term care. More than two-thirds of the states in 1982 applied for waivers to extend Medicaid coverage to community-based long term care (State Health Notes, 1982). Of the 32 states to apply for the waivers, 19 have been approved, 3 disapproved, and 21 left pending. While these actions may be positive, they also reinforce the perception that the public sector is responsible for funding the bulk of human services, particularly in social service areas, and potentially in the long term area.

Conclusion

The data and discussion presented in this chapter suggest tentative answers to some of the most important questions raised. In terms of whether the private nonprofit service delivery sector can exist without government support, our conclusion would be yes, but in a fashion decidedly different from the past and with decided consequences for the poor and elderly. Based on the fact that the government share of funding for health and human services exceeds by two to three times that provided by private giving, the voluntary sector clearly has not operated separately from the public sector.

As to whether the current fiscal problems are a result of the policies of the current administration, we have indicated they are not. However, the fiscal policy of the current administration has exacerbated those preexisting problems and will most likely continue to do so.

In response to the question of whether the private sector can (or will) compensate for the withdrawal of federal funds, the answer appears to be a decided no. Factors that contribute to this conclusion include general economic conditions, federal cutbacks, increasing state and local taxing and spending limitations and fiscal pressures, diminishing foundation assets, reduced individual giving (that provides 90 percent of all giving), and tax incentives that are expected further to reduce private giving (President's Task Force on Private Sector Initiatives, 1982; Clotfelter and Salamon, 1981). The likelihood of the private sector's continuing traditional giving patterns that are more oriented to religion, education, and health than to social services will mean that the needed human services programs, particularly for low-income and elderly individuals, are likely to suffer most, since these programs have been both hard hit by federal cutbacks and of relatively low funding priority in the private sector.

Perhaps the major issue concerns where, indeed, the responsibility for the public good rests. While arguing, on the one hand, that the private sector can provide services better and with more accountability than government, the same sector indicates that filling the funding gaps left by federal cutbacks is tantamount to private sector assumption of public sector responsibility. These very issues raised by the private sector in part explain the importance of federal-level commitments and national policies to address unequal resources and the political disposition of the different levels of the public-private partnership.

References

American Association of Fund-Raising Counsel, Inc. (AAF-RC). *Giving USA: 1981 Annual Report*. New York: AAF-RC, 1981.

Berger, J. "New Directions in Giving." *Hospital Forum*, 25, No. 1 (January/February 1982), 13-22.

Castelli, J. "Reaganomics Ripples: Charity Groups Sink Under Budget Cuts." *Sacramento Bee*, June 20, 1982.

Clotfelter, C.J., and L. M. Salamon. *The Federal Government and the Nonprofit Sector: The Impact of the 1981 Tax Act on Individual Charitable Giving*. Washington, DC: Urban Institute, 1981.

Douglas, J. *Toward a Rationale for Private Nonprofit Organizations: A Review of Current Theory*. New Haven, CT: Institution for Social and Policy Studies, Yale University, 1980.

Ellwood, J. W., ed. *Reductions in U.S. Domestic Spending: How They Affect State and Local Governments*. New Brunswick, NJ: Transaction, 1982.

Estes, C. L. *The Aging Enterprise*. San Francisco: Jossey-Bass, 1979.

Florence V. Burden Foundation. *Grantmaking for the Elderly: An Analysis of Foundation Expenditures*. New York: The Foundation, 1980.

The Foundation Center. *The Foundation Directory* (8th ed.). New York: The Center, 1981.

Goddard, S. "Accountability with Independence — Toward a Balance in Government/Independent Sector Financial Partnerships." Speech delivered at the annual meetings of the Independent Sector, San Francisco, October 1, 1982.

Hansmann, H. B. "The Role of Nonprofit Enterprise." *Yale Law Journal*, 89, No. 5 (1980), 835-901.

Independent Sector. *Americans Volunteer 1981: A Summary Report*. Washington, DC: Independent Sector, 1981.

Klemmack, D. L., and L. L. Roff. "Predicting General Comparative Support for Government's Providing Benefits to Older Persons." *Gerontologist*, 21, No. 6 (December 1981), 592-599.

Lipscomb, G. "The Case of the Triple Whammy." *Grantsmanship Center News*, 9, No. 5 (September/October 1981), 18-25.

Lyman, R. W. Statement given before the Task Force on Entitlements, Uncontrolla-
   bles, and Indexing, Commission on the Budget, House of Representatives:
   "Impact of the Omnibus Reconciliation Act and Proposed Fiscal Year 1983
   Budget Cut in Entitlements, Uncontrollables, and Indexing," February 22, 26;
   March 1. Washington, DC: U.S. Government Printing Office, 1982.

Magat, R. "Putting Nonprofits on the Academic Map." *Grantsmanship Center
   News,* 9, No. 4 (July/August 1981), 42-47.

Menchik, M. D., and A. H. Pascal. *The Equity Effects of Restraints on Taxing and
   Spending.* Santa Monica, CA: Rand Corporation, 1980.

Milofsky, C. *Not for Profit Organizations and Community: A Review of the Sociological Literature.* New Haven, CT: Institution for Social and Policy Studies, Yale
   University, 1979.

Minkler, M., and S. R. Blum. "Community Based Home Health and Social Services
   for California's Elderly: Present Constraints and Future Alternatives." Commissioned paper for the California Policy Seminar, Berkeley, February 1981.

Nathan, R. P., et al. "Initial Effects of the Fiscal Year 1982 Reductions in Federal
   Domestic Spending on State and Local Governments." In *Reductions in U.S.
   Domestic Spending.* Ed. J. W. Ellwood. New Brunswick, NJ: Transaction, 1982.

Nielsen, W. A. *The Endangered Sector.* New York: Columbia University Press,
   1979.

O'Connell, B. Speech delivered at the annual meetings of the Independent Sector,
   San Francisco, October 25, 1982.

Palmer, J. L., and I. V. Sawhill, eds. *The Reagan Experiment.* Washington, DC:
   Urban Institute, 1982.

Pifer, A. "The Trends of the 1980's: Where Are They Leading Us?" *Philanthropy
   Monthly* (April 1981), 20-28.

President's Task Force on Private Sector Initiatives. *Building Partnerships.*
   Washington, DC: Author, 1982.

Rose-Ackerman, S. "United Charities: An Economic Analysis." *Public Policy,* 28,
   No. 3 (Summer 1980), 323-350.

Salamon, L. M., and A. J. Abramson. *The Federal Government and the Nonprofit
   Sector: Implications of the Reagan Budget Proposals.* Washington, DC: Urban
   Institute, 1981.

———. "The Nonprofit Sector." In *The Reagan Experiment.* Ed. J. L. Palmer and
   I. V. Sawhill. Washington, DC: Urban Institute, 1982.

Smith, B. L. R., and N. M. Rosenbaum. Statement given before the U.S. Senate
   Committee on Labor and Human Resources, Subcommittee on Aging, Family
   and Human Services: "Voluntarism in America: Promoting Individual and
   Corporate Responsibility," April 22. Washington, DC: U.S. Government Printing Office, 1982.

Smith, D. H. "'United Way' Is the Name, Monopoly Is the Game." *Business and
   Society Review* (Spring 1978), 30-34.

Smith, L. "The Unsentimental Corporate Giver." *Fortune,* 104, No. 6 (September
   21, 1981), 121-140.

State Health Notes. "Survey on Medicaid Changes." No. 30 (October/November
   1982), 1-6.

Sternberg, S. "The Realities of Corporate Giving." *Issues and Strategies* (Spring 1981), 19-27.

Swan, J. H., C. L. Estes, J. B. Wood, M. Kreger, and J. Garfield. *Fiscal Crisis: Impact on Aging Services*. Final Report. Prepared for the U.S. Administration on Aging under Grant No. 90-AR-006. San Francisco: Aging Health Policy Center, University of California, 1982.

Teltsch, K. "Charities' Appeals for Funds Rising Sharply in New York." *New York Times*, December 12, 1982, p. 22.

Troy, K. *Annual Survey of Corporate Contributions, 1982 Edition*. New York: The Conference Board, 1982.

U.S. Conference of City Human Services Officials. *Human Services in FY 82: Shrinking Resources in Troubled Times*. N.p.: The Conference, 1982.

U.S. Congressional Budget Office (CBO). *Long-Term Care for the Elderly and Disabled*. Washington, DC: CBO, 1977.

Wexler, N. "Corporate Charity." *New Republic*, April 5, 1980, pp. 19-22.

CHAPTER 11

THE FUTURE FOR AGING AND PUBLIC POLICY
Two Perspectives

Carroll L. Estes
Robert J. Newcomer

We conclude this book with a chapter that presents the views and interpretations of the senior authors. In the conceptualization and writing of this book we found the purpose to be twofold. One goal was to present a synthesis of the research conducted by the Aging Health Policy Center over the past eight years, objectively interpreting these findings and their implications for future policy for the aged. A second objective was to use this book as a vehicle for interpretation and perspective on American social policy and the influences on it. We have worked together for years with differing perspectives. Rather than attempt to create an amalgam of our differences, we have found it useful to prepare separate conclusions. We think these divergent viewpoints have relevance to the complexity of issues discussed throughout the book. Perhaps in our diversity, we can help you draw your own conclusions.

Perspectives of a Pluralist

ROBERT J. NEWCOMER

It has been well documented that the health and social service system is not functioning as well as many would like. There is less consensus about what is causing this poor functioning, and even less

Authors' Note: The authors wish to acknowledge the invaluable contributions of Lenore Gerard, Philip R. Lee, and Jane Sprague Zones in the preparation of this chapter.

concerning solutions. A major theme of the book has dealt with one proposed solution — the delegation or transfer of authority from the federal government to state and local government or to the private sector. The media and public debate concerning this possible direction of future health and social service policy has tended more commonly toward the use of labels and rhetoric than a reasoned consideration of which authority might be decentralized and the appropriateness of these actions in terms of problems allegedly addressed by this action. Decentralization, as we have discussed it, can include a transfer of all or some financial responsibility. It can also include responsibility for all or some goal setting, service selection, or eligibility determination. At a more mundane level it can simply refer to program management and administration changes.

Personal ideologies and cultural values have important influences on decision making. This is especially true in how a problem is defined, how multiple solutions are viewed, and how a choice is made as to which problems to address. In assessing the advantages and disadvantages of various decentralization proposals, or any other proposals, I have found it helpful to disaggregate the problem into its causal elements. The more refinement possible in this area, the easier it becomes to design solutions. However, not all causal factors are amenable to corrections, and others can be addressed through multiple approaches. Further complicating decision making is that one factor may ameliorate one condition and have adverse effects on other elements.

An issue as complex as the organization and financing of our health and social service system is fraught with multiple causality and interactions among various system components. Recognizing this, I am somewhat humbled by the presumption of drawing any conclusions about appropriate or inappropriate courses of change. In fact, I have no specific directions for change to propose. My contribution to the solution will be to ask that we step back from our current debates and reassess whether we are talking about the right issues.

Simplifying the situation greatly, discussions of fiscal conditions and the historical and projected costs of health and social services have made the point that our current approach to services for the elderly has some flaws. The system is heavily biased toward the acute health care industry, which is growing at unacceptably high rates. Other needed services are not being developed, and populations with less intensive service needs are being either ignored or forced to pay exhorbitant proportions of their service costs out-of-pocket. Our choices are: ignoring these problems and continuing to expend the resources demanded by the current delivery structure; making modest efficiency reforms without structural change; transferring the cost burden without structural change; or reformulating the system itself.

The major reforms considered in this book fall largely under the categories of "efforts at modest efficiency" and "transferring the cost burden." In my opinion, decentralization proposals do not address major reformulation of the health and social service system. My comments thus take two forms. The first is to consider whether or not the reforms now being debated are focusing on the most important issues. The second is to consider the merits of decentralization reforms within the existing program structure.

Three fundamental conditions have dominated the evolution of policy and services for the elderly over the past fifty years.

(1) We have been unwilling to impose incentives or sanctions that would produce a rate of capital formation sufficient to meet the income needs of the population as it retires. Instead, we have elected to finance retirement from existing revenues. One consequence of this action is that a large proportion of the elderly population lives at or near the poverty level, and we have chosen to meet their service needs through some form of subsidization of service cost — again, from current resources. (Although recent changes in tax laws have encouraged more savings for retirement, neither is this a mandatory program nor does it affect those who cannot afford savings.)

(2) The health care system has been characterized by a fee-for-service structure in which the provider rather than the payee is the decision maker relative to the range and cost of services received. Public attitudes toward physicians in particular have largely accepted this system. Government's role has been one of generating the funding, attempting to control abuse and fraud, and encouraging expansions of care when the private market has not responded to needs (such as long term care and rural health services).

(3) Our social service system is characterized by funding and operation at largely symbolic or token levels, rather than being adequate to the needs of the public. Moreover, we have used this system (a) as an inefficient method for passing on income subsidies to those with low incomes, (b) as a battlefield for absorbing the attention of public advocates, and (c) as a diversion from conditions 1 and 2.

How does this relate to the issue of new federalism and service decentralization? First, the biggest problem with the new federalism proposals is that they have absorbed a tremendous amount of energy and deflected debate away from what I see as more fundamental reform — such as abandonment of the fee-for-service, provider-dominated approach to health care. Further deflecting focus from such basic issues has been the erosion of federal and state-level social service budget allocations. In its characteristic way, advocacy for the aged has given major priority to maintaining social service funding levels. Advocates have not taken time to reassess the utility to these approaches, or to consider that health care costs are a major factor affecting the reduced availability of social service costs. In short, the new federalism proposals have been articulated and discussed as if they involved fundamental change. Instead, they essentially transfer administrative responsibilities while maintaining the existing service structure.

The health care delivery system we have in the United States today has evolved over a number of years. Any changes in it will carry risks. The incomes of many people and institutions will be affected, mistakes will be made, and adjustments will be necessary in any new alternatives adopted. Although caution is indicated, we cannot allow all attention to focus on incremental changes. Minor changes such as further decentralization should be tried and monitored without as much agony in getting them going. If this can be more easily done through demonstrations or limited programs rather than through wholesale nationwide programs, then let us do it that way. The time spent on the debate of incremental adjustments by our legislators and public advocates would, in my view, be better spent scrutinizing existing policy and arguing about the equitability of our current system, as well as considering the means of effecting fundamental reform in the distribution of resources now going to the health sector, and the means to a more direct income subsidy to those who need it. Until basic issues are addressed and resolved, public policy for the aged will continue to involve minor tinkering and adjustment.

Having reached the conclusion that new federalism decentralization reforms are not of a fundamental nature, it remains appropriate to consider the effect of these changes on the operation of the current system. Of the concerns addressed in this book — the definition of national, state, and local responsibility; the capacity and structural incentives of government; equity; accountability; and democratic participation — for me the most important practical aspect is whether there is the fiscal capacity within our current state tax structures to accommodate an increase in fiscal responsibility for health and social services.

It seems apparent that unless there are major changes in how the Medicaid system (in particular) would work and who would be eligible for these services, state governments simply cannot assume an expanded financial burden for this program. In other words, continued or expanded federal fiscal involvement in health care programs is essential. Within this context, would a transfer of more administrative responsibility to states have any advantage? There is reason for cautious optimism here. Clear historical evidence shows state willingness to go beyond federal minimum requirements in service eligibility and service provision. There is also evidence of a willingness to innovate in service system reform — particularly in reimbursement systems for hospitals and physicians, but also in a variety of other services. The federal Medicare program has been much slower to adopt similar cost-saving approaches.

Critics of expanded state responsibility argue that states are unequal in their ability (as evidenced by their variation in eligibility criteria and program policies) to fulfill expanded responsibilities. While this is certainly true, often overlooked in these comments is that all states are operating at least at the minimum levels required under federal policy. Higher performance from states is possible to achieve through several means: higher federal minimum requirements, more federal financial resources, training of state program officials, and judicial oversight. There is nothing inherent in new federalism that would prohibit the exercise of these options by the federal government. A clear definition of federal, state, and local responsibility can be achieved by establishing federal minimums and giving the states options to go beyond these. (This sounds like our current system, doesn't it?) For the most part, policy debate would be more fruitful if it concentrated on establishing the federal minimum instead of arguing the upper limits of state authority.

The last three issues of equity, accountability, and democratic participation are important to any critique of new federalism reform or of our existing health and social service structure. Being an avowed pluralist, I am inclined to believe that the questions of equity and institutional accountability are resolved over time through constant negotiation. The level of this negotiation (federal versus state versus local), as well as its democratic quality, is ultimately determined by the issue and the decision to be made. The only real absolute in this process is the process itself.

Norton Long (1958), in a classic article, characterized politics as an ecology of games. This imagery provides a simple and convenient way of viewing the array of institutions and their interactions in the policy arena. Taking some liberties with Long's model, I have framed an illustration of the institutions or players in the health and social services game. These include federal, state, and local government; banking; insurance; health providers; and so forth. One assumption of the pluralist model is that there are norms, rules, and reward structures that largely govern the behavior of each separate set of players. Moreover, each set of players is usually assumed to operate without direct consideration of the other players. Interaction or conflict can occur among the players when there is an overlap of resource demands or other circumstances among one or more of these sets of players.

The Medicaid program illustrates such an interaction. All levels of government are involved directly or indirectly in this program, as are the health industry, insurance, and banking (through outstanding loans to hospitals and others). Any change from the status quo will affect all of these players — hence the use of the term "ecology." Through a series of accommodations by all players and games, the whole system eventually adjusts and is stable until new problems or changes occur.

A dilemma facing us as social critics is that we can compress a long history of an evolving issue into a brief diagnosis of its problems. This compression often leads us to think that changes can be made quickly. I do not think it is that simple. Health and social services policies have been evolving to their present form for over fifty years. During that time the roles and relationships of the various players and games involved in these policies have adapted. Some groups, of course, fared better under the rules than others; hospitals, physicians, and insurance companies, for example, have fared better in total dollars and per capita income than have social service providers or consumers paying for services.

Nevertheless, our society (in fact, much of the world) came to accept these disparities while the total supply of resources continued to grow rapidly enough for all major players to get what they had come to define as their fair shares. As funds have become less and less available, the ecology of games has been disrupted. Within this transition period a new negotiation of resource distribution will begin to emerge.

Since we can no longer afford the old structure, it will apparently have to make some accommodation. Cost, however, has not been the only problem with the system; another has been gaps in needed services, especially in long term care. These issues must and will be resolved to the advantage of the public, which is both the consumer and the taxpayer for health and social services. The concerted involvement of all levels of government will enhance the molding of the next service system equilibrium.

This point of transition in which we now find ourselves, though anxiety producing, is nevertheless a point of opportunity. While new directions are being debated, considered, experimented with, and accepted or rejected, there is an opportunity to assess where we are and where we are going.

The only way to experiment with public policy is to put a program in place. Over the years, national policy has benefited from the experience of states. The new federalism proposals, though likely to improve program management, cannot realistically be expected to accomplish much else. Expansion of state financial responsibility, for example, will not solve the problem of financing health and social services. Expansion of administrative responsibility will not, in and of itself, reform the health care system. My feeling is that for the short term we should experiment with greater state administrative control, but within specified federal minimum requirements. A more serious concern is that our public decision makers stop using this administrative realignment issue as a means to deflect attention and consideration away from fundamental change. There, my colleagues in aging, is our biggest challenge.

Perspectives of a Political Economist

CARROLL L. ESTES

Decentralization, new federalism, and recent reductions in the federal role in domestic social policy serve important political and economic functions. This shift has six deleterious results.

First, decentralized and highly discretionary nonnational programs tend to neutralize and weaken political mobilization of the powerless by shifting the focal point for social action from a more easily mobilized national effort to the hundreds and thousands of state and local jurisdictions. Such a shift makes mobilization difficult or impossible. This weakens the capacity of all but the most well-organized, stable, and well-funded organizations to build and maintain momentum. The net effect is to blunt the power and potential of national movements in favor of interests with the economic resources (such as chambers of commerce and organized medicine) to build and sustain widely dispersed influence on multiple governmental levels. To influence policy for the aged in decentralized programs, it becomes necessary to address officials in hundreds of different agencies in the fifty states and, in some cases, in thousands of localities. Further, within each of the major decentralized programs affecting the elderly — Medicaid, block-granted social services, mental health services, the Older Americans Act, and state-determined aspects of SSI eligibility and supplementation — the advocacy efforts that must be mounted across many agencies and political jurisdictions compete not only with similar advocacy efforts of other disadvantaged populations (such as poor children and the disabled), but also with the extremely well-organized and economically dominant corporate and provider interests.

Second, the decentralization in recent policies provides a mechanism for the devolution of responsibility for policymaking from government (the public sector) to the private sector through interest group influence (Lowi, 1971). Old age policies, particularly those for the sick and poor aged, will increasingly be mediated in important and largely unknown ways by business and provider interests. This will occur because block grants and new federalism provide extremely broad powers to the states in language that may have many interpretations, thus opening major opportunities for political actors, powerful interests, and state and local administrators to "make policy" in the implementation process. Further, extreme fiscal pressures on many states and localities are likely to exacerbate the political nature of the decisions reached, as each organized interest exerts itself as forcefully as possible to prevent cutbacks or other negative policy shifts.

When legislative enactments set few central directions (for example, block grants) and implementation policies are worked out through a decentralized system of independent agencies, those who are well organized and well informed have a clear advantage over the general public. Although decentralization policies sometimes generate new agencies, the political establishment is usually affected only during the first round of organization:

> Once new groups have been formed, they take on all of the oligarchic trappings of previously organized groups, and the character of true representation in the society has hardly been affected at all. Thus,

decentralization through the delegation of power to lower levels almost always results in unequal access and group domination of the public situation [Lowi, 1971, p. 78].

In other words, decentralization is one mechanism for delegating critical program and policy decisions to progressively lower levels of authority. Decisions then come to represent a combination of interest group pressures and low-level bureaucratic processing, rendering a weakened public interest. The decentralization that increases interest group access and pressure at every level of government may, in this and myriad other ways, eclipse once nationally guaranteed basic protections for the average citizen. (Heidenheimer et al., 1975).

Third, the decentralization of social programs under current new federalism policies places human service demands on the most fiscally vulnerable levels of decision making. State and local governments have to balance their budgets annually (no deficit spending is permitted, as for the federal government) and are subject to (1) shrinking federal funding; (2) diminished state revenues due to cuts in individual and corporate taxes (often indexed to federal income taxes, resulting in additional tax reductions due to massive federal tax cuts) and to unemployment and the recession; (3) the constraints of state-imposed taxing and spending limitations; and (4) reduced local tax revenues due to property tax cuts. In California, for example, state and local revenues have been reduced by $66 billion since 1978. In 1983 California and its counties will receive $13 billion less than would have been available without the tax cuts. Although no other state crippled its fiscal capacity to the same extent, many not as fiscally strong as California have nonetheless reduced taxes. The recession has seriously compounded the effect in many states.

With decentralization, decisions about services for the poor are located precisely where pressures to control social expenses are greatest and necessarily the most conservative. As Friedland et al. (1977) and David and Kantor (1981) have shown, the need to maintain both state and local economies creates pressures on these governments to minimize business taxation and to provide other economic incentives to prevent business from relocating to more economically favorable sites. Public state and local resources may thus be seriously affected not only by federal economic policies but also by private market considerations over which state and local public officials have little control (Matheson, 1982).

That decentralization, particularly to localities, is biased *against* redistributive policies has been shown: "Constrained by their relatively weaker market position . . . the local political economy . . . imposes enormous pressures to use . . . funds to protect and enhance the urban economic base" (Kantor and David, 1982, p. 16). Nathan (1982) even observed that, without central policymaking, there may be competition between the states and localities to *reduce* benefits for the most unpopular disadvantaged groups.

Fourth, decentralization supplants national policy goals and commitments with the more autonomous and variable state and local policy choices, particularly with regard to programs for the poor of all ages. There is little assurance of consistency or uniformity of policy and little assurance of equity for powerless groups across different states. That the poor will be treated differently by different states has been shown by our own and others' research (see Chapters 6 and 7; David and Schoen, 1978; David, 1975; Bovbjerg and Holahan, 1982; Palmer and Sawhill, 1982).

Issues of national priorities and central program goals that assure equity and social justice are among the most significant in understanding the consequences of public policy determination by decentralized processes. A serious question concerns how much state and local commitment to long-term planning and coherent public policy can realistically be expected in the face of the growing fiscal constraints and intensified political pressures that occur when decision making and resource allocations are brought closer to home. How likely are program and allocation decisions to be politically or economically motivated rather than based on need under such conditions? How compatible is decentralization with the defense of basic social justice if it results in the replacement of national goals by the diversified (and essentially unverifiable) outcomes of state and local political maneuvering? Because decentralization tends to produce fragmentation in problem solving, it weakens the impact of programs on both the personal lives and the aggregate social condition of the elderly.

Fifth, as policy choices about human service cutbacks are increasingly made at the state and local levels, these cutbacks and their impact on the poor and aged will be extremely difficult to document. The reduction of comparable program data concerning block grants and other policy shifts of the Reagan administration, as well as the reduction of uniform federal data (theoretically to reduce government red tape and intrusion), serve the political function of obfuscation.

Insufficient, noncomparable, or nonexistent national data to indicate what is occurring will render impossible any accountability for actions taken or their consequences.

This is why some observers have expressed concern that decentralization has the potential to erode civil rights and other safeguards that were previously assured by federal standards and requirements for public accountability. The question raised is: Who is accountable to whom and for what in a national program that is predicated essentially on self-evaluation of performance and a principled refusal to set uniform standards?

Sixth, and critically important, decentralization assures that the dominant economic and political interests will not be challenged by the multiple and divergent state and local policies that are variably created and inconsistently implemented. Both the increasing number of policy decisions made by administering agencies and the heightened intensity of interest group and private interest politics tend to minimize even the influence of political leaders on public expenditures and priorities. The loss of congressional initiative and power to the executive branch and to private economic interests is a trend noted by C. Wright Mills (1956). We know from past experience that policies determined through private negotiations are likely to be less representative of the public interest than those emerging from the more accessible legislative and electoral processes that they replace.

Similar considerations led Alford and Friedland (1975) to conclude that our government is structured in a way that protects dominant interests from political challenge — that political fragmentation neutralizes the weaker, nondominant interests and bolsters the government's fiscal and policy dependence on the needs and wants of private economic power, thereby limiting legislative or electoral control over the structure of expenditures and revenues (see also Heidenheimer et al., 1975). Alford and Friedland (1975, p. 447) point out that, through successful pressures for favorable taxation, the "fiscal capacity of all units of government is contingent upon the locational, production and investment decisions of increasingly concentrated corporations." Relocation flexibility and financial resources are used by corporate capital to restrain both taxes and regulation (for example, on plant closings) that it claims will drive business to seek other locations with better tax advantages. Because local taxing systems are extremely vulnerable to economic threats and to restraints imposed by private capital, they are less influenced by the electorate than by business. Alford and Friedland (1975, p. 448) sum up the problem: "As long as state revenues depend (solely) on taxes, the autonomy of the state is limited by the necessity to avoid any policies that impact upon capital accumulation and growth."

Who Wins and Who Loses: The Effects of Decentralization

My concern is with the effect of the recent decentralization policy shifts on meaningful citizen participation and on the public interest. In this context, the question for Reagan's new federalism is: Decentralization to whom? It does not appear to be to the citizen, to the worker, or to the older person (particularly the elderly poor). It does not appear to be to the "community" or to those who are collapsing under the weight of unemployment and a changed economic base. Rather, there appears to be a shift of power to the private sector, particularly to the interests of corporations, major providers, and the intergovernmental lobby. Further, with the loss of categorical programs, crucial budgetary decisions affecting state and local government tend to be less influenced by Congress, while the power of the White House over vital appropriations is strengthened (Beer, 1978) through such mechanisms as block grants.

Decentralization favors the trade associations and other powerful interest groups that gain access to and comprise "third-party government" (Beer in U.S. House, 1981). Concerning the critical question of whom these groups represent, I am inclined to agree with Samuel Beer's (1978, p. 20) uneasy conclusions about the intergovernmental lobby (as well as what he called the professional bureaucratic complex) — that they tend to reflect "dilutions of the popular will [because] the new structures have a strong connotation of corporate rather than personal representation." The reasons this would be so have already been elaborated. They relate to the structural segregation and protection of key economic policies from popular control through national regulatory agencies and their relationship to regulated industry and to appointive bodies, such as the autonomous Federal Reserve Board, and through the threat of business relocation or closure if favorable tax treatment is not forthcoming. The closed and protected nature of the determination of major economic policies may be starkly contrasted with that of policies dealing with human services. The latter are largely left to the more accessible, easily politicized, and vulnerable state and local arenas.

The popular American version of how policy is made portrays the policy process as essentially an open (and implicitly "fair") competition for anyone who wishes to organize through interest groups and voluntary associations (Dahl, 1956). Mills (1956), Lowi (1971), and others have cited major inadequacies in this benign view of politics: (1) It erroneously equates organized interest group participation with democratic participation, giving preference to group (as opposed to individual) action; (2) it justifies and equates the equal availability of access to all parties with interest group politics, ignoring the fact that many citizens (such as the unemployed) with important concerns are not organized and are thus excluded from the political process; and (3) it assumes that whatever finally results from interest group bargaining represents some magical formulation of consensus or will of the people, instead of the imposition of the will of the most powerful on those who are least powerful.

A challenge to the view of interest group politics as a harmless, friendly, and consensual representation of the public is presented by Piven and Cloward in their analysis of the policy shifts of the 1980s. In their book, *The New Class War* (1982), they have argued that the goal of Reagan policies is to dismantle the welfare state, reflecting nothing less than a war of capitalism (especially monopolies and multinational corporations) against democracy (basic entitlements of citizenship). Arguing that Reagan has "declared a new class war on the unemployed, the unemployable, and the working poor," Piven and Cloward's thesis (1982, pp. 1, 7) is that "the programs that provide us a national minimum income floor are being cut back as one part of a larger strategy to increase business profits [and] to promote a massive upward redistribution of income."

Increasing profits and redistributing income upward are not the only reasons the Reagan administration has for attacking social spending. The key reason, Piven and Cloward (1982, p. 13) argue, is that "income maintenance programs . . . limit profits by enlarging the bargaining power of workers with employers." The reason for cutting social programs, particularly programs that affect the working poor and welfare recipients, is that such cuts weaken the bargaining power of workers and exert a "downward pressure" on their wages. The relationship between unemployment and lowered wages is relatively easy to understand. When there are unemployed workers with low (or no) benefits to ease their situation, both the employed and the unemployed are likely to accept low (or lowered) wages and benefits than they would if there were adequate welfare state benefits for the unemployed, the working poor, and the unemployable. The "reserve army of labor" that Marx argued was essential to capital's exploitation of labor has been augmented significantly by recent policy choices increasing unemployment while reducing social programs that ease its burden.

A question of growing significance is whether (and if so, how) it is possible for both a market economy and a democracy to coexist. Are there unresolvable conflicts between advancing the public interest, as the democratic process would seem wont to do, and advancing private profit, as a market economy is designed to do (Myles, 1983; O'Connor, 1973; Castells, 1982)?

The Uncertain Future of
Aging Policy

The poor elderly have traditionally been both the victims of public policy and the recipients of programs designed to serve either the aged (such as Social Security and Medicare) or the poor (such as SSI and Medicaid). Today, their future seems more uncertain than at any time in the past fifty years. In my view, there are four major questions for the future of aging policy under the current conditions of austerity. They revolve around the power struggles now being played out and those yet to emerge between federal, state, and local public officials, corporate elites, labor, the elderly, and other organized interests. They address the serious consequences of austerity for the aging.

The structural character of the economic crisis raises important and critical questions concerning political advocacy. Theorists have argued that conventional interest group pluralism will increasingly fail in terms of governmental response to numerous political demands (O'Connor, 1973; Castells, 1980; Garfield, 1980, 1981). The political initiatives commonly employed by interest groups in the past will tend to be defused and neutralized by the reality of fiscal constraint and its political environment. Therefore, efforts and activities aimed at ameliorating the fiscal crisis itself will be of the utmost importance. This could be accomplished partly through coalitional efforts to preserve or expand available revenues for governments under financial stress (O'Connor, 1973; Castells, 1980; Garfield, 1980, 1981).

Our research on fiscal crisis (see Chapter 5) indicates some positive effects of local-level advocacy efforts by aging organizations in opposing cutbacks. Aging groups, however, reported less success than did others (especially unions) that engaged in coalition-forming and other aggressive tactics. Although public participation is likely to be limited under conditions of fiscal strain (Estes, 1979), there is evidence that organized citizen efforts may have an impact (Juster, 1976; Waldhorn et al., 1975). Where participation (for example, opposition to cutbacks) is combined with influence, as our study findings show (Swan et al., 1982), advocacy can be important for public policy in stemming or reducing the impacts of proposed cutbacks or policy shifts.

Thus, the first question for the future of aging policy concerns the extent to which aging interest groups will ally with a broader base of action and expand their concerns to encompass more generic issues such as revenue reform, corporate taxation, and labor control of pension funds. Single-interest aging-based politics may have been an efficacious strategy to follow over the past thirty years. However, there is evidence that unless advocates for the elderly now address broad policy issues, many of which may not deal directly with aging issues, the elderly are likely to find their future shaped by the advocacy of others. For example, our findings show that across-the-board cuts and reductions in public employment at the state and local levels, as well as other nonaging-specific service cuts (such as those in health services) are associated with cuts in services to the elderly. We also found that area agencies on aging were the *least* likely of all the community agencies studied to oppose cutbacks that were not specifically or overtly targeted to the elderly (Swan et al., 1982) — apparently not recognizing that broad cuts may affect the elderly.

The second question affecting the future of aging policy concerns the extent to which governors, mayors, and other state and local elected officials are likely to "accept" the federal retrenchment and shift of governmental responsibility to state and local governments, especially when their political futures become increasingly uncertain and the social problems they confront become increasingly difficult. As our research has shown, there were significant erosions in the revenue bases and discretionary general funds at both the state and local levels *prior* to the cutbacks and additional revenue losses incurred with federal tax and spending legislation in 1981-1983. The political "hot seat," which state and local officials will increasingly occupy as the full impact of the federal and state cutbacks are felt "at home," may well make these representatives of the "intergovernmental lobby" willing participants, or even front-liners, in resistance to efforts to dismantle the welfare state (Piven and Cloward, 1982).

The third question about the future of aging policy is whether the interests of the wealthy and the middle class (particularly the mythical average worker who has a long, steady, secure, and uninterrupted work career) will continue to dominate public policy for the aging or whether the interests of all working people (the marginally employed, those disabled in the course of their working lives, the working poor, and women) will be given due consideration. Will aging advocates join what Piven and Cloward (1982) have called the "new class war"?

It is well known that, among national aging organizations, few (and these are the least powerful) have been identified primarily with the low-income elderly, the minority elderly, or older women. When times were better, it was in all probability easier to provide constituency support for improving benefits to a broad base of the elderly, including lower-class older persons, women, and minorities. However, as financial and political pressure mounts, the question remains as to whether Piven and Cloward (1982) are correct in arguing that middle-class dependency on the benefits of the welfare state (through Social Security, for example) is likely to ensure support for the survival of the welfare state or whether it will occur in such a form that class and age differences in public policy become even more pronounced. Equally important is the choice of political strategy — that is, whether the poor and downwardly mobile elderly and other disadvantaged groups (such as older women) will organize or align themselves with their counterparts of other generations or persuasions.

The fourth question is both the most important and most problematic, for it concerns the extent to which (and the manner in which) the human consequences of austerity and aging are felt and experienced. It is critically necessary to obtain an accurate portrayal of the human consequences of these shifts in the best way that social science can offer.

Two things are clear: First, public policy for the elderly mirrors the structural arrangements of American society and the distribution of political, economic, and ideological opportunities and resources within it; second, both the treatment of older people in society and the experience of old age itself are related to an economy, the boundaries of which are no longer limited to considerations of the United States alone but include worldwide economic and political conditions and considerations (Amin et al., 1982; Mandel, 1978; Castells, 1980).

As inequities are exacerbated in younger age groups in society, they will be exacerbated in old age. Such inequities will then be added to those already created by social policies for the aged that have had the net result of *increasing* the disparities between different groups of elderly (Crystal, 1982; Nelson, 1982, forthcoming; Estes, 1982).

As various researchers have shown, public benefits to the elderly have increased, but they have not been targeted to help those who need them most. Speaking of "two worlds" of aging, Crystal shows that the gap is widening between the best-off and the worst-off. One world is inhabited by those who are poor, sick, and incapacitated; the other, by those who are economically and physically well off. His argument is that policy for the aging subsidizes the larger population, who are healthy and financially well off, at the expense of those who are poor and chronically ill. There are, in fact, two "highly unequal" classes of aged, both largely dependent on direct and indirect public aid (Crystal, 1982, p. 9). These two classes, or two worlds, of aging are separate and unequal — one is comfortable, the other miserable and destitute.

Crystal's (1982, p. 30) most important contribution is the observation that, "despite the general improvement and the increasing reliance on public programs, the distribution of income among the elderly population remains highly skewed, with the bottom group getting a small share not only of total income but of government benefits." In spite of the much-heralded decline in poverty in the 1970s (a decline that stopped in 1978 and since has been reversed), the substantial gap between the mean and median income of the elderly has not been diminished. "The distribution of assets is even more highly skewed" (Crystal, 1982, p. 30). Thus, a relatively small percentage of elderly receive substantial public benefits (the high-income group), while nearly 40 percent are poor or near-poor (Lehrman, 1980), and the remainder are able to live modest lives.

As Crystal (1982, p. 32) has noted, "the number of elderly with high income increased substantially in recent years, producing a skewed income distribution with the mean income considerably higher than the median." In 1980 the mean income for the elderly family was $16,918, while the median income was only $12,881. For individuals, the mean income was $7,176, compared to a median income of $5,095 (U.S. Bureau of the Census, 1982; Crystal, 1982). This means that *half* of all elderly individuals survived on *less* than $5,095 in 1980, even with the income assistance of the beleaguered Social Security and Supplemental Security Income (SSI) programs.

An important and unrecognized fact is that the decline in poverty of the 1970s was not evenly distributed. There are significant disparities in income by race and living arrangements as well as by sex in old age. The decline in poverty was greater for older persons living in families than for those living alone, for whites than for nonwhites (13.6 percent of white elders are poor compared to 38.1 percent of black elders), and for men than for women (41 percent of single older women are poor compared to 15 percent of men). There are also disparities in pensions, which tend to be accorded to stable white male workers in middle- or upper-income jobs. Forced (and early) retirement is more typical for low-income retirees (Crystal, 1982).

Income disparities in old age emerge from and reflect differential lifetime opportunities for paid employment that is both permanent (not sporadic) and "covered" by Social Security as well as for private pensions. These income disparities are even greater if unequally distributed tax subsidies (an indirect federal expenditure for the elderly) are considered as well. As Nelson (forthcoming), Crystal (1982), and Olson (1982) have shown, tax benefits for public and private pensions, including those for federal workers, railroad employees, and veterans; tax credits for the elderly; and the benefits of recent federal tax legislation all favor those elderly who are in the higher-income brackets rather than those in the medium- or low-income brackets. If one goes beyond income to examine the distribution of wealth, the disparities in economic capacity among different sectors of the population become stunning (and outrageous).

Contrary to popular perception, Ryan (1982, p. 14) observes that "the great majority [of all ages] are just scraping by, a small minority are at least temporarily comfortable, and a tiny handful of persons live at levels of affluence and luxury that most persons cannot even imagine." Ryan's (1982, p. 14) description of inequality and of wealth in American society is compelling in this regard:

> About one out of every four Americans owns nothing. Nothing! In fact, many of them *owe* more than they have. . . . The persons in the next quarter own about 5 percent of all personal assets. In other words, half of us own 5 percent, the other half own 95 percent. But it gets worse as you go up the scale. Those in the top 6 percent own half of all the wealth. . . . Those in the top 1 percent own one-fourth of all the wealth. Those in the top ½ percent own one-fifth of all the wealth. The very rich put their wealth into the ownership of things that produce more wealth — corporate stocks and bonds, mortgages, notes, and the like. Two-thirds of their wealth is in this form and the top 1 percent owns 60 percent of all that valuable paper. The rest of it is owned by only an additional 10 percent, which means that nine people out of ten own none of it.

In discussing public policy for the aging, Nelson (1982, p. 18) describes a similar situation in which there are three tiers of public policy, based on "highly political and subjective standards of entitlement: (a) a standard for the poor, (b) a standard for the middle and the lower middle class, and (c) a standard for the high income elderly." The standard for the poor is subsistence; the standard for the middle and downwardly mobile lower-middle-income elders is social adequacy; and the standard for the high-income older people is the maintenance of their high income both before and after retirement. This has prompted Nelson (forthcoming) to ask the very important question, Is it "appropriate to use billions of tax dollars to maintain high income life-styles of an elite American elderly when millions of other elderly are in poverty or in near poverty?"

How has such a blatantly unfair situation occurred? As I argued in *The Aging Enterprise* (1979), a substantially classless view of old age has been incorporated into public policy (on the false assumption that broad benefit policies for the elderly, including tax credits, are equally beneficial to all older persons). This camouflages the existing inequitable distribution of public benefits to the elderly. As described in Chapter 1, policies that most benefit those who are considered deserving (the upper-income and downwardly mobile middle-income groups) tend to be "national" policies (such as Social Security and Medicare). These policies are easily protected, uniform, and visible. Policies for the "undeserving," on the other hand, tend to be state-level policies. They are highly variable and inequitable from state to state and are under increasingly extreme fiscal pressure with cutbacks at all levels of government.

An analysis of the distribution of public benefits, including both direct programs and indirect tax expenditures (such as tax credits and subsidies), illuminates the great disparity between the rich and everyone else. Public policy supports a class-based and class-biased treatment of older persons to such an extent that I believe many Americans would be shocked to realize its full magnitude (Nelson, 1982, forthcoming; Tussing, 1971; Crystal, 1982; Estes, 1982). The increasing concentration of wealth (Ryan, 1982), the increasing monopolization of business and markets (O'Connor, 1973; Castells, 1980), and the increasing disparity between the rich and the rest of the population (Ryan, 1982) are, in my view, shameful facts of American life.

The 1980s have commenced with vigorous power struggles between the proponents of class privilege and the proponents of the rights of citizenship (Myles, 1983). For the former, "rights" may be only that which is earned, ignoring the inherent disadvantages of large sectors of the population in comparison with others. For the latter, the belief is that citizenship confers inalienable rights and responsibilities, including entitlement to basic health and welfare. I count myself among the latter.

References

Alford, R., and R. Friedland. "Political Participation and Public Policy." *Annual Review of Sociology,* 1 (1975), 429-479.

Amin, S., et al., eds. *Dynamics of Global Crises.* New York: Monthly Review Press, 1982.

Bachrach, P. *The Theory of Democratic Elitism: A Critique.* Boston: Little, Brown, 1967.

Beer, S. H. "Federalism, Nationalism, and Democracy in America." *American Political Science Review,* 71, No. 1 (1978), 9-21.

Beer, S. M. "Federalism: Lessons of the Past, Choices for the Future." In *Federalism: Making the System Work.* Ed. S. M. Beer et al. Washington, DC: Center for National Policy, 1982.

Bovbjerg, R. R., and J. Holahan. *Medicaid in the Reagan Era.* Washington, DC: Urban Institute, 1982.

Castells, M. *The Economic Crisis and American Society.* Princeton, NJ: Princeton University Press, 1980.

————. *City, Class and Power.* New York: St. Martin's Press, 1982.

Connolly, W. E. *The Bias of Pluralism.* New York: Atherton, 1969.

Crystal, S. *America's Old Age Crisis.* New York: Basic Books, 1982.

Dahl, R. A. *A Preface to the Democratic Theory.* Chicago: University of Chicago Press, 1956.

David, S. M., and P. Kantor. "Urban Policy in the Federal Systems: A Reconceptualization of Federalism." Paper presented at the annual meeting of the American Political Science Association, New York, September 25, 1981.

Davis, K. "Equal Treatment and Unequal Benefits: The Medicare Program." *Milbank Memorial Fund Quarterly/Health and Society,* 53, No. 4 (1975), 449-488.

————, and C. Schoen. *Health and the War on Poverty: A Ten-Year Appraisal.* Washington, DC: Brookings Institution, 1978.

Estes, C. L. *The Aging Enterprise.* San Francisco: Jossey-Bass, 1979.

————. "Austerity and Aging." *International Journal of Health Services,* 12, No. 4 (1982), 573-584.

————. "Social Security: The Social Construction of a Crisis." *Milbank Memorial Quarterly/Health and Society,* forthcoming.

————, and P. R. Lee. "Policy Shifts and Their Impact on Health Care for Elderly Persons." *Western Journal of Medicine,* 135, No. 6 (1981), 511-517.

Friedland, R., R. R. Alford, and F. F. Piven. "The Political Management of the Urban Fiscal Crises." Paper presented at the annual meeting of the American Sociological Association, Chicago, September 1977.

Garfield, J. "Progressive Approaches to Tax Reform Revenue Generation, and Budgetary Priorities." Paper presented at the annual meeting of the American Public Health Association, Detroit, October 20, 1980.

————. "Political Action and the Fiscal Crisis: Labor and Community Mobilization in Post-Proposition 13 San Francisco." Paper presented at the meeting of the American Public Health Association, Los Angeles, November 3, 1981.

Heidenheimer, A. J., H. Heclo, and C. T. Adams. *Comparative Public Policy.* New York: St. Martin's Press, 1975.

Institute of Medicine. *Health Care in a Context of Civil Rights.* Washington, DC: National Academy Press, 1981.

Juster, F. T., ed. *The Economic and Political Impact of General Revenue Sharing.* Washington, DC: National Science Foundation, 1976.

Klemmack, D. L., and L. L. Roff. "Predicting General Comparative Support for Government's Providing Benefits to Older Persons." *Gerontologist,* 21, No. 6 (1981), 592-599.

Lehrman, R. "Poverty Statistics Serve as Nagging Reminder." *Generations,* 4, No. 1 (May 1980), 17.

Long, N. "The Local Community as an Ecology of Games." *American Journal of Sociology,* 64 (1958), 251-261.

Lowi, T. *The Politics of Disorder.* New York: Basic Books, 1971.

Mandel, E. *The Second Slump: A Marxist Analysis of Recession in the Seventies.* London: NLB, 1978.

Matheson, S. M. Presentation at the 14th Annual Conference of State Medical Directors, Salt Lake City, April 26, 1982.

Mills, C. W. *The Power Elite.* New York: Oxford University Press, 1956.

Myles, J. F. *Old Age in the Welfare State: The Political Economy of Public Pensions.* Boston: Little, Brown, 1983.

Nathan, Richard P. "'Reforming' the Federal Grant-in-Aid System for States and Localities." In *Policy Studies Annual Review,* Vol. 6. Ed. R. C. Rist. Beverly Hills, CA: Sage, 1982.

Nelson, G. "Social Class and Public Policy for the Elderly." *Social Science Review,* 56, No. 1 (1982), 85-107.

————. "Tax Expenditures for the Elderly." *Gerontologist,* forthcoming.

O'Connor, J. *The Fiscal Crisis of the State.* New York: St. Martin's Press, 1973.

Olson, L. K. *The Political Economy of Aging.* New York: Columbia University Press, 1982.

Palmer, J. L., and I. V. Sawhill, eds. *The Reagan Experiment.* Washington, DC: Urban Institute, 1982.

Piven, F. F., and R. Cloward. *The New Class War.* New York: Pantheon Books, 1982.

Ryan, W. *Equality.* New York: Vintage, 1982.

Swan, J. H., C. L. Estes, J. B. Wood, M. Kreger, and J. Garfield. *Fiscal Crisis: Impact on Aging Services.* Final Report. Prepared for the U.S. Administration on Aging under Grant No. 90-AR-0016. San Francisco: Aging Health Policy Center, University of California, 1982.

Tussing, A. "The Dual Welfare System." In *Social Realities.* Ed. L. Horowitz and C. Levy. New York: Harper & Row, 1971.

U.S. Bureau of the Census. *Money Income and Poverty Status of Families and Persons in the United States: 1981.* Washington, DC: U.S. Government Printing Office, 1982.

———. *Money Income and Poverty Status of Families and Persons in the United States: 1980.* Washington, DC: U.S. Government Printing Office, 1981.

U.S. House, Committee on Government Operations. *Current Condition of American Federalism.* Washington, DC: U.S. Government Printing Office, 1981.

U.S. House, Committee on Post Office and Civil Service, Subcommittee on Census and Population. *Impact of Budget Cuts on Federal Statistical Programs.* Washington, DC: U.S. Government Printing Office, 1982.

Waldorn, S. A., et al. *Planning and Participation: General Revenue Sharing in Ten Large Cities.* Menlo Park, CA: Stanford Research Institute, 1975.

NAME INDEX

Achenbaum, W. A., 60, 61, 63
Aday, L. A., 50
Alford, R., 18, 47, 212, 260, 261
Altmeyer, A. J., 66
Amin, S., 263

Ball, R. M., 29, 85
Banfield, E. C., 54
Banta, D., 212
Beer, S. M., 42, 43, 260
Benjamin, A. E., 215, 216, 217
Benton, B., 135
Berger, J., 227
Berry, B. J. L., 118
Bishop, C. E., 180
Bloom, B. S., 209, 210
Bovbjerg, R. R., 34, 167, 171, 174, 25
Brodsky, D., 74
Brody, S. J., 223
Brown, L. B., 222
Buckley, J. L., 75
Butler, L. H., 219

Callahan, J., 178
Castelli, J., 232, 233
Castells, M., 262
Chelimsky, E., 51
Clarke, G. J., 47
Clotfelter, C. J., 241, 244
Coelen, C., 177
Collins, R., 17
Connolly, W. E., 18
Cook, F. L., 29, 32, 114
Coombs, S., 190
Crystal, S., 32

Dahl, R. A., 261
David, S. M., 46, 47, 49, 257, 258
Davidson, S. M., 69
Davis, K., 33, 258
Derthick, M., 74, 136

Douglas, J., 228
Downs, A., 223

Ellickson, P. L., 119
Ellwood, J. W., 242
Enthoven, A. C., 98
Estes, C. L., 18, 32, 33, 47, 51, 69, 73, 75, 79, 85, 114, 117, 136, 152, 163, 190, 200, 235, 263, 267

Feder, J., 97, 98, 104, 211, 216
Fetter, R. B., 103
Fischer, D. H., 62, 64, 67
Fisher, C. R., 93, 94, 96, 97, 183
Freeland, M. S., 92
Friedland, R., 47, 117, 257

Garfield, J., 262
Garfinkel, S., 160
Gilbert, N., 136, 152
Glenn, K., 101
Goddard, S., 233
Gordon, D., 115, 118
Gutowski, M. F., 51, 152

Haas, J. E., 220
Hale, G. E., 44, 60
Hansmann, H. B., 227
Harrington, C., 101, 104, 162, 172, 181
Harris, L., 29
Heidenheimer, A. J., 257, 259
Holahan, J., 211
Howell, J. M., 118, 119
Hudson, R. B., 71, 85, 202

Juster, F. T., 263

Kahne, H., 89
Klemmack, D. L., 114, 243
Kutza, E. A., 62, 105

SUBJECT INDEX

Accountability, definition and methods, 51-54; in private nonprofit sector, 233; in Title XX social services, 136, 150-151

Access to social services, 149

Advocacy, and Economic Crisis, 262-263; in Older Americans Act, 203

Aging, and austerity, 21, 23; as a biological phenomenon, 19; and class basis of public policies, 31-35; and debate over public expenditures, 21-24; definitions of the social problem of, 17-20; and the federal budget, 29-30; federal programs for, 73; and fiscal crisis, 20, 127; fundamental conditions shaping policy and services, 251; future policy of, 262-268; and new federalism, 21; and social security crisis, 21; societal perceptions of, 18; "two worlds" of, 265

Austerity, 13, 20-23, 76-78, 262-264

Block grants, 34, 77, 52-53, 134, 148. *See also* Social services, Older Americans Act

Certificate of need, 213, 215-217

Chronic illness, 157

Class basis of policies, 31-35, 261, 264, 267. *See also* Social justice

Class and fiscal cutbacks, 128

Class privilege, 267

Community-based care, 160, 184

Comprehensive Employment Training Act (CETA), 230

Comprehensive Health Manpower Training Act, 209

Comprehensive Health Planning Act of 1966, 213

Conference Board, 238, 21

Continuum of care, 182

Cost containment. *See* Cost control

Cost Control, in Medicaid program, 171-184; in Medicare program, 92. *See also* Medicare program, Medicaid program

Crisis in Social Security, 21, 29, 79, 84-85, 86-88; elimination of the minimum benefit, 32-33, 86; expenditures, 83; legitimacy of public support, 27-29. *See also* Social Security

Data reductions, 53-54

Decentralization, 54-55; and fiscal capacity, 46; and health and social services, 251-254; myth of, 43; and Older Americans Act, 187-189; political and economic aspects of, 255-258; and social services, 148

Defense spending, 24-27. *See also* Expenditures

Deficit spending, 115

Deservingness. *See* Legitimacy of aged

Disability insurance, 86

Distributive justice. *See* Social justice

Ecology of games, 253

Economic crisis and political advocacy, 262

Economic Opportunity Act of 1964, 69

Economic Recovery Tax Act of 1981, 20, 241

Equity, considerations in policy, 252-253; distribution of public resources, 33-35; and distribution of social services, 151-153; effects of cutbacks on certain classes, 128; equity of access defined, 50; and Older Americans Act, 203; private,

eligibility standards, 167-171;
expenditures, 159, 163-166; policy
changes, 166-171; reimbursement
rates, 176-181; service expenditure
patterns, 163-166

Medicare program, catastrophic
insurance proposal, 98; changes for
1982 and 1983, 93-95; cost-sharing,
94-97; description of, 92-93;
disparities in benefits, 33, 97; health
maintenance organizations, 95,
99-100, 107; integrated financing of,
105; means-test proposal, 104;
Medigap, 96; passage of, 68-69;
proposed changes for 1984, 95;
reimbursement policies, 100-104;
and the Social Security crisis, 21; as
a target for cost containment 92-93;
vouchers, 98-99; 107

Medigap, 96

National Commission on Social
Security, 86-87, 91. *See also* Social
Security crisis

National Governors' Association,
47-48, 115

National Health Planning and
Development Act of 1974, 74, 213.
See also Health Planning

New class war, 261, 264

New federalism, 21, 54, 70, 76-80; and
decentralization, 255-259; and
health planning, 222-223; and
Henny Penny school, 42; and
National Governors' Association,
48, 78; and the Older Americans
Act, 199, 202-203; Reagan
reductions and the private sector,
233; and redistribution of power, 55;
as a source of policy bias, 46

Nursing Homes, and certificate of need
review, 215-217; costs, 159;
reimbursement rates, 180-181

Older Americans Act, advocacy role,
203; aging network, 194, 200;
amendments to 1973, 189;
appropriations, 190-191;
conformance with federal
directives, 200-201; cutback effects,
203; decentralization, 187-188,

190-191; equity, 203; and federalism,
199, 202-203; and health planning,
219-222; legislative history, 69,
189-191; spending patterns of
agencies, 197; spending patterns of
Title XX social services, 198; state
and local roles, 194-198, 201-202;
targeting, 198-199

Omnibus Budget Reconciliation Act of
1981, 20, 33, 53, 77, 86, 90, 93, 124,
138, 163

Out-of-pocket expenses. *See* Payments

Payments, hospital national average per
day, 178; out-of-pocket, 96, 107, 160,
182

Personnel, 229

Policy, definition of bias, 46-47;
outcomes, 47; process and health
planning, 212; redistributive policy
issues, 45-47

Poverty. *See* Income of aged

Power. *See* Decentralization, New
federalism

President's Commission for the Study of
Ethical Problems in Biomedical and
Behavioral Research, 49

Private nonprofit sector, definition of,
228; reductions in funding, 230-231;
social services, 229

Professional bureaucratic complex, 260

Professional standard review
organizations, 172

Redistributive policy. *See* Social justice

Reform in federal domestic social policy,
41-42

Reimbursement in Medicaid, 176-181

Roosevelt and the New Deal, 65-67

Social justice and decentralization, 258;
Rawls's concept of, 49;
redistributive policy issues, 45-47.
See also Equity

Social Security program, Amendments,
22, 67; crisis in financing, 84-85;
disability insurance, 86; enactment
in 1935, 65-67, 210; expenditures, 83;
Medicare and Medicaid, 68-69;
minimum Social Security benefits,
32, 86; public confidence in, 29;

ABOUT THE AUTHORS

A. E. BENJAMIN, Jr., Ph.D., Adjunct Assistant Professor, Department of Social and Behavioral Sciences, and Associate Director of the Aging Health Policy Center, School of Nursing, University of California, San Francisco. Dr. Benjamin is co-principal investigator with Dr. Budetti on a study of health planning and the elderly, does research on long term care, and has written on health planning, income assistance, and long term care for the elderly.

CARROLL L. ESTES, Ph.D., Professor of Sociology, is Chairperson of the Department of Social and Behavioral Sciences and Director of the Aging Health Policy Center, School of Nursing, University of California, San Francisco. Dr. Estes conducts research and writes about aging policy, issues in long term care for the elderly, and the effects of fiscal crisis and new federalism policies on aging services. The author of *The Aging Enterprise* (1979) and *The Decision Makers: The Power Structure of Dallas* (1963), Dr. Estes is president of the Western Gerontological Society and immediate past president of the Association for Gerontology in Higher Education.

LENORE GERARD, B.A., Staff Research Associate, Department of Social and Behavioral Sciences, Aging Health Policy Center, School of Nursing, University of California, San Francisco. Ms. Gerard has extensive experience in health policy and aging following work as a health economics assistant in the Institute for Health Policy Studies, School of Medicine, University of California, San Francisco. She is involved in legislative research, writing, and analysis of issues concerning political economy, health, and aging.

CHARLENE HARRINGTON, R.N., Ph.D., Adjunct Associate Professor, Department of Social and Behavioral Sciences, and Associate Director of the Aging Health Policy Center, School of Nursing, University of California, San Francisco. Dr. Harrington has had twenty years of active experience in the health care field, including direct community health nursing, and has administered state and regional health planning and regulatory agencies. She currently directs research projects examining trends in long term care service expenditure and utilization and has written extensively on nursing homes and long term care.

PHILIP R. LEE, M.D., Professor of Social Medicine, Department of Medicine, and Director of the Institute for Health Policy Studies, School of Medicine, University of California, San Francisco. A former Assistant Secretary of Health in the U.S. Department of Health, Education, and Welfare (1965-1969), and former Chancellor of UCSF (1969-1972), Dr. Lee conducts research and writes about a wide range of health policy issues, including long term care for the elderly, prescription drugs, primary health care, and health promotion and disease prevention.

277

DAVID A. LINDEMAN, Research Associate, Department of Social and Behavioral Sciences, Aging Health Policy Center, School of Nursing, University of California, San Francisco. Mr. Lindeman is a doctoral candidate in social welfare at the University of California, Berkeley. His areas of expertise include social services, health planning, data systems, and research methods.

ROBERT J. NEWCOMER, Ph.D., Adjunct Associate Professor, Department of Social and Behavioral Sciences, and Deputy Director of the Aging Health Policy Center, School of Nursing, University of California, San Francisco. Dr. Newcomer directs the Center's major studies of aging policy, including research projects related to long term care, the effect of new federalism policies on aging services, and self-help and the elderly. Dr. Newcomer is also Director of the National Policy Center on Health funded by the Administration on Aging and co-editor (with Lawton and Byarts) of *Community Planning for an Aging Society.*

ALAN PARDINI, M.S., Senior Research Associate, Department of Social and Behavioral Sciences, Aging Health Policy Center, School of Nursing, University of California, San Francisco. Mr. Pardini is currently involved in an analysis of federal health and social service programs and policies affecting older persons. His previous research dealt with national policies in health services planning and health personnel.

JAMES H. SWAN, Ph.D., Senior Research Associate and Adjunct Assistant Professor, Department of Social and Behavioral Sciences, Aging Health Policy Center, School of Nursing, University of California, San Francisco. Dr. Swan directed a project with Dr. Estes assessing the impact on aging services of fiscal crisis at the state and local levels.

JUANITA B. WOOD, Ph.D., Senior Public Administration Analyst, Department of Social and Behavioral Sciences, Aging Health Policy Center, School of Nursing, University of California, San Francisco. Dr. Wood is Project Director of the nonprofit sector study and also teaches a graduate seminar in field research in the School of Nursing and co-teaches a seminar in health care access for the disabled in the School of Medicine, University of California, San Francisco.